CURVEBALL

CURVEBALL

SPIES, LIES, AND THE MAN BEHIND THEM: THE REAL

REASON AMERICA WENT TO WAR IN IRAQ

BOB DROGIN

EBURY
PRESS

1 3 5 7 9 10 8 6 4 2

Published in 2007 by Ebury Press, an imprint of Ebury Publishing

A Random House Group Company

Copyright © Bob Drogin 2007

Bob Drogin has asserted his right to be identified as the author of this Work in accordance with the Copyright, Designs and Patents Act 1988

The Random House Group Limited Reg. No. 954009

Addresses for companies within the Random House Group can be found at www.randomhouse.co.uk

A CIP catalogue record for this book is available from the British Library

Mixed Sources
Product group from well-managed forests and other controlled sources
www.fsc.org Cert no. TT-COC-2139
© 1996 Forest Stewardship Council
FSC

Printed and bound in Great Britain by Clays Ltd, St Ives PLC

ISBN 9780091923037 (hardback)
ISBN 9780091923020 (paperback)

To buy books by your favourite authors and register for offers visit
www.rbooks.co.uk

For Francoise

curve ball or curve•ball (kûrv' bôl)

n. 1. *Baseball* Any of several pitches that veer to the left when thrown with the right hand and to the right when thrown with the left hand.

2. *Slang* Something that is unexpected or designed to trick or deceive: That last question on the exam was a real curve ball.

Idiom: pitch/throw (someone) a curve ball *Slang*
1. To mislead; deceive. 2. To cause to be surprised, especially unpleasantly so.

—*American Heritage Dictionary of the English Language,*
Fourth Edition (Boston: Houghton Mifflin, 2004)

CONTENTS

AUTHOR'S NOTE

Curveball is a true-life spy story, a nonfiction account of one of America's worst intelligence failures.

Yet it needs a caveat. Clandestine operatives are trained to spread falsehoods as part of their tradecraft. Intelligence agencies spin or hide the truth as a matter of policy and law. And spy services, even close allies, routinely conceal information from each other. In this case, the layers of secrecy and deception created a Rashomon effect: each group saw Curveball through a different lens.

I have tried to unravel the intrigue and navigate the distortions that plagued this case. I base my narrative on the facts as best I could determine and confirm them. Like any author, I flesh out the written record and the memories of participants to bring life to the page. I rely on my own observations, on thousands of pages of public and private documents, and on my research and interviews with more than eighty current and former intelligence officers, government officials, scientists, and other sources in Germany, Great Britain, Iraq, the United Nations, the United States, and elsewhere. I draw heavily on my earlier reporting and that of my colleagues at the *Los Angeles Times*.

Unless otherwise indicated, all quotations are directly from my interviews. All thoughts attributed to individuals are taken from interviews, a colleague with firsthand knowledge, or the written record. Dialogue that does not appear in quotation marks represents my understanding of a given conversation. I use endnotes to cite material published by others. In some cases, I use the notes to provide further detail or context for the text.

Several participants agreed to cooperate only if I promised not to identify them by name because they work undercover, are bound by secrecy agreements, or are discussing sensitive sources and methods. As a rule in these cases, I err on the side of caution. I conducted some interviews on background, meaning I could use the information but not identify the source. I refer to some intelligence officers by their first names to protect their anonymity. In a few cases, I resort to pseudonyms to shield them further. Some participants refused to talk or could not be located. Curveball remains under the protection of the German intelligence service. Ahmed Hassan Mohammed is not his real name.

KEY CHARACTERS

CIA AND OTHER U.S. INTELLIGENCE AGENCIES

GEORGE TENET: Director of central intelligence.

JOHN McLAUGHLIN: Deputy director of central intelligence.

JAMES PAVITT: Head of the CIA clandestine service.

TYLER DRUMHELLER: Chief of the CIA European division.

ALEX STEINER: Head of DIA operations at Munich House.

BERNIE MUELLER: U.S. intelligence officer in Munich.

LES: CIA doctor who meets Curveball in 2000.

BETH: Senior CIA analyst for biological weapons.

MARGARET: CIA operations group chief for Germany.

STEVE: McLaughlin's executive assistant.

CHRIS: CIA operations officer who interviews Curveball in 2004.

GERMAN FEDERAL INTELLIGENCE SERVICE (BND)

AUGUST HANNING: President of the BND.

WERNER KAPPEL: Senior BND official.

SCHUMANN: Cover name for Curveball's case officer.

MEINER: Cover name for Curveball's chief debriefer.

HANS PIEPER: Meiner's supervisor.

HORST SCHNEIDER: Schumann's supervisor.

ERNST UHRLAU: Germany's national intelligence coordinator.

GRADL: Cover name for BND resident agent in Washington.

IRAQIS

AHMED HASSAN MOHAMMED: The Iraqi defector code-named Curveball.

AHMED CHALABI: Head of the Iraqi National Congress.

LT. GEN. HUSSEIN KAMIL: Saddam Hussein's son-in-law.

LT. GEN. AMIR HAMMUDI HASAN SAADI: Saddam Hussein's scientific advisor.

DR. RIHAB RASHID TAHA: Senior biowarfare scientist, also known as Dr. Germ.

MAJOR MOHAMMED HARITH: Defector who was deemed a fabricator.

RED RIVER: Informant for British intelligence.

IRAQ SURVEY GROUP

DAVID KAY: CIA-appointed chief of the Iraq Survey Group.

MAJ. GEN. KEITH DAYTON: Top DIA officer in Iraq Survey Group.

HAMISH KILLIP: British expert on Curveball.

JERRY: CIA bioweapons expert.

TIM: CIA bioweapons expert, also known as the Kid.

RITA: CIA analyst and head of the Curveball team.

MARTHA: CIA bioweapons expert.

MOHAMMED: CIA operations officer who meets Curveball's parents.

UNSCOM

SCOTT RITTER JR.: Weapons inspector.

ROLF EKEUS: Chief weapons inspector.

RICHARD SPERTZEL: American biowarfare expert.

UNMOVIC

HANS BLIX: Chief weapons inspector.

DIMITRI PERRICOS: Deputy chief U.N. weapons inspector.

KAY MEREISH: Senior biological inspector.

JAMES CORCORAN: Chief intelligence liaison.

ROCCO CASAGRANDE: Director of biological laboratory in Baghdad.

U.S. GOVERNMENT

GEORGE BUSH: President of the United States.

RICHARD CHENEY: Vice president of the United States.

COLIN POWELL: Secretary of state.

LAWRENCE WILKERSON: Powell's chief of staff.

CONDOLEEZZA RICE: National security advisor.

DONALD RUMSFELD: Secretary of defense.

STEPHEN CAMBONE: Undersecretary of defense for intelligence.

PROLOGUE

For a few wild months, the HVT Bar served as the secret social hub for American spies in Iraq.

It opened without fanfare late one night in early May 2003, shortly after the American-led invasion, in a distant corner of the newly captured Saddam Hussein International Airport. The saloon was dark and dingy, hidden in a grubby two-room guardhouse. Inside, a brace of captured Iraqi grenade launchers and assault rifles adorned one wall, like souvenir hockey sticks in a sports bar. Lightbulbs dangled from the ceiling, casting harsh shadows, and hard rock pounded from speakers. The air buzzed with backslapping camaraderie and whispers of intrigue; it smelled of rank sweat and cigarette smoke. The liquor was cheap, the beer ice cold, and the white wine, by all accounts, the color and taste of camel piss. It was a dive of distinction.

Few outsiders knew of the HVT Bar and, given the location, fewer still could get in. This was no surprise. It was the Central Intelligence Agency's private nightspot. The speakeasy pulsed in the heart of the Baghdad station, the CIA's newest overseas base and the center of a surreal secret world.

The agency had decided to build the station, as it called its major outposts, in the airport compound previously reserved only for "Very, Very Important Persons," meaning Saddam Hussein. The tyrant had not dared leave Iraq during his reign. But he built a majestic domed reception hall and opulent marble outbuildings to mark rare visits from Arab royalty and heads of state. The CIA, unchallenged rulers of the global intelligence netherworld, chose the regal V.V.I.P. complex as the spoils of a war for which it was largely responsible.

Work bustled on all sides those first few weeks. Looters still ran free elsewhere in Iraq, ransacking ministries and pillaging factories. But inside the guarded CIA compound, technicians planted a lush high-tech jungle of antennas and satellite dishes. They uncoiled power lines and communications cables like tendrils across the gravel. Crews rushed to renovate offices and warehouses, kicking up thick clouds of dust. Late one afternoon, Army demolition experts destroyed a cache of Iraqi munitions discovered in concrete bunkers down the road. But they miscalculated badly and the deafening explosions shattered the panoramic windows in the V.V.I.P. lounge and sent people diving for cover. The plate glass was quickly replaced, but a week or two later, overeager engineers blew the CIA windows into shards again. Such was the price of progress.

Equipment and supplies poured in. The incoming CIA planes were easy to spot. Military aircraft corkscrewed carefully down over the runway to evade portable surface-to-air missiles or other ground fire from outside the airport walls. The slow but safe descent, round and round in a tightening downward spiral, took at least twenty tedious minutes. The CIA contract pilots, macho men to the core, preferred to just plummet from ten thousand feet or so, screaming out of the crystalline desert sky like a Dauntless dive-bomber at Midway. Grinning madly, the pilots finally pulled out, engines howling in protest, at the last possible, stomach-churning, ass-puckering moment and roared down the runway. "Thank you for flying CIA," the pilot would languidly drawl as dazed passengers staggered to the exit.

The agency's unmarked L-100 turboprop cargo planes disgorged pallets of CIA food rations and water bottles and hulking steel shipping containers that were hardwired inside with special computers and communications gear. They even flew in a prefabricated SCIF, or sensitive compartmented information facility. It was the latest plug-and-play model. Once installed behind a thicket of razor wire, the CIA computer jocks crammed elbow to elbow inside could safely transmit information considered so sensitive that even its classification level, far above Top Secret, was secret.

The CIA also airlifted in a fleet of bicycles so staff spooks could pedal down the dusty runways and access roads for exercise. The U.S. intelligence budget is classified, but presumably somewhere in the estimated $45 billion that Washington spent that year on spying on its friends and enemies—far more than Germany, say, allocated for its entire national defense—was a line item for ten-speeds.

The Pentagon barred U.S. troops from consuming alcohol in Iraq. So the HVT Bar was strictly off-limits to the soldiers and

Marines moving up to the Baghdad airport and the archipelago of bases and camps sprouting nearby. The ban even extended to military personnel from the Defense Intelligence Agency, or DIA, and other Pentagon-based agencies that vastly outspend and outnumber the CIA in the U.S. intelligence community.

No one at the CIA complained, of course. Most agency operatives mocked the DIA as rank amateurs and wannabe spies, able to shoot and salute but not think. The rivalry between the two spy services was legendary. A few Special Forces teams and the odd Ranger sometimes bellied up to the bar but that was fine. Like most things in the CIA, if you got in the door, normal rules didn't apply. After all, spies were trained to lie, cheat, and steal.

The HVT Bar rarely opened before 11 p.m. But several dozen hard-working spooks usually packed the after-hours saloon: case officers, weapons analysts, code breakers, safe-crackers, linguists, British and Australian operatives, and of course, the CIA's covert ops teams. Known as Secret Squirrels, they had roared around Iraq in pickup trucks before and during the invasion, scouting targets, causing havoc, and having a swell time.

According to "rumint," or rumors intelligence, more than one affair caught fire in the gloom at the HVT (far more salacious rumint focused on a senior CIA official spotted in flagrante delicto in the executive garage back home; it was the talk of the agency). Most HVT regulars simply let off steam around a foosball table, liberated from somewhere in Baghdad, which appeared one night in the back room. It proved so exhilarating that a loaded foosball fan fired his loaded Glock pistol in the excitement, puncturing the wall and nearly another player. After that, the CIA station chief cracked down and ordered HVT patrons to check weapons at the door.

Contract security guys known as knuckle-draggers served as volunteer bartenders. Many were retired former field operatives who earned their chops and their pensions in the squalid streets of Somalia or Kosovo or a hundred other places. Some had even survived the cutthroat corridors of CIA headquarters back in Langley, Virginia. The agency had surged for the war in Iraq—alarms clanged battle stations, all hands on deck—and veteran troopers heeded the call. A CIA bar was an honored ritual in the agency's cultish lore, a trophy in every war. In Afghanistan, after CIA paramilitary forces helped oust the Taliban, the new Kabul station proudly partied at "The Talibar."

The HVT stood for High Value Target, the video game euphemism that U.S. authorities bestowed on those they most sought to capture or kill. In time, one could even buy a souvenir T-shirt at the bar. It read HVT BAR in bold black letters on the front and showed Saddam and three of his top aides, their grizzled faces fanned out as four aces, on the back. Pentagon wags had listed the fifty-two most wanted Iraqis like cards in a deck. But the joke quickly lost its punch. Most of the key cards, including Saddam, the Ace of Spades, still roamed at large.

By early summer, hundreds of American, British, and Australian intelligence officers were swarming into Baghdad. The majority set up shop at Camp Slayer, a bizarre sprawl of Arabian Nights palaces and Hieronymus Bosch bunkers across the airport from the CIA station. It was a wondrous place. Intelligence teams moved into marble guest-houses, lakeside cabanas, and a fabulous former whorehouse. They hauled in plush carpets, garish paintings, and gilded thrones, plundered from the dictator's former digs. Most of the hooches had no electricity, air-conditioning, or running water, and a creepy colony of bats blackened the sky at dusk. But early post-Saddam Iraq felt like a carnival, and it was grand.

Some of the Secret Squirrels took over a cave complex at Slayer. From afar, it looked like Tora Bora in the desert. Craggy rocks and deep ravines climbed the side of a short, steep hill. But like so much in Iraq, it was all illusion. It was a children's playground, a mini-mountain redoubt of poured concrete over a metal frame, like a Hollywood film set. The team loved living like the Flintstones. They camped in the fake rock rooms and wriggled down child-sized tunnels and slides. They scrawled "Yabba Dabba Do!" graffiti on the ersatz boulders and hung a sign on the concertina wire out front: "Welcome to Bedrock."

Later, that first summer in Iraq would seem almost a time of innocence. No one in U.S. intelligence yet realized they were in the eye of the storm, the calm between the fast fury of the spring invasion and the ferocious insurgency that would explode in the fall. Americans still were welcomed in Iraq. CIA officers could do anything, talk to anyone, drive anywhere. And the first priority was clear.

The CIA had issued fierce warnings before the war: Saddam's regime was churning out poison gases and lethal germs, and was racing to build a nuclear bomb. President George W. Bush had launched the war to rid the world of Iraq's weapons of mass destruction. But postwar searches found no such arms, no such threat. And week by week, as

CIA-led weapons hunters based at Slayer dashed back and forth across the baking desert, the doubts and disappointments grew more palpable. Few believed all the prewar warnings were 100 percent accurate; intelligence rarely was. But inside the smoky HVT Bar, in beach chairs along the lakeside, even back in the cubicles at Langley, some CIA officers quietly began voicing darker suspicions. How much of the intelligence was wrong?

Then, a triumph. U.S. forces in northern Iraq recovered two truck trailers loaded with laboratory equipment. CIA and DIA experts crawled all over them, testing, probing, and measuring every pipe and puddle. Their conclusion: the mobile labs were designed to cook up a witch's brew of pestilential germs. At the end of May, President Bush claimed the trailers provided vindication for his war. "We found the weapons of mass destruction," he crowed with evident relief.

But that claim crumbled into the sand as well. By early fall, as one inquiry after another fell short, as the once impregnable intelligence that led to war proved as false as a desert mirage, the weapons detectives increasingly focused on a young, fancy-struck Iraqi engineer. His role had been hidden before the war. But nearly all the intelligence now seemed to hang on him. One very peculiar man, it appeared, held the key to Saddam's missing arsenals of WMD and America's ill-conceived war in Iraq. And the secret CIA world would never be the same.

MUNICH
1999-2001

CHAPTER 1

Staring out the window, Ahmed Hassan Mohammed could see little of his new home.

In the spring or summer, arriving passengers at Munich's Franz Josef Strauss International Airport normally glimpse the rugged foothills of the Bavarian Alps jutting above the horizon. The distant mountains gleam softly in the morning light, and shimmer in the rich pastels of the setting sun.

But in November 1999, when Ahmed's plane landed, gray mist usually veiled the view. On most days, heavy clouds swirled across the leaden sky. Rain pelted down from passing squalls and driving storms. Sharp gusts skittered across the runway puddles and flattened the nearby grass. Droplets streamed down the windows like tears.

Ahmed's plane flew from North Africa, and the stale air in the cabin would smell of sweet anise and cheap cologne. Foreign workers heading home traveled heavy and happy. They forgot their dismal jobs and cramped flats. They shrugged off the suspicious eyes and sudden silences in German shops. Their bags betrayed their new riches. They hauled television sets and fancy stereos. They dragged cheap suitcases, cardboard boxes wrapped with rope, and plastic sacks full of duty-free cigarettes. But the return flights, like this one, from the desert villages and urban slums of Algeria, Tunisia, and Morocco, seemed sadder. The men brought back stuffed dates and preserved lemons, kif candy and almond cookies. They suffused the plane with the scent of regret and wrenching farewells.

The airplane aisle filled quickly as passengers climbed out of their seats and yanked overstuffed bags down from overhead bins. They pulled on worn leather coats and thick ski parkas. They pushed their tired children and each other toward the exit door and shuffled down the metal stairs. Ahmed followed.

Airport workers in neon yellow slickers scurried near the plane. Utility vehicles painted cautionary orange chugged and hauled silver containers bulging with bags. Boxy white Sky Chefs delivery trucks disgorged supplies or took others on. Airport vans, all the same olive green, rushed in one direction and then back again. Ahmed couldn't help but notice. Germany was so orderly. So color-coordinated. So different from the cacophony of life back home. An elongated blue bus, the two parts joined by a black rubber accordion neck, pulled up beside the plane. On the side, black letters read "Flughafen München." Munich Airport.

He boarded the bus to the terminal for international arrivals and was swept along as the throng pushed inside. White acoustic tiles and the drone of hidden machinery suddenly muffled the crowd's chatter. He stepped on a moving sidewalk that glided silently past glittering ads for gold watches, sleek cars, and high-priced appliances. Gorgeous women, tall and young, beckoned to him from the posters. The light was blindingly bright.

The long hall emptied into a smaller area, where other passengers already were shuffling into lines in front of four booths. A large sign on top read, *Passkontrolle—Alle Pässe*. Ahmed didn't speak German, but a translation was posted underneath in English and he could read and write enough of that. *Passport Control—All Passports*. Each booth featured a large glass window at eye level, but the lower portion was frosted white so someone waiting in line or even standing a foot away could only see the face and chest of the federal border police officer sitting inside. The officer wore a starched, military-style khaki shirt and a white plastic ID card in a red border hung from the right pocket. Small stars embroidered his shoulder boards. A patch on the left shoulder read "Polizei."

The long line moved slowly, but the traveler was patient. He knew how to wait in submissive silence for hard-eyed men in military uniforms. Finally his turn came. He steeled himself and stepped up to the window. The officer inside could extend his right arm and his open palm would appear in a small, semicircular opening. Ahmed handed his dark brown passport to the pink fingers that suddenly poked out.

The document was from Iraq, issued in Baghdad. Leafing through the stiff pages, the officer could see several large, colorful visas, plus the usual entry and exit stamps. Small countries invariably issue the biggest, most florid visas, perhaps to compensate for their insignificance. These showed he had visited Turkey and, more recently, Jordan, Cyprus, Morocco, and Spain, traveling for about six months. His passport held no visa for Germany.

Just outside each booth, a rectangular mirror hung on a metal arm from the ceiling. It was positioned so the border officer could tilt his head and peer up to his right, and get a clear view of the applicant waiting in front of him. This one didn't stand out.

He was a good-looking man, solidly built, of olive complexion and medium height. He looked in his late twenties, perhaps a little older. He had jet black hair, parted on the left, and a thick shock draped low on his forehead. His eyes were large and heavy-lidded, pensive and brooding, set far apart. A broad, hawkish nose sat over full lips and a strong chin. A full mustache curled around the corners of his mouth like a sneer. It seemed notable only because most Iraqi men raised shaggy brush mustaches to mimic Saddam. Perhaps he was cold, or tense, but the traveler seemed to tremble. Later, German intelligence authorities would say he often quivered with nervous energy.

The border officer studied the document and then looked up at the Iraqi. Ahmed would have stared back. He usually held people in a frank gaze, tilting his head just so. It conjured an impression of serious endeavor. If he flashed a shy smile, as he often did, the officer would have noticed teeth stained with tobacco tar. Ahmed didn't just smoke. He embraced the habit, almost tenderly. He carefully cupped his lighter with his slender fingers, as if facing a vigorous wind. Then he flicked the blue flame alive, closed his dark eyes, and leaned back, letting the smoke wreathe up to caress his face.

No record was kept of their conversation, but it would be brief and to the point.

Where is your visa? The border officer spoke in English. Few Iraqis knew decent German.

Please, I want political asylum. He replied in slow, thickly accented English. Few Germans spoke any Arabic.

The officer was not, as one might think, surprised. Germany was the travel hub of modern Europe and its economy was booming. Every day—every hour—refugees showed up from one hellhole or another and appealed for safe haven from war, famine, ethnic persecution, and political oppression. Nearly half of all refugees who applied for asylum in the promised lands of Western Europe filed their claims in Germany.

Immigration records showed 7,476 people sought asylum in Germany the month Ahmed arrived. A total of 95,113 flooded in that year.

Most fled the vicious civil war in the Balkans, then rupturing along ethnic fault lines. But southern Germany also was refuge of choice for Iraqis on the run. Thousands flowed in each year, wave upon wave of businessmen, engineers, scientists, and soldiers, all fleeing Saddam's tyranny. More than sixty thousand Iraqi refugees and émigrés lived in Germany, and at least half of them clustered around the cities of Munich, Nuremberg, and Augsburg in the southern state of Bavaria.

They had good reason to come. Germany provided greater benefits to refugees than nearly any other nation in Europe. It was especially tolerant and benevolent to those seeking sanctuary from the misery of Iraq. Saddam's secret police picked up and tortured people at whim, or shot them in front of their homes and hung the bodies from lampposts. The U.N. had imposed strict military and economic sanctions, and guilt-stricken postwar Germany wasn't going to forcibly repatriate anyone to one of the most repressive regimes on the planet.

The border officer pressed a button on his desk, and another man in a starched khaki shirt appeared and escorted the traveler across the hall to a small office with a desk. Ahmed sat down on a hard metal chair, and an Arabic translator soon arrived so the German officer could ask a series of questions and take down the answers. German officials later would describe the story that Ahmed blurted out in a smoker's voice, thick and gravelly.

I am from Baghdad, northeast Baghdad. I live with my mother and father. I am a chemical engineer. I attended the University of Baghdad. I worked at the government Chemical Engineering and Design Center. I worked in a program to help Iraqi farmers. We improved their seeds.

Yes, I am married. No, she is still in Baghdad. Ahmed Hassan Mohammed is a false name. I used this passport to escape Iraq. I cannot go back. I am against Saddam. They know this. I had serious problems with the authorities. If I go back, they will put me in prison and torture or kill me.

The lengthy interview and paperwork took several hours but the translator finally wrote out careful instructions and helped Ahmed buy the necessary bus and train tickets at a kiosk just outside the customs hall so he wouldn't get lost. Clutching the slips of paper and his bag, he walked purposefully through the huge airport to reach the bus stand outside.

He boarded the local bus to the town of Friesing, about twenty minutes away past dark russet fields lined by thick hedgerows. He got out at the town center and entered a small Tyrolean train station with carved wooden benches and a red-gabled roof, like a model for a toy train set. He descended into a small tunnel under the tracks, and climbed back up into the biting wind on Platform 4. A red suburban train soon roared up and when the door slid open, he entered the second-class compartment and found a seat. The doors whooshed to a close, and the train roared away again on the two-hour journey to Nuremberg.

From the train, Ahmed could see rolling hills, ice-flecked rivers, and desolate winter fields of rapeseed and flax. The view was surprisingly rural. Horses grazed in small paddocks, stamping their feet and snorting steam in the cold air. Every so often, the train entered a deep forest glen, and the light grew dim and mossy under broad chestnuts and oaks, or stately stands of fir and spruce. Back in the open, tall cable pylons counted off in strict cadence for a few miles beside the tracks before they pivoted away into a side valley. A power plant cooling tower, shaped like an hourglass, puffed in the distance. Further along, low-lying fog shrouded an entire field or a farmhouse. But the mist soon freed other pastures and outbuildings, ghostly and drained of color.

The villages along the tracks all seemed alike: spotless streets lined by tidy stucco houses under steep roofs of rust red tiles. Soon small towns and then cities appeared, with glass-fronted offices and department stores along busy shopping districts. Burly men in green loden coats hunched against the chill. Stylish women hurried down the cobblestone street, faces red and raw in the wind, pulling children with mittens. Teens conspired and smoked in doorways. Mostly, however, Ahmed saw turrets and spires poking into the pewter sky. They were medieval church towers, neo-Baroque clock towers, and ornate bell towers. He was used to the simple, unadorned minarets of the mosques back home, where the devout muezzin calls the faithful to prayer five times a day.

Ahmed was not especially faithful. Not about Islam. Not to his native country. Certainly not to the long-suffering wife he had abandoned back in Baghdad. Faith was a luxury in his life. Life under Saddam was too fragile and too dangerous for such naive virtues. Iraqis made painful moral compromises every day to survive. But that was the past.

Ahmed intended to start a new life in Germany. He was certain of that. He would find a huge house and buy a gleaming Mercedes sedan with buttery soft leather seats. As an engineer, he liked huge cars and machines, the bigger the better. He would find work as a high-paid chemical engineer in a color-coordinated factory. Go to beer halls. Learn German.

The last leg of Ahmed's journey was not far, perhaps twenty minutes or so by bus from the Nuremberg train station to the western suburb of Zirndorf. But the scenery shifted dramatically. Zirndorf perched on the upper lip of a wide valley. Down below he could see factories and industrial yards stretching into the winter haze. A bitter wind whipped up over the ridgeline, and scraps of paper and loose trash tumbled along the dirt verge. Auto garages and repair shops, smoky pilaf and kebab cafés, and shabby apartment blocks crowded the street.

Rounding a bend in the road, Ahmed finally approached his destination. The Zirndorf refugee center stood atop a small hill, stark and severe, protected by high walls and a metal gate. A police post guarded one side of the driveway. Across from it, a two-story building stood behind a chain link fence topped by barbed wire. A tarnished brass sign identified it as the Hauptstelle für Befragundswegen, or the Main Office for Questioning. It meant nothing to him.

He walked up the driveway to a small guardhouse beside the gate and slid his passport and airport documents through a slot under the window. After a few moments, the sentry returned his papers and signaled for him to pass. He pressed a button and the gate clicked open. Ahmed gratefully pushed through a turnstile enclosed in a steel cage. It was clear no one could come or go from Zirndorf, as the refugee center was known, without permission.

Inside the courtyard, he could see three imposing barracks aligned in soldierly rows. They looked as inviting as penal blocks. Off on the left, a small Catholic church appeared abandoned and forlorn. Few people used the old church anymore. Most recent refugees were Muslims but the center had no mosque. Across from the church, a gaudy Bavarian clock tower overlooked the compound from atop the administration building. But both hands were missing from the face, as if time no longer mattered.

Ahmed walked to the administration building and pushed the metal door open. The walls were moldering yellow plaster and the halls reeked of curry and sweat, of too many people in too small a place. But the German staff seemed efficient. After checking his papers, they took his picture and issued him a color photo ID in a plastic sleeve. They led him to a supply room and gave him a bar of soap, a toothbrush, and other toiletries. They furnished him coarse sheets, a small pillow, and a thin blue blanket. They brought him to another room stuffed with donated clothes, and let him choose a warmer coat, boots, and anything else for the winter.

They showed him the small coffee shop, where strict rules against fighting, alcohol, and other infractions were posted in eight languages above a black stand-up piano. It was battered, and badly out of tune, apparently the victim of a rule breach or two. A refugee had painted a mural on the wall of smiling African women in bright wraparound dresses, with rich head-ties of stiff brocade, a colorful reminder of another world, another time. An old TV blared loudly in the corner, and the multi-language warning tacked to the front was mangled if clear in English: *Don't Tuch It!*

The staff assigned Ahmed a bed upstairs with other single men. He climbed the broad stone staircase and looked in. His room contained six bunk beds, three on each side wall. A small metal table sat between them. Graffiti scarred the walls, the only decoration. A yellow bulb hanging from the ceiling reflected dully on the door, and it took a moment to realize it was heavy galvanized metal, several inches thick, secured with reinforced locks.

Zirndorf had five hundred beds for refugees and one cafeteria, back down on the first floor. Years ago, mobs of hungry men fought to squeeze through the single narrow door that led to the dining hall. To ease the crush, authorities installed floor-to-ceiling steel bars and chicken mesh to funnel diners into single-file lines. The angry crowds thinned out over time but the barred pens and coops remained. Zirndorf looked more like a prison than a place of refuge.

The Nazis built Zirndorf early in World War II to house motorized military police, and the nearly two-foot-thick stone walls somehow survived the British and American air raids that obliterated most of Nuremberg. After the war, Zirndorf lay deep in the American occupation zone. U.S. authorities turned it into an interrogation center and holding camp—the largest in the country—for Soviet bloc defectors and refugees. As the Cold War raged on, decade after decade, tens of thousands of East Germans, Hungarians, Poles, Czechs and other asylum seekers passed through the dismal compound as authorities weighed their words and their fates.

After the Berlin Wall fell in 1989, Zirndorf became a focal point for the flood of hope released by the collapse of communism. Refugees poured in as borders and regulations fell across Eastern Europe. When those rivers began to ebb, other streams suddenly swelled. In the mid-1990s, the aging barracks overflowed with families fleeing the bloodletting in the Balkans. Mostly men came, but some brought fearful women clutching wide-eyed children, and they jostled for room with runaways from Algeria, Belarus, Congo, Eritrea, Iran, Iraq, Libya, Mongolia, Sudan, and almost everywhere else. The dispossessed of the world, it seemed, passed through Zirndorf.

The administrators tried to keep abreast of headlines since each new civil war or blast of ethnic cleansing sent another wave crashing their way. But they also kept a weather eye on older animosities. So they assigned Iraqis separate rooms from Iranians, their traditional enemies. They housed Serbs apart from Croats, and kept Muslims who only ate halal foods separate from pork eaters. After several racial altercations, they learned to separate Russians from Africans. And they isolated the Gypsies, known as Roma, from everyone.

Newcomers got free medical care and a small stipend, just cigarette money, really. They could take classes to study local food and culture, or study introductory German: *Guten Morgen. Willkommen in Zirndorf!* The computer-literate could work on a couple of aging desktops. Ahmed had heard of e-mail and Internet Web sites, of course, and now he could try them firsthand. His physical freedom was sharply restricted, however. He could walk to nearby parks or cafés. But strict rules barred refugees from going into Nuremberg or anywhere else unless they obtained a special written pass.

More important, Ahmed and the others could only stay at Zirndorf for ninety days. Each month, authorities hauled hundreds of refugees to grim government-run group homes and barracks, especially in the harsh factory towns of the former East Germany, to await word of their asylum applications. A year or three might disappear in paperwork, interviews, and hearings. If the authorities ultimately granted political asylum, if they determined the applicant had a well-founded fear of persecution, they issued a small three-page residence permit. It permitted the bearer to find work, travel outside the country, and stay indefinitely in Germany. After five years, he could apply for citizenship.

But German immigration officials granted asylum, on average, to only one in twenty-five applicants. They rejected nearly all the rest as economic migrants who simply sought a better life in the West. Such ambition was understandable. It was even laudable. But it wasn't permitted. So rejected applicants appealed to higher courts. Five years would pass, maybe seven. In many cases, courts finally ordered them to leave the country or face deportation. But most refugees found ways to prolong their appeals. And German immigration authorities tended to be tolerant, rarely forcing them out.

As a result, several hundred thousand refugees lived in legal limbo. Some stayed in the bleak halfway houses and depressing dormitories. Others submerged deeper into the shadows, struggling to survive in the margins. Laws sharply limited how and where they could work.

The Federal Employment Ministry acknowledged their plight the month Ahmed arrived. "In the future," the ministry announced, "asylum seekers and recognized refugees will be able to submit applications for work permits after two years instead of four to six years." Even then, they were permitted to work only if no German or another citizen of the European Union had applied for the job. It usually meant menial labor at minimum wage or less. Refugees worked at McDonald's and Burger King, or scrubbed lavatories and scraped gum as airport cleaning crews. Some sold flowers in bars at night, going table to table with plaintive looks and wilted bouquets.

For Iraqis on the run, the route to Zirndorf was more a maze than a pipeline. Most spent weeks or months en route, escaping to Turkey or Jordan and then slipping across porous borders in Eastern Europe with the help of human smugglers. No matter how they came, however, most Iraqis insisted that they simply climbed into the back of a closed truck and were driven straight to Germany and never knew the route. That way, they couldn't be pushed back to the last country they had transited. Nearly every Iraqi asylum seeker shared that one constant. They lied to immigration and intelligence authorities about their travels. "We hear all kinds of stories," explained Robert Dirrigl, the deputy director of Zirndorf. "Most of them are not true."

After their initial processing, Iraqis were usually ordered to appear at the fenced-off building back down the driveway. The main office for questioning housed a special team from the Bundesnachrichtendienst, the Federal Intelligence Service. The BND, as it was known, was Germany's primary spy service.

BND officials knew that Germany's generosity to Iraqis was much admired in the Arab world. Enterprising Egyptians, Palestinians, and others often posed as exiles from Saddam's regime in hopes of gaining quick asylum. So the intelligence officers first sought to ensure the applicant was not a pretender. They had a checklist of questions.

What is the color of the Iraqi dinar? Describe the coins.

You say you are from Diwaniya. What is the distance from there to Najaf? How far is it to Baghdad? What road do you take? How long does it take?

Once satisfied that the applicant was indeed an Iraqi, they pulled out more relevant queries.

What was your job? Were you a member of the Ba'ath Party?

Did you serve in the army? Where did you serve? Who were your officers? Did you work for the government? What was your role?

It usually proved a futile exercise. Many Iraqis could describe the inside of a jail cell or torture chamber. But few knew useful intelligence about Saddam's regime. In the vast majority of cases, the interviewers said thanks and sent the asylum seeker back up the driveway to resume his long wait.

The BND provided a far warmer welcome to the rare refugee who offered solid intelligence about Saddam's inner circle or his security apparatus. Even more prized were those few who brought credible eyewitness details about Iraq's efforts to build illegal weapons of mass destruction. Those refugees were escorted to the front of the asylum line at Zirndorf and given red-carpet treatment.

"If they had good information, the Germans gave them a fabulous package," said a U.S. intelligence official who worked in Germany at the time. "They got a stipend, a house, a job. Germany was the best in Europe. Not only was it the best program, but there was a huge Iraqi population around Munich. Everybody knew about it back in Baghdad."

Bitter cold gripped Zirndorf by the time a visiting BND team scheduled an interview with Ahmed. It was nearly Christmas 1999 about six weeks after he had arrived. Someone finally had reviewed the Iraqi's paperwork and noticed that he was a chemical engineer who worked for a military commission in Baghdad.

"We said, 'Okay, let's talk to this guy,'" a BND supervisor later recalled. "We were trolling for sources. And we fished him out of the net." No one foresaw a special prize. Saddam largely had faded from the headlines in late 1999. "Iraq was not a prime target for us."

But Ahmed obviously was primed for them. He told the BND officers that he was miserable in the ghastly confines of Zirndorf. He recoiled at the prisonlike bars, the clanging metal doors, and the strict rules about coming and going. He dreaded the notion of winding up in a flophouse and flipping bratwurst or cleaning toilets for the rest of his life. It wasn't the freedom he expected, the bold new life he had planned for so long.

Thanks to misinformation in the refugee rumor mill, Ahmed feared that the Germans might deport him back to Iraq. Even if he didn't get thrown out, he knew he might wait years for asylum, especially after a Zirndorf official told him "the end of the line is over there" behind all the other friendless refugees clogging the system. Most important, Ahmed had learned that he could shorten the wait if he gave the Germans the information they sought.

The room was small and stuffy when Ahmed finally sat across a table from the BND team at the federal questioning center. But he motioned them closer to take them into his confidence. He wanted to share a secret. He would enlighten them about his vital job back in Baghdad, he said. He was ready to trade his valuable information for his fantastic asylum package. He was all set for his munificent stipend, fancy manor house, and silver Mercedes. He would happily assist his new German friends, he vowed.

He began to tell them of Saddam's secret program to churn out what BND reports later memorably would describe as *Biowaffen*.

In English, it meant germ weapons.

CHAPTER 2

Ahmed knew nothing about the BND. Few outsiders did.

It had emerged from the Nazi horrors of World War II. Maj. Gen. Reinhard Gehlen was one of Hitler's top spymasters, responsible for subversion and sabotage against the Soviet Union. But disaster loomed in early 1945. American and British armies were racing the Red Army toward the final battle in Berlin. So Gehlen prepared to switch sides.

He ordered his top deputies to hide their intelligence files in the Bavarian Alps. The men shed their Nazi uniforms, hid in a cluster of mountain chalets, and waited out the war. That May, with most of the Third Reich in flames or in ruins, Gehlen and his aides surrendered to U.S. troops and handed over their archives. In exchange for their secrets, he and five aides were put on a plane to America. They underwent a year of comfortable debriefings at Fort Hunt, Virginia, and visited the Grand Canyon as Gehlen's former colleagues in the German high command were being hanged at Nuremberg.

By then, Washington was struggling against a new enemy. The newly created CIA, America's first peacetime spy service, scrambled for intelligence against the Soviets. Gehlen insisted his old Nazi network could help. He was flown back to Germany, and his American-sponsored group soon claimed to run thousands of spies behind the Iron Curtain. Gehlen took over a twenty-five-acre estate with bronze statue gardens, a swimming pool, and elegant villas in the small town of Pullach, just southeast of Munich, as his headquarters. Martin Bormann, Hitler's chief deputy, originally had designed the housing compound for members of the Nazi elite. That seemed fitting. Gehlen's spy service had become a ratline for Nazi commanders. More than one hundred SS and Gestapo officers won release from internment camps to join him. They included at least five associates of Adolf Eichmann, who directed the mass murder of European Jews.

The CIA's unsavory partnership with former Nazi officials carried a heavy cost. The Soviets and their supporters portrayed Europe's anti-communist movements as Nazi successors. Even worse, Soviet spies riddled every level of the Gehlen organization. Scores of sensitive operations and hundreds of legitimate spies were betrayed or killed.

The scandals worsened after the CIA relinquished control to the newly sovereign West German Federal Republic in 1956. Heinz Felfe, a former Nazi SS officer, was chief of counterespionage for the BND, the new name for Gehlen's group. He enjoyed almost unlimited access to U.S. military and intelligence operations in Western Europe. But he also served as one of Moscow's most important spies.

After West German authorities arrested Felfe in 1961, a then secret CIA damage assessment called him "the most knowledgeable of all BND officials on CIA operations against the Soviet targets in East and West Germany." Losses were "of the broadest scope." Felfe caused most U.S. eavesdropping operations against the Soviets to end in "complete failure or a worthless product." He compromised "all major" spying operations and betrayed "a majority" of American field agents and spies in East Germany, including over one hundred CIA staff officers.

But Germany was still the front line in the Cold War. Unforgiving forces of faith and betrayal, of light and darkness, struggled for supremacy in the shadows. Both sides poured spies into the battle. An estimated 25,000 men and women worked for the CIA and Pentagon-funded intelligence services in Germany. Secret postwar protocols governing intelligence activities gave the CIA, in particular, almost unlimited legal authority.

"I was just a kid but we could do almost anything," recalled Milt Bearden, who first arrived in Bonn in 1965 as a newly minted CIA case officer. "We were given a little book that basically said in English, French, and German, 'Leave him alone. He's a spy. If you have any questions, call this number.' We called it our 'Murder, Rape, and Get Out of Jail Free card.'"

If the CIA could do anything, the BND couldn't catch a break. The discovery of an East German spy at the top levels of government forced popular West German chancellor Willy Brandt to resign in scandal in 1974. His successor, Helmut Schmidt, publicly belittled the BND as "a band of dilettantes" and complained that the national spy service "only reported what he had already read in the newspaper." Franz Josef Strauss, then minister president of Bavaria, memorably dismissed another BND scandal involving a secretary who sold 1,700 classified reports to the KGB, the Soviet foreign intelligence service. "Ninety percent of what the intelligence agencies report is rubbish anyway," he said.

If anything, CIA officials held a lower opinion. They maligned German intelligence as unreliable and untrustworthy. As far as CIA officials were concerned, moles and traitors lined the BND halls at Pullach. "We wouldn't do a joint operation with the Germans against the KGB," recalled a senior CIA operations official. "You might as well just run it directly with the KGB. You're giving it to them anyway." He refused even to read German intelligence reports, figuring they were filled with misinformation.

Tensions boiled over in the mid-1980s. BND officials chose a politically connected operative as their resident agent in Washington, their most prestigious overseas post. He was handsome and debonair and carried himself with aristocratic bearing. CIA officials were unimpressed. They viewed Juergens, the BND cover name for the German spy, as uncooperative and unsympathetic to American needs.

One night Juergens was arrested in the men's room of a gay bar in Washington. Supposedly he was drunk and passed out. He was accredited as a diplomat so the State Department and FBI counterintelligence got called in. CIA officials warned their BND counterparts that Juergens could be blackmailed as a homosexual if the scandal leaked to the press. The Germans got the hint and recalled him to run a subdepartment in Pullach. He had followed his father and grandfather into German intelligence, and colleagues respected him. He had served bravely in Tehran during the 1979 Islamic revolution, when American hostages were seized, and later worked with the CIA against the Soviet army in Afghanistan. His BND friends were outraged at what they considered a CIA dirty trick.

"They were convinced the CIA got him a lot of whiskey until he passed out and then carried him to a gay bar," said Erich Schmidt-Eenboom, a former German military intelligence officer and author of several books on the BND. "They didn't believe that he was homosexual because he used to sleep with all his female secretaries in every office he worked. He was notorious for it. So all the senior people in Pullach were convinced he was set up. They saw it as what happens to German station chiefs who are not friendly to Americans."

The collapse of East Germany, ironically, only reinforced the distrust. Soviet bloc spies had completely penetrated the upper echelons of West German intelligence. The damage became clear when Gabriele Gast, the top BND analyst for the Soviet Union and Eastern Europe, was arrested. Gast had prepared the daily intelligence briefing for Chancellor Helmut Kohl. But she secretly shared the gleanings with Markus Wolf, the notorious East German spymaster. Gast handed Wolf everything from NATO military deployments to White House plans for summits with Soviet leaders. Communist agents bugged every phone line in Kohl's offices and even the pay phones outside. U.S. intelligence officials were flabbergasted as they surveyed the wreckage. Gast's treachery, one official said, was "like having Santa Claus on the payroll of the Kremlin."

Bearden returned to Germany as CIA chief of station in 1992. The Cold War was over, the Soviets vanquished. U.S. military and intelligence bases were closing or shrinking in Germany. The CIA quietly shifted its station from Bonn to newly reunified Berlin and tried to adjust to the uncertain new world. But one thing did not change—the perks.

"The chief of station got the best residence in Dahlem," one of Berlin's most exclusive and expensive suburbs, Bearden recalled wistfully. "The Germans had to provide cut flowers and firewood for all the fireplaces, and Rosenthal china and crystal for the dining room. It was part of the postwar agreements."

The benefits wouldn't last. Resentment toward the CIA had been seething for years inside the BND. Now senior officers let loose with incendiary complaints. Analysts protested that arrogant CIA experts patronized and insulted them. Case officers ranted that their CIA counterparts stole their sources and sabotaged their operations. Berlin finally issued an ultimatum: the CIA and other U.S. services must end all unauthorized operations on German soil. No more Get Out of Jail Free cards or anything else.

The acrimony inevitably spilled into the public. In 1996, the president of the BND, Konrad Porzner, abruptly quit after complaining that Kohl's aides refused to discipline two officials who allegedly sold German intelligence files to American operatives for envelopes full of cash. The following year, the Germans booted out a CIA case officer who had tried to recruit a German government expert on Iran. That hit the press. So did a 1999 report that U.S. operatives had bugged the German embassy in Washington. Soon after, German authorities expelled four more CIA case officers. They had tried to recruit a German officer in Munich who supposedly could help them penetrate a terror network. The CIA team made two critical mistakes. They didn't notice that German agents tracked their every move. And they tried to force the target to take a lie detector test.

A polygraph measures physical signs of anxiety—elevated blood pressure, heart rate, breathing, and perspiration—that may accompany deceptive behavior. The science is extremely dubious. Most U.S. courts disallow the results, and German law bars polygraph tests outright. Germans consider forcibly strapping people to wires and interpreting the chicken scratches on paper a reminder of the barbaric "science" the Nazis used to practice.

"It was a harebrained scheme, and it embarrassed a lot of people," a CIA official said of the botched recruitment. "We reaped the whirlwind of all the bad blood with the BND. The old guys remembered how poorly we had treated them. And the younger ones heard of it."

Another dispute became far more public and far more emotional.

In the early 1990s, a resourceful CIA operative secretly snatched up nearly the entire archives of the Stasi, East Germany's foreign espionage service. Operation Rosewood, as the action was called, was an intelligence coup, not least because the CIA officer supposedly paid only $1.5 million, a steal, to a former KGB officer. The computer discs identified thousands of Stasi agents and collaborators in West German politics, business, labor unions, and media. A master list named Stasi spies, informants, and surveillance targets elsewhere around the globe, including the United States. The files also pointed to spies at U.S. military installations in Europe, and the U.S. embassy in Bonn.

German authorities demanded return of the trove, or at least a copy. George Tenet adamantly refused after he was named director of central intelligence in 1997, giving him command of the CIA and responsibility for all U.S. intelligence. But the CIA allowed a BND officer to review some of the material at Langley. He notified Pullach that the CIA had begun to blackmail Germans into spying for America by threatening to expose their Stasi past. CIA officials staunchly defended their actions when the dispute leaked to the press. Disclosure of the Rosewood files would jeopardize lives of CIA officers and their agents, they warned, and would scuttle sensitive intelligence operations.

German editorial writers fulminated and elected politicians accused Washington of protecting the former East German police state just as the CIA once embraced Nazi war criminals. The German government demanded access to the Stasi files to document decades of organized terror and to help reconcile the divided and still suspicious nation.

The CIA continued to refuse. In early 1999, the new German chancellor, Gerhard Schroeder, accepted an invitation to the White House to meet President Bill Clinton. The election of the former Marxist firebrand, onetime chairman of the far-left Young Socialists, now leader of the Social Democrats, had ended the era of compliant postwar German governments that tamely followed America's lead.

Schroeder let it be known that he intended to return home with a deal for access to the Stasi files. He sent his chief of staff to Washington to make the final arrangements. But Schroeder's deputy ran smack into what he later called a barrier of mutual distrust. At the CIA's insistence, White House officials refused to even discuss the matter.

Schroeder, aides told reporters, was "outraged" by the refusal to surrender files that Germany considered its rightful property. The impasse, they said, threatened to undermine cooperation with the CIA on other intelligence issues. They publicly warned "that the time may be coming to curtail operations of U.S. intelligence agencies in Germany."

The Rosewood clash deepened the fault lines between the CIA and the BND. "There was visceral, mutual antagonism," a senior CIA official said. "The BND doesn't like the CIA and vice versa," agreed a senior German intelligence officer. "There is an adversarial relationship. Neither side trusts the other."

The abysmal relations had not improved eight months later when Ahmed arrived in Munich.

CHAPTER 3

The chief of the BND team who first interviewed Ahmed at Zirndorf had expected another tedious session with another dreary Iraqi. Instead, he filed an urgent report back to Pullach.

The BND headquarters had changed considerably from the early days. Gehlen's regal mansion and lush lily ponds had given way to a warren of low-slung offices with white cantilevered roofs and covered walkways. The drab industrial design had all the charm of a lackluster community college.

Officials at Pullach passed a copy of the Zirndorf report to a little-known BND office on Neumannsgasse 2 in central Berlin. The secluded side street ended at a broad canal that fed the River Spree. The lack of normal traffic focused attention on those few people who approached the heavy door halfway down on the left. Armed guards stood just inside behind a bulletproof gate.

The Zirndorf report was rushed up to a large corner office occupied by a senior operations officer. Tall and elegant, with silver-tinged hair and a baritone voice, Werner Kappel wore well-tailored suits and gold-rimmed glasses. Kappel artfully called himself an intelligence bureaucrat, not a spy. In truth, he was an intellectual. He read German romantic poetry by Heinrich Heine and nineteenth-century philosophy and sociology. He especially liked to quote Max Weber's theories on rationalizing behavior. It helped ground him for the alternate realities of his day job. Truth, he would say, was a matter of perception. People hear what they want to hear.

Each day, Kappel sat at his polished desk and read "eyes only" and other classified reports from BND stations around the world, as well as the spy services of other governments. The early report on Ahmed from the Zirndorf team was marked for his special attention. He studied it carefully.

"If someone says, 'I am a general, or a physicist, or a member of Saddam's staff and I know about Saddam's weapons and had to leave Iraq,' then we are informed," he said later. "Most of these people are not of interest. But sometimes there are jewels."

Ahmed, he and his aides decided, was such a gem.

The BND was organized into directorates, each with a distinct role.

Directorate Five supervised counterintelligence. They vetted staff and battled to stop leaks and uncover double agents, the bane of the BND since the Gehlen era.

Directorate Four provided the lawyers, payroll clerks, logistics masters, and others who handled the administration of spying.

Directorate Two handled what it euphemistically called "technical procurement." Its operatives collected and analyzed signals intelligence, known as "sigint." They intercepted telephone calls and other communications, installed electronic bugs and wiretaps in foreign embassies and institutions, inserted special codes in computer software to read e-mails, and so on.

Directorate Three held the largest staff and was the pride of the service. These were the subject experts and analysts. They boasted an array of specialties, from American folk culture to nuclear engineering. They compiled information flowing in from spies to satellites, then evaluated its significance for policy makers. They also ran a twenty-four-hour situation center to monitor the crisis of the day under flickering TV and videoconferencing screens.

Far smaller in size and reputation was Directorate One. It handled "humint," or human intelligence. The office focused mostly on military issues and, since the scandals of the Cold War, did not emphasize recruiting and running foreign agents as spies. A hundred or so BND case officers operated overseas under diplomatic cover, usually as political officers stationed in German embassies. But a core group provided operational support at Pullach, and in early January 2000, shortly after the Zirndorf interview, they were given responsibility for handling Ahmed's case.

The chief of Directorate One chose the head of his counterproliferation division as Ahmed's case officer. He would help the edgy Iraqi adjust to his new life in a strange land and his new job as an informant for German intelligence.

The case officer stood straight-backed and tall, with bright sharp eyes and a thick black mustache. Already in his late fifties, he had spied for Germany across Africa in the 1980s and then returned to Pullach to focus on Soviet weapons programs near the end of the Cold War. He spoke several languages, including decent English, but no real Arabic. He was most fluent in the pitiless vernacular of spying: the necessary use of dishonest means—theft, lies, blackmail, and worse—to get at the truth.

Like everyone else at the BND, the newly assigned handler used an alias, called a work name, to shield his identity during clandestine operations. The BND issued him a separate cover name to use on written reports and cables, further cloaking his identity. Even at the BND, most people knew Ahmed's chief case officer only by his cover name, Schumann.

Schumann's special skill was persuading informants to talk. He leaned forward, nodding with sympathy, eyes fixed in sincerity, his whole body offering empathy. When it was his turn, he spoke gently and softly. He reassured people wracked by guilt and doubt. He coaxed them to trust him. He eased their insecurities and appealed to their vanity. Over time, he became their confessor, mentor and friend. And then, he calmly seduced his charges to commit treason against their native lands. He tutored them in treachery and betrayal. He didn't call it that, of course. But that was his job.

Soon after Schumann took over the case, he helped move Ahmed out of the drafty dormitory and gloomy detention of Zirndorf. The spy service usually installed new defectors in an inexpensive apartment or small hotel. The BND especially liked furnished flats near the busy universities and technical colleges that flourished in the suburbs around Nuremberg.

The city bustled with 400,000 native Germans and nearly ninety thousand foreigners, including thousands of Turks and Iraqis. Most of the city's medieval center was carefully rebuilt after the war, and tourists flocked through the thick stone gates and down the tight, winding streets. They caroused in crowded beer cellars, dark grottoes with vaulted ceilings and long wooden tables. They jammed shops selling plump sausages, tangy gingerbread, and handmade toys. The constant roil of nationalities and ethnic types, the crush of foreign tourists and students, the confusing Babel of languages, wove a curtain of anonymity. Strangers didn't stand out.

Schumann helped arrange for a special team of "babysitters" to keep an eye on Ahmed. Five to eight recently retired intelligence officers normally were hired under special contract to keep a new informant out of trouble, and cater to his needs, if not his whims. Few amenities were out of bounds.

"They say, 'Would you like to watch TV? What would you like for dinner? Would you like to go to a restaurant? Would you like a woman?' Most of the Arab defectors say, 'I want a big, fat blond woman.' And they usually get one. The BND provides the prostitute," said Erich Schmidt-Eenboom, the former German intelligence officer.

The agency maintained a small Nuremberg spy base to support local clandestine operations. But Schumann began to debrief Ahmed at a separate fortresslike facility on the city's outskirts that was infamous in international spying circles. It was called the Joint Interrogation Center.

During the Cold War, American, German, British, and French intelligence teams interrogated hundreds of high-level Soviet bloc defectors at the Nuremberg center. The Soviets, in turn, directed one of their most important American spies there. The head of the interrogation center, U.S. Army colonel George Trofimoff, delivered fifty thousand pages of highly classified documents to the Soviets over twenty-five years. In 2000, Trofimoff became the highest-ranking U.S. military officer ever to be convicted of espionage.

Trofimoff was an "agent in place," meaning he spied for years without arousing suspicion. But his kind of espionage is rare. Few people are willing to commit treason as a career. There's almost no real in-country recruiting in totalitarian countries. The CIA had no one in the inner circles at the Kremlin, in North Vietnam or in North Korea.

So intelligence services reach out to paid informants, and information brokers and foreign spy services. And they depend on people coming to them. The walk-ins. The defectors. The runaways. That's the nature of Orwellian societies. But those who trade secrets for money or a passport present other problems.

"Defectors defect because they are defective," explained Volker Foertsch, former head of BND counterespionage. "They are not just trying to escape a regime. They are trying to escape something terrible in themselves, in their own lives. They are almost always unhappy people. They have problems with women, with their careers, with rotten marriages, with money. And they are uneasy about being a traitor. It gets on their nerves. It is not easy to live a double life.

"Not every defector lies. But after a while, they typically fear that they lose value. They are very dependent people. So they begin to

exaggerate, and tell you what you want to hear. They are totally dependent on the people they're talking to for their future well-being. They
want to please their masters. Psychologically, they have to do something
to enhance their value. So they begin to stretch the truth."

During debriefings, a truly skillful liar plants seeds of truth in his
story. He spins deceit around verifiable kernels of fact, adding false
details that cannot be checked. He builds a maze of twisting passages
and dead ends, but always around a vibrant core. And sometimes, his
case officer goes astray in the hunt. He gets lost in the labyrinth of lies.
He makes excuses and defends his informant beyond reason. He
inadvertently collaborates in a fraud. It's a common problem. All spy
services worry when a case officer "falls in love" with his source.

Over the years, the BND issued extensive written guidelines on
how to handle defectors and their lies. Beware of fabricators and con
artists, of charlatans and middlemen, the rules warn. These rogues hear
gossip in a souk or café, clip stories from a magazine, or read an
academic report on the Internet. And they will keep peddling fresh
tidbits of intelligence until the money stops.

"An initial impression can sometimes develop that it's going to be
an especially easy, risk-free kind of intelligence windfall," one set of
classified BND guidelines warns. "It appears that all the usual difficul-
ties connected with making such contacts simply fall away. In fact,
however, those who offer their services to the BND unsolicited can be
especially risky cases."

Case officers should take special guard against such "carriers of
disinformation," the rules advise. "Provocateurs, swindlers, or black-
mailers are especially significant. People with this kind of background
appear frequently as interesting informants."

After two decades at the BND, after his tours as a German spy in
Africa and as a manager in Pullach, Schumann knew the risks as he
began his first formal debriefing of his eager new Iraqi contact on a
cold day in January 2000.

The protocol for the introductory interview of an informant was
always the same. Engage your subject. Be relaxed. Keep it light at first.
Convince him to trust you. Let him talk. Draw him out. Be neutral. This
is just the first meeting. You can go back later to resolve contradictions
or problems.

After introducing himself, Schumann carefully ran down a standard
checklist of about twenty questions for Ahmed.

What's your full name? Date of birth? Where were you born? Current address? Do you have a family? Where are they? What kind of identification do you have? What languages do you speak?

Ahmed replied sharply and tersely, almost chopping off each question in mid-sentence. His fingers drummed the table and his toe and heel tapped a tattoo on the floor. Although he spoke in Arabic, he stared intently at Schumann's mild face and aimed his remarks directly at him, not the translator. He chain-smoked, but seemed to spit the smoke out in a rush. He looked impatient, as if he couldn't wait to get past the small talk. Perhaps he was just enthusiastic.

Schumann continued his line of inquiry, watching the Iraqi closely.

Who else knows you're here? Does your government know that you left? What will happen when they find out?

He reached the last queries on his list.

Do you have special information for us? Why did you contact us?

It was as if the German had lit a bomb. Ahmed erupted in a burst of manic energy.

Puffing madly on his cigarettes, pacing the room, waving his arms in excited arcs, the Iraqi rattled off multipart names of two dozen Iraqi officials, a bewildering array of government and military companies and commissions, project code numbers and obscure locations. He outlined detailed engineering equipment and procedures. He cited pipe diameters, temperature ranges, reagent mists, and fluid dynamics. He spoke of growth media and fermentation rates. He seemed determined to share every meticulous detail, pouring them out in a relentless, roiling torrent.

The translator was stunned, overwhelmed by the flood of technical terms and engineering jargon. And Schumann was lost. What did it all mean? He was neither an engineer nor a microbiologist. He had no training in turning bacteria, viruses, and toxins into military weapons. He didn't know what to ask.

After the meeting, Schumann went back to Pullach and did something that speaks to his professionalism. He decided he wouldn't fake it. Ahmed's information sounded far too consequential. Schumann was honest enough to know he needed help and self-confident enough to ask. He asked his superiors in Directorate One for backup. They were surprised, but agreed to approach Werner Kappel, the Weber-quoting intelligence manager up in Berlin.

"They said, 'This material is exciting, it is of utmost importance,

and we don't understand it. We need to bring in the subject experts,'"
Kappel recalled. "That is not the norm. It is very unusual. Normally,
collectors do not bring in analysts for interrogations."

But he swiftly approved the request. Directorate Three, the analysis and evaluation wing, assigned a senior analyst to work with
Schumann. He reported to the science and technology division. He
specialized in biowarfare.

If Schumann knew little about germ weapons, his new partner—a
shy, pallid biologist known here as Meiner—was said to be ill at ease
with people. He had a double chin, thinning brown hair, and the sad
eyes of someone who seemed to wish he were somewhere else. Like
many intelligence analysts, he was a frustrated academic, resentful that
he was denied the easy life and deference due a university professor.
Deep in his Pullach cubicle, far behind the BND's brick walls and
encrypted computer networks, he normally assessed and wrote papers
that only a handful of people ever read. He mostly focused on developments in biotechnology and microbiology, from advances in stealth
viruses to recombinant DNA.

Meiner, however, had zero experience with the intense rigor of
interrogation.

He was a scientist. In the world he inhabited, people reached
conclusions through testing hypotheses, seeking proofs, and submitting
results to peer review. He knew nothing of the psychological seduction
and constant inveigling needed to question a vital new defector. But he
swallowed his trepidation and accepted the post.

The CIA would call him the quarterback. British intelligence might
call him the vicar. Kappel called him the chief interrogator. Whatever the
title, Meiner would run the marathon meetings with Ahmed and ask the
technical and scientific questions. He would provide extensive oral briefings and written reports on the case to higher-ups in Pullach and Berlin,
including August Hanning, the BND president, and his top deputies.

They uniformly deemed Ahmed's information high-priority from
the start. Most defectors meet one or two case officers. Meiner's bosses
at Directorate Three helped him assemble a team of a dozen biologists,
chemists, physicists, psychologists, and others to generate queries and
analyze answers. They funneled most of their questions to Meiner to
ask, although task force members took part in some of the debriefings.

"We put our best resources on this," Kappel said. "We knew
precisely the importance of what he was saying."

Schumann still handled the nontechnical side of the case. He asserted his right to join every debriefing of Ahmed and every meeting about him, no matter how trivial. Fiercely protective of his charge, he scrutinized everyone who sought access and every report they issued. He was "very territorial," said Horst Schneider, a BND operations officer who helped supervise Schumann on the case. "He was always present. This was his source. This was his baby."

If Schumann followed the BND guidelines, his first step was to try to unravel Ahmed's motivation for coming forward. What drove him to cooperate with German intelligence? What spurred him to betray his country and abandon his family? What did he want in exchange?

"You must gain a full picture of the person's life," said Foertsch, the former counterintelligence chief. "You try to find out who he is, what his life is really about, and what makes him tick. You go into the details about the person at first, not where is this factory or that one. Who are his friends? Where did he work? How did he get here?"

In Ahmed's case, the answers were not immediately clear.

The Iraqi shrugged apologetically when Schumann politely asked exactly how he traveled to Germany. He gave indistinct answers when his case officer pressed him to explain how he got the money to pay his airfare, hotels, and other expenses during the months he spent en route to Munich. He mumbled uncomfortably when his handler demanded to know whom he met, where he went, and why.

No matter how Schumann implored or scolded him, Ahmed peered blandly back, a thin-lipped smile frozen on his face. Given the Iraqi regime's corrosive corruption, they guessed that he had stolen government funds and feared a confession might spoil his asylum plea. In Iraq it probably would mean a death sentence. They advised Pullach that he most likely bought his passport on the black market and relied on human smugglers to make his way to Germany like other Iraqi refugees. They gave up trying to sort out his unexplained journey and his mysterious finances. At some point, one official said with a shrug, it "just goes off into that Arab murkiness where there is no bottom line."

Another problem seemed far more important anyway.

CHAPTER 4

Saddam was using German-manufactured equipment to build his WMD, Ahmed told the BND.

The handlers passed the news to their supervisors at headquarters in Pullach and it shot up the chain of command. Alarms ring in official Berlin if a German company or business assists an outlaw regime. "We were very concerned about this," Kappel admitted. "There were political ramifications if German companies were involved."

Within the government, the BND reported to Schroeder's national coordinator of intelligence, Ernst Uhrlau. He was a political appointee with little background in intelligence. He began his career as a lecturer in the police academy in Hamburg, Germany's main commercial port. After two decades in local law enforcement, he was named Hamburg's chief of police. He was a cop at heart, not a spy.

A trim, white-haired figure in his mid-fifties, Uhrlau had established his intelligence command post in a corner office in the new federal Chancellery in Berlin. The building is the seat of executive power, comparable to the White House. Nine stories high, across from the national parliament, the gleaming marble and concrete facade is dominated by a colossal round window. The huge porthole on the shiny white Chancellery is so striking, and so instantly familiar, that even Schroeder's aides joked that they worked from a giant washing machine.

Uhrlau was not amused. His glasses rode low on his nose and he glared over them with an icy impatience that intimidated his staff. He spoke in mirthless, clipped sentences, and his tirades were infamous. Once, during a meeting in his office, he abruptly rose from his black conference table, strutted to the door, and loudly dressed down a passing aide, his outburst echoing among the suites that ringed the central atrium.

"This is how I control these people," he grunted in satisfaction to a surprised CIA officer in the room.

Many in the BND returned his apparent disdain. Morale plummeted under Uhrlau's imperious command. Senior German spies derided him as a political hack who failed to appreciate the subtleties and intricacies of intelligence. Nor, they complained, did he understand the outside world. Until he was named minister, U.S. officials said, he had never visited the United States.

In early 2000, shortly after Ahmed began assisting the BND, aides briefed Uhrlau about the Iraqi's allegation that German companies provided designs or equipment for Saddam's germ weapons. But Uhrlau, they said later, threw a fit.

If news got out, political opponents would skewer him and the Schroeder government. BND officials never forgot when Kohl, the previous chancellor, publicly chewed them out for gross incompetence over outraged press reports that German companies had built a poison gas factory for Colonel Muammar Qaddafi, the military strongman in Libya. "Auschwitz in the Sand," the headlines had called it.

Iraq was much worse. Before the Persian Gulf War in 1991, dozens of West German companies sold blueprints, components, raw material, and expertise that aided Saddam's efforts to produce poison gases and to develop nuclear weapons, as well as ballistic missiles to deliver them. After the war, U.N. investigations showed that no other country had provided more help to Saddam's weapons programs. The so-called German connection sparked a scandal that no one in Berlin wanted to repeat. Prosecutors had lined up all through the 1990s to investigate some of Germany's largest and most respected corporations.

Some fifty-six separate inquiries or trials were launched, although only half a dozen led to prison terms. Other nations denounced Germany's weak export control laws. Under intense pressure, the government finally had closed the legal loopholes and stiffened enforcement.

"The Germans had the best machine tools, the most expertise and a business culture based on export," explained David Albright, a Washington-based nuclear expert who studied the German cases. "Plus they had a tolerance of criminal behavior when it came to exports."

But belated legal reforms, and stiff U.N. weapons sanctions, didn't stop the problem. Other scandals hit the headlines shortly before

Ahmed flew into Munich in 1999. In April that year, a pair of engineers in Pforzheim, known chiefly for producing gold jewelry and cuckoo clocks, helped sell sophisticated drilling equipment to Iraq. When their case came to trial, prosecutors revealed that Iraq planned to drill the barrel of a huge, long-range "supergun" that could fire shells filled with chemical or biological agents.

"Guns of this caliber are capable of carrying weapons of mass destruction," they charged. The two men were convicted of breaching German export laws and the U.N. weapons embargo.

Ironically, the BND also furnished equipment to Iraq. Under a covert program code-named Yellow Line, German authorities quietly approved the delivery of advanced antennas, high-end computers, plus sophisticated encryption and communications hardware to a middle-man in Jordan who passed it to Saddam's intelligence services. The BND wasn't interested in the money.

"We always put back doors in the German equipment," said Schmidt-Eenboom, the former intelligence officer. The reconfiguration, called a Trojan horse, created a secret channel so BND eavesdropping experts could tap Iraqi communications.

The stealthy sale proved so useful that the Germans did it again after U.S. and British air strikes targeted scores of Iraqi intelligence facilities, military installations, and communication sites over four days in December 1998.

"The Germans were not unhappy," said Schmidt-Eenboom. "Because they destroyed German antennas and other equipment, and the Iraqis were forced to buy our equipment again."

But Uhrlau, the national coordinator of intelligence, constantly groused that public criticism unfairly focused on German sales in Iraq. He and his aides blamed the CIA for refusing to share details about illegal trafficking by U.S. companies.

"We were not at all happy with U.S. cooperation on proliferation," said Kappel. "We provided a lot of information concerning German companies. We never got anything, not one report, concerning American companies. It was a one-way street. They wanted our information but would not give us theirs. It made no sense. U.S. companies were deeply involved. So we were not happy."

BND officials saw no reason to publicize Ahmed's embarrassing claims about German involvement in germ weapons. They could not confirm his claim. And no one wanted another scandal. The BND advised the foreign affairs committee in parliament in closed session of the problem. But senior BND officials decided to bar the CIA from talking to their new source.

The question was what they would tell the Americans.

CHAPTER 5

The answers came in reports addressed to flowers and shrubs.

Like any large organization, the BND stamped a distribution list atop any important document. But they cloaked the identity of each recipient with code names. Somewhere along the line, they chose garden flora to mask the major American intelligence and law enforcement agencies.

They marked *Hortensia 1,* a bright pink and blue hydrangea that grows best in acidic soil, on reports aimed at the CIA. They wrote *Hortensia 3* on papers for the eavesdroppers and code breakers at the National Security Agency. Documents for *Heckenrose,* a wild rose known for barbed thorns, went to the local FBI office.

But the BND stamped *Hortensia 2* on reports based on Ahmed's interviews. These were funneled to the local operations base of the Defense Intelligence Agency, or DIA, the chief intelligence wing at the Pentagon. They would handle the defector's case for U.S. intelligence.

During the Cold War, the American, British, French, and West German governments quietly cooperated in collecting and assessing information from Soviet bloc defectors. U.S. officials assigned the job to the DIA, which vastly outnumbered the CIA in Germany. Later, after the Soviet threat ended, the French pulled out of the program. The British left a token officer in place so the BND still shared reports with London's Secret Intelligence Service, better known as MI6. But the DIA remained a hands-on partner. They regularly joined BND counterparts to debrief those seeking political asylum in Germany in the 1990s.

"We got the pick of the litter," recalled William Davis, a former senior DIA officer. "The Germans would say, 'Who do you need? Who do you want? Who are you fighting?'"

The BND and the DIA seemed natural allies. They each employed about six thousand people, about a third the size of the CIA, and shared similar missions and military cultures. Most important, they both distrusted the civilian CIA. The BND animus was entrenched after so many years of humiliation and abuse. But many at the Pentagon intelligence shop also resented the CIA as elitist and arrogant. The rivalry seemed especially toxic in Germany, where senior DIA officers viewed the CIA as a virtual enemy camp.

"We were often in open warfare with the CIA over intelligence operations and sources in Germany," said Davis. "The CIA got access to everybody we had. We didn't get access to almost anybody they had."

CIA officers, in turn, viewed their military rivals as too rule-bound, too rigid in their thinking. They mocked DIA reports as unreliable and their tradecraft as amateurish.

"As a general rule of thumb, the CIA tends to look down at the DIA," a CIA operations officer said. "Of course, we tend to look down at nearly everyone. But the sense we all had was that DIA officers were way below the caliber you'd find at the agency. They are not the A team."

The DIA traditionally focused on assessing foreign military threats. But it also embraced espionage after 1993 when the Pentagon reorganized rival military branches for human intelligence into a unified command called the Defense HUMINT Service. The new DIA service set up shop in an anonymous high rise in Clarendon, Virginia, a bedroom suburb of Washington. By the time Ahmed applied for asylum in Munich six years later, Defense HUMINT ran spy bases around the globe.

Their most important operations base in Germany occupied a neo-Baroque manor in Bogenhausen, a stylish residential district in east Munich that is a short drive from the BND headquarters at Pullach. The Nazis supposedly seized the mansion from a wealthy Jewish family, who then disappeared in the Holocaust. After the war, a U.S. Army intelligence commander confiscated it from a ranking Nazi officer, and the U.S. military never let go. The operations base changed names several times over the years, but insiders invariably called it Munich House. It was a relic of the Cold War glory days, a legend in intelligence circles.

Munich House sat on a quiet corner compound across from a leafy park that provided a perfect setting to arrange clandestine conversations that, afterward, never occurred. A concrete wall, topped by a wrought iron palisade, protected the manor. Set well back, shrouded by shade trees, the house exuded old-world elegance. Tall columns with

Ionic capitals flanked front and rear porticoes. Carved wreaths topped pilasters on the oatmeal-colored walls. No name hung on the mailbox.

Inside, graceful French doors in the foyer swung open to a formal dining room converted to a conference room. A brick-lined wine cellar, once perhaps filled with grand cru vintages, now held heavy steel vaults and secret coding and communications gear. A sweeping staircase in the front hall led to offices with rich mahogany paneling on the walls and lush Oriental carpets on the floors. Most had working fireplaces that roared in the winter.

About thirty DIA staffers, mostly retired noncommissioned U.S. military officers, worked at Munich House in late 1999 when Ahmed arrived in Germany. But a smaller group of Defense HUMINT operatives, about a half dozen in all, handled most of the paperwork on his case. They were the first to read the *Hortensia 2* reports about the Iraqi engineer.

One of their first official moves would forever brand the young case with the stigma of ridicule. One would like to think it was accompanied by knowing winks and conspiratorial laughter. It wasn't. In the early spring of 2000, after the BND had run their first formal debriefings of Ahmed and shared their first *Hortensia 2* reports, the Defense HUMINT team issued the high-level new defector his improbable code name: CURVE BALL. It first appeared in a Munich House report sent through U.S. intelligence channels.

The DIA normally used codes based on colors and numbers to protect the identity of its confidential informants. In DIA files, Germany was Red and Berlin was 798. So Red 798-001 was DIA source 001 in Berlin. But this defector belonged to the Germans, not the DIA. After his first interview, the BND files referred to the Iraqi only with their code, V for defector followed by eight numbers. The Defense HUMINT team at Munich House would not use the BND code. So they issued their own.

It wasn't unusual. Intelligence services regularly assigned randomly generated code names, or cryptonyms, when they shared an informant's information with another spy service. In this case, BND officials at Pullach liked the catchy American name and adopted it for ease when discussing the defector with Washington and London. The CIA and MI6, who employed their own complicated internal codes, followed suit to avoid confusion. Most classified U.S. reports soon restyled the name as Curveball.

The apparent reference to a baseball pitch with topspin, one that falls away at the plate to deceive the batter, was a fluke, a coincidence. During the Cold War, the CIA and its allies in West Germany had used the crypt Ball to identify Soviet bloc defectors who furnished weapons secrets. A series of Ball sources followed, including one called Match Ball.

Precisely who chose Curve Ball from the old files has never been clear. No one later would admit patrimony. After the invasion of Iraq, a blue-ribbon commission in Washington would investigate the prewar intelligence, including the Curveball case. The investigators never could pin down who was responsible. "Everyone denies they came up with the name," a senior investigator said with a laugh. "It's a bit of a mystery. No one would cop to it. Maybe the Germans did it. Or the British."

The Germans denied it later. "It is not a German name," Kappel, the senior BND official, pointed out. A British intelligence officer also sniffed at the baseball term. "We would have called him Googly," a sidewinder in cricket. "It wasn't ours."

In any case, U.S. intelligence authorities wrestled with a more pressing problem. In a few cases, perhaps once or twice a year, German intelligence officials refused to let the operatives at Munich House meet an important defector or asylum seeker. The BND wouldn't even share transcripts or videotapes of their debriefings. They sent just edited summaries.

The DIA tagged those files as Blue instead of the usual Red.

"If the Germans thought something from an Iraqi would jeopardize their economic interests, or would reflect badly on Germany, they would not give us direct access," said Davis, the former senior DIA officer. "It was rare, but we had a few Blue cases. We tended not to rely on those sources. It is very hard to assess someone if you don't see his face, his style, his mannerisms, what he's saying, how he responds. All of that is very important in judging someone's credibility."

The Munich House team normally reported an official brush-off to DIA headquarters in Washington.

"They'd say, 'Look, the Germans have a Blue source. Here's what they tell us he said. Do you have any questions?' They usually didn't. We had no need to do anything else. We weren't required to evaluate the source. How could we if we didn't meet him?"

As far as is known, no one in U.S. intelligence asked to meet Curveball when he first arrived. His importance wasn't immediately clear. Saddam's weapons barely merited mention in the annual CIA and DIA threat assessments given to Congress, or in the U.S. presidential campaign then underway. In any case, *Hortensia 2* reports poured out of Pullach. The file was growing steadily.

But in the early spring of 2000, the DIA tasked Munich House to arrange a routine interview. The Germans initially agreed, and two DIA officers, including a microbiologist, caught a flight to Munich. So an American request went to the liaison officer at Pullach to set up a joint debriefing.

The BND handler had to give his okay, however. And Schumann, Curveball's case officer, adamantly refused.

He argued emphatically against letting U.S. intelligence share his source. He and his colleagues were perfectly capable of debriefing an important defector without American help. He bore an old grudge against the CIA and he picked at it like a scab.

"They always want to steal our sources," Schumann grumbled to a colleague. "They think Germany is still occupied, and we are just a support service. The Americans think they are still big brother and we are little cousins."

Higher-ups at the BND still were nervous about Curveball's claim that German companies helped Saddam build germ weapons. But when Schumann went ballistic about protecting his source, he gave them a convincing reason to deny Americans access to their defector.

Curveball hates Americans, they told the visiting DIA team. He absolutely refuses to meet any Americans. He won't even consider talking to them. Sorry, they said, but he's completely off limits. Plus he speaks no English.

"Curveball did not want to speak to Americans," Uhrlau, the national coordinator of intelligence, explained later. "We can't then bring an American in and violate his trust. The informant would have the impression he is being lied to."

The two DIA officers flew home empty-handed. Munich House messaged Washington with the disappointing news.

Curveball is Blue. We can't meet him. We have to depend on the Germans.

CHAPTER 6

At first, Curveball was ingratiating with his German handlers.

He placed his right hand over his heart and murmured traditional greetings through the Arabic translator. He inquired respectfully about their health and their families. He seemed eager to start. He had picked up a few odd words of German along with his broken English and he cobbled together a few pidgin sentences. He punctuated them with nervous smiles and a flurry of excited hand gestures.

Schumann and Meiner didn't always get his point. But they nodded enthusiastically and grinned back, and he relaxed a bit. He loved Cokes, they quickly discovered, so they stocked his refrigerator and brought some to the offices and safe houses that they used for meetings. They set ashtrays out and usually sat around a table. In some cases, but not all, they ran concealed tape recorders and video cameras.

Mostly, in the beginning, they just listened.

The young engineer marveled at his new world. The U-Bahn, or underground, was a special wonder. The tunnels were spotless and the subways sleek and fast. That was no surprise. Each passenger purchased a paper ticket from a machine or manned booth. But it was an honor system. Amazing. No one stood at the gate and demanded to see if he bought the right ticket or, indeed, any ticket at all. How could that be?

Above ground seemed even odder. In spring, when the fragrance of linden trees filled the air and café tables overflowed onto sunlit plazas, pale young *fräuleins* emerged from cocoonlike offices and shed their clothes in public. In Munich, they sunbathed topless or nude near the white swans in Englischer Park, or on the gray stone embankment of the rushing Isar River. Men crossing footbridges downtown could stop—did stop—and watch. Such sights were unimaginable along the Tigris in Baghdad.

So were the German red-light districts. They pulsated with stripper bars, vast multifloored brothels, and garish shops filled with sex toys. His head swam just looking in. He had never seen anything like it. Entire cable TV channels were dedicated to nothing but soft porn and lurid ads for multilingual escort services and phone sex. Curvaceous women cavorted in bubble baths and stripped to thumping music on pool tables and soccer fields. On channel after channel, for hour after hour, they flashed their breasts and their phone numbers at him.

Curveball was not a religious or prudish man, he assured his handlers. He had left his wife in Baghdad, but she was still his wife. He admitted with a blush that he also had bedded a non-Iraqi "girlfriend," as he put it, during his travels to Munich. His smirk suggested he suffered no regrets. Still, he seemed shocked by the wanton, erotic offerings of his new home.

For solace, or as a diversion, he could surf the Internet. He grew excited at the possibilities. Back in Baghdad, security agents opened mail, tapped telephone lines, and kept detailed records on people's political views. Even minor dissent was illegal. Government thugs tortured or executed people for the crime of "insulting" the president or Ba'ath Party rule. Security agents watched every street, office, and school, every hotel and coffee shop to report on what people said.

Now he could read anything, watch anything, and print anything he chose. Small cybercafés and computer shops were starting to open between the beer halls and book stalls near the university. They charged little for access. He could hover in them for hours, chain-smoking and staring intently at the screen as his fingers flicked across the keys. Even Arabic Web sites were opening online. He could play computer games, read up on chemical engineering, and study the latest depressing news and reports on Iraq. Conditions back home were deteriorating by the day. But here, on his computer, he could get lost, as if in a dream. Sometimes, late at night, he might be the last to leave, red-eyed and exhausted.

Schumann and Meiner paid close attention, like indulgent parents watching an excited child describe his first day at school. He seemed happy to please them. He flattered them with compliments, and gifted them with his grin. Schumann soon gave supervisors a brief profile of his creative new source. Curveball appeared shrewd, "self-assured," and "personable." He was charming and intellectually agile, perhaps "a genius." He enjoyed a caustic sense of humor. But he could be "calculating" and cunning, even manipulative. Still, Schumann concluded, Curveball "seems to be settling in."

His father, Curveball indicated, was the kind of man who prayed at the local Sunni mosque and read his newspapers while drinking glasses of sugary tea in a local café. But he seemed a spectral figure in the backwash of Curveball's life. His mother was more animated, more vibrant. She pushed her two sons to attend school, to make something of their lives, to make her proud. He doted on his mother and missed her, he confessed, and he telephoned her after he left Iraq. He was estranged from his older brother, he told the Germans, and they had very little contact.

His family was neither poor nor rich, he said. They normally gathered for their evening meal after the baking heat of day finally began to ease. The government blamed U.N. sanctions for growing food shortages, and issued each family rations of wheat flour, rice, sugar, tea, and cooking oil. But one could find much more on the black market, and women like his mother worked magic with their aluminum pots and propane stoves. They ground chickpeas and sesame seeds into hummus, grilled tender chicken or lamb chunks on skewers, and baked crisp flat breads called *samoons*. They fried fava beans and cooked *kubba*, minced meat with nuts, raisins, and spices.

On special days, open-air cafés and restaurants beckoned on the banks of the Tigris. Waiters served heaping platters of amber rice and *masghouf*, a succulent river fish grilled on a spit. They brought out salvers of sweet pomegranates, sliced apples, and iced watermelon. Eucalyptus and date palms shaded the metal tables and everyone ate their fill as the coffee-colored current swirled silently by.

Curveball recounted how he grew up oblivious to politics in a lively Sunni neighborhood in northeast Baghdad. It was a maze of sun-blasted streets, honking horns, and flat-roofed homes behind thick masonry walls. His parents rented an apartment in one of the ubiqui-tous ocher-colored apartment blocks that fill the city.

The cramped flat was up several flights of musty stairs, with terra-cotta floors that were cool and pleasant to the touch. Furnishings were austere, an old couch and a few tattered carpets mostly, with family pictures on a shelf. Tenants fought a losing battle each day against clouds of desert sand, fine as talcum powder, which blew in through gauzy curtains and filled every crevice and crack. He had his own bedroom.

Curveball attended the University of Baghdad. The broad urban campus was lined by tall date palms, an oasis in the busy city. It nestled near foreign embassies and one of Saddam's huge palaces on the east side of a hairpin bend in the Tigris that sticks like a thumb into the city center. The university not only was Iraq's largest educational institution, it once was the nation's finest, respected as a center of learning in the Arabic-speaking world. But those glories had faded under Saddam.

The dictator's oldest son, Uday Hussein, took a special interest in the school and kept an office on campus. He chose deans and faculty for their loyalty to the regime, not their teaching skills or intellect. Students and basic studies were disregarded. Classrooms fell into disrepair. Students struggled with too few textbooks or out-of-date manuals. Laboratories often lacked basic equipment. Computers were rare. Even typewriters were a luxury.

Still, it was Iraq's only school to offer a degree in chemical engineering, Curveball's chosen profession. In Iraq, an engineering diploma provided the same crude utility and raw access as a law degree in Washington. It opened doors and conferred rank irrespective of ability. Saddam's diktats and decrees were law in Baghdad. So engineers, not lawyers, were kings. Saddam issued the top engineers in his regime a new Mercedes or other luxury car every two years, plus a driver. Engineers got a title, like doctors or generals. They signed "Maj. Gen. Eng.," or simply "General/Engineer."

But not all engineers are equal. Chemical engineers contend their discipline is the most demanding by far. Academic studies combine chemistry, physics, biology, and mathematics. Courses may include computational and applied mathematics, fluid mechanics, heat and mass transfer, thermodynamics, chemical kinetics, and chemical reactor design. Coursework is grueling.

Curveball was determined to help bring Iraq into the modern world despite the privations and U.N. sanctions. He freely admitted another incentive. He longed for that new Mercedes, for a chauffeur to drive him to meetings, for the status it would carry. He studied hard in his tiny bedroom, cramming late at night for brutal tests and exams. He spent hours in the labs and a thinly stocked library. His diligence and hard work paid off, he boasted.

I graduated first in my class.

Chemical engineers tend to work in industry and factories, not with test tubes in laboratories. They design and build complex systems, then operate and maintain them. In the West, they hold senior jobs in the oil and gas industry, pharmaceuticals, or other high-tech fields. Saddam's corrupt, impoverished Iraq had fewer options, but in the fall of 1994, shortly before Curveball graduated, he found one.

I was recruited by the government's Military Industrialization Commission to work on a special project.

It was an impressive first job for a young engineer. The director, Lt. Gen. Hussein Kamil, was the son of Saddam's first cousin. That got him a job as one of the dictator's motorcycle outriders. But Kamil was ambitious and smart. He married Saddam's eldest daughter, Raghad, after serving as her private bodyguard during a shopping spree to London.

Kamil's career soared. He lunched with his father-in-law several times a week and proved slavishly loyal. Kamil was given command of secret police and security organizations, including the Special Security Organization and the Republican Guard, two of the most powerful groups in the police state. He possessed a volcanic temper and a sadistic streak that terrified his aides. "No one . . . could control him and everyone feared him," one subordinate said.

Kamil took over the Military Industrialization Commission in August 1987. It supplied everything from soup to tanks for Iraq's military and intelligence services. He soon oversaw at least sixty research centers, arms factories, and trading companies, as well as a global web of front companies, bank accounts, and proxy agents for illegal imports. More important, Kamil was in charge of producing Saddam's weapons of mass destruction, including germ weapons.

He worked from a plush penthouse suite atop commission headquarters, an imposing high rise building in central Baghdad. There was no mistaking its importance. Commandos brandishing assault rifles stood guard at the end of the driveway. They checked employee ID badges and saluted smartly as cars with dark windows rolled by. Men with briefcases clattered up and down the front steps, rushing for appointments. Most of them, one visitor later recalled, wore thick, drooping mustaches that matched the large portrait of Saddam hanging in the lobby.

Like much of official Iraq, the commission building looked run-down when Curveball first was hired in late 1994. Cracks marred the rich marble and grime dimmed the windows. Iraq's basic economy was collapsing. Prices doubled every three months. Generators couldn't keep up with the rolling brownouts. Lights flickered and died. And air-conditioning stuttered and stopped in the furnace of the Baghdad summer. People sweltered and swore at their desks.

I was assigned to the Chemical Engineering and Design Center. I worked there for four years.

The eight-story design center rose several blocks away from Kamil's headquarters. When Curveball arrived, several hundred engineers, architects, and technicians worked at drafting tables and desks inside. Kamil regularly reorganized and renamed his companies to confuse outsiders. The Chemical Engineering and Design Center later was renamed the Al Zahrawi Center in the Sa'ad State Company, but its role didn't change. It designed and built civilian and military engineering projects, including specially modified tank carriers and other military vehicles.

Each morning, Curveball put on a white shirt like every other engineer and left his parents' home. He climbed onto a crowded minibus to get to work. He showed his ID to guards in wine red berets. He usually climbed the stairs since the elevators rarely worked. At the start, he worked with about two dozen other people in the fermentation design office. Bathed in fluorescent light, they shared a crowded cluster of scuffed metal desks and filing cabinets stuffed with blueprints. Later, he would move to other offices in the building, he said.

Once, he recalled, Kamil visited their office. He swaggered by in a uniform heavy with medals, surrounded by scurrying aides and bodyguards. All conversation suddenly ceased, all movement stopped at his approach, as if he were a black hole that sucked in energy and light. Engineers froze at their desks, secretaries blanched, and bureaucrats arched backward against the walls, trying to become invisible. The building itself seemed to hold its breath in fear until Kamil departed.

Some of his colleagues at the Chemical Engineering and Design Center were crooks, Curveball confided. They showed up late or not at all because they held second jobs or paid off a supervisor. Or they ran corrupt schemes on the side, diddling the system with endless scams.

Curveball seemed sympathetic. Everyone cut corners and worked deals to survive, he explained. They had no choice. No one could live on a normal salary. Government gangsters ruled their lives. Every petty bureaucrat and pock-faced pen pusher demanded a bribe. Every contract and license required a kickback. Even honest people were forced to twist the truth to get by. And some people took dreadful risks.

Curveball said one co-worker was so brazen, or perhaps so

desperate, that he cheated the regime. He secretly rented out the four-wheel-drive Land Cruisers, swanky Mercedes sedan cars, and other government vehicles assigned to the engineering design center. One could only imagine Kamil's wrath if the man were caught.

The vehicle scam was a minor part of Curveball's manic, caffeine-fueled account to the Germans. But American intelligence officials were impressed when they read the Munich House report about the rental car rip-off. It was an audacious scheme and a telling detail, they reasoned. "It adds credence to his story because only someone inside would know this," a senior CIA official said.

Once he started work, Curveball said, he was assigned to "seed purification," Kamil's latest project.

Iraq's farmers desperately needed help. Watered by two rivers, the rich soil of ancient Mesopotamia was the supposed cradle of modern agriculture. But drought and mismanagement under Saddam, and years of wars, took a terrible toll. Irrigation systems collapsed. Salinization ruined vast tracts. Farmers lost crops to mold, rot, rust, and fungi. Iraq was forced to import nearly all its food staples except fruit and vegetables.

Now Kamil aimed to help. Curveball and his colleagues were ordered to design machinery to spray fungicides on corn, wheat, barley, and other seed stocks. They would install sorting and treatment systems at crop warehouses across the country. After considering several designs, Curveball said, the engineers decided to reverse-engineer a system already operating up in Tikrit, the ancestral home of Saddam's clan. It was manufactured in Germany.

Curveball celebrated his good fortune. He finally had gotten his chance to help Iraq emerge from hardship. His parents depended on him, and now his country could too. He would not let them down.

CHAPTER 7

Curveball did not disappoint his German handlers either.

Far from it. His account only reinforced what Western intelligence services understood about Saddam's corrupt regime and its long-hidden arsenal of terrible weapons.

After the 1991 war, the U.N. Security Council had ordered Iraq to surrender its WMD. Inspectors from the United Nations Special Commission, called UNSCOM for short, soon found and demolished Iraq's major poison gas factories and thousands of chemical munitions. They crushed hundreds of ballistic missiles and launchers. The U.N.'s International Atomic Energy Agency, the IAEA, dismantled a nascent nuclear arms program. Despite countless frustrations, the U.N. experts were racking up steady gains by early 1995, shortly after Curveball began working for Kamil's commission.

Saddam's biological weapons were the major exception. They remained a complete mystery.

Unlike chemical or nuclear arms, deadly microbes are relatively inexpensive to produce, easy to hide, and simple to replenish. They can spread death and disease in invisible clouds that waft on a summer breeze. They can wipe out a city or terrorize a population. In theory, they are weapons of mass extermination.

Saddam's aides repeatedly denied building such weapons. U.N. biological inspectors, who worked closely with the CIA and other spy services, found tantalizing tips but no solid proof. It was maddening. They knew the evidence could be hidden in plain sight.

Nearly every instrument in a bioweapons program has civilian uses, from medicine to pesticide. The same fermentor used to grow anthrax bacteria can brew anti-flu vaccine. And even a basic biological laboratory with off-the-shelf beakers, autoclaves, and other equipment can produce pathogens. Skilled scientists are the key. And Iraq had plenty, mostly trained in Germany, England, and the United States.

When Curveball joined Kamil's commission, U.N. biological experts in Iraq were focusing on a suspicious laboratory complex southwest of Baghdad called Al Hakam. Kamil's aides insisted that the heavily guarded facility only produced a single-cell protein used as a supplement in cattle feed. The Chemical Engineering and Design Center designed the project to help Iraqi farmers, they added. The U.N. inspectors were unconvinced but couldn't crack the story.

But in March 1995, Israeli intelligence provided the U.N. with proof that Iraq had secretly imported forty-two tons of powdered nutrients, known as growth media, that are used to nourish and grow bacteria. It was a breakthrough clue. In hospitals, doctors use growth media to culture germs to identify diseases. Iraq bought enough microbial food in one year to supply its hospitals and tiny biotechnology industry for decades—or to brew thousands of gallons of biological poisons.

Meeting in a conference room near Baghdad University, several U.N. experts confronted a group of Iraqi generals and scientists with shipping documents and receipts for the unexplained imports.

"Where is all this stuff?" demanded Terence Taylor, a British bioweapons expert.

The Iraqis replied that they had distributed supplies to hospitals but the bulk was destroyed during local food riots. They produced documents saying so. Taylor took a quick look and tossed them on the table with disdain.

"They're forged," he declared.

"They're not forged," the Iraqi group leader countered. "They're reconstructed."

The Iraqis began to retreat. In July 1995, they admitted for the first time that the regime had researched anthrax, botulinum toxin, and other deadly agents before the 1991 war. They still denied building weapons, however. A stern-faced, British-trained microbiologist named Rihab Rashid Taha had directed the program.

Taha wore her hair in a dark swirl that encircled her face and plucked her eyebrows to match, each a perfect half-moon over turbulent eyes. Her face seemed set in a perpetual scowl, like a cartoon villain. British tabloid writers couldn't resist. They dubbed her "Dr. Germ." Taha married General Amer Rashid, chief of Iraq's ballistic missile program. He became "the Missile Man."

Kamil was Taha's boss. But on the night of August 7, 1995, he abruptly fled to Jordan. He brought his brother, who had also married one of Saddam's daughters, their wives and children, and bags stuffed with an estimated $25 million pilfered from commission accounts. Kamil had lost a power struggle with his chief rival, Saddam's son Uday.

Since Kamil knew some of Saddam's most important secrets, regime officials panicked in Baghdad. They abruptly blamed him for lying to the U.N. about WMD, and especially germ weapons. They escorted Rolf Ekeus, the chief U.N. weapons inspector, to Kamil's chicken farm a short drive west of Baghdad. Ekeus found 143 metal boxes in a shed out back. Nearly one million pages of documents, photographs, microfilm, and other records lay inside.

Most of the haul contained records from the chemical, nuclear, and missile programs. The biology file was more meager, an odd mix of receipts, travel vouchers, and other litter, like "the contents of someone's bottom desk drawer," as one official described it. An old red photo album from Al Hakam drew their interest, however. Neatly mounted inside were color pictures of fermentors, freeze dryers, munitions, and dead animals, including donkeys and monkeys covered with lesions. It was not standard research.

Ekeus demanded answers when he and two other U.N. officers met with Kamil shortly after the Iraqi arrived in Jordan. For the first time, Kamil admitted that he had produced horrific germ weapons. But he insisted he had ordered all the records, supplies, and munitions destroyed after the 1991 war rather than risk their discovery.

"Nothing remained," declared the Iraqi.

Kamil, who supposedly laughed when visiting torture cells, added another denial. "I was not involved in any of their wrongdoing," he told Ekeus, "I led a quiet life. I never tried tea or coffee, smoked a cigarette or drank alcohol."

That fall, Saddam sent word that he would pardon his son-in-law for spilling regime secrets, robbing its coffers, and absconding with his daughters and grandchildren. Kamil inexplicably fell for the ruse and returned home. Authorities immediately placed him and his brother under house arrest. Saddam's daughters divorced the pair days later. Soon after, armed commandos attacked Kamil's compound and killed them both.

In the aftermath, Baghdad gave the U.N. what it called a "full, final and complete declaration" of its bioweapons program. It was incomplete and inaccurate in parts, but the document caused shock waves in Washington. It was clear that the CIA and other Western spy services had grossly underestimated the size, sophistication, and lethality of Saddam's biowarfare program.

According to the document, in the months before the 1991 war, Iraqi scientists churned out 8,445 liters of *Bacillus anthracis*, which causes anthrax, 19,180 liters of *Clostridium botulinum*, a nerve toxin, plus smaller quantities of aflatoxin, a carcinogen, and several other agents. Technicians poured about half the soupy bio-agents into 157 aerial bombs and twenty-five Scud missile warheads, and stored the rest. None was ever used.

Al Hakam, the big complex in the desert, had been Iraq's largest and most advanced bioweapons factory. Taha simply had converted the equipment to produce cattle feed after the 1991 war to deceive U.N. inspectors. The Chemical Engineering and Design Center had designed the subterfuge. No one had recognized the evidence in clear view all along.

The news stunned CIA analysts. Anthrax posed appalling dangers. If an infectious dose of *Bacillus anthracis* is inhaled—less than one-millionth of a gram will do—the spores germinate in lymph nodes. The infection causes vomiting, fever, and shock. Respiratory collapse and agonizing death are certain without aggressive medical care.

Clostridium botulinum creates a deadly neurotoxin. If ingested, it blocks biochemical action in nerves that activate muscles. After a day or so of painful paralysis, the lungs essentially freeze up and the victim suffocates. But the toxin is difficult to use as a weapon. Few U.N. experts believed the Iraqis had overcome the challenge. Still, they couldn't take a chance.

Aflatoxin, the third Iraqi bioweapon, was more puzzling. Aflatoxins are chemical poisons produced by certain fungal species. The mold normally infects wheat and rice, or grows on peanuts. In humans, extended exposure may increase the risk of lung or liver cancer. A long-term carcinogen like cigarette smoke is not a battlefield weapon. But no one knew what the Iraqis had in mind.

In any case, using a living organism in a weapon is not simple. Unless properly designed, aerial bombs, artillery shells, and missile warheads will burn off a living payload when they explode, or just splash it into the ground. And Iraq's weapons were poorly designed. The R-400 aerial bomb that carried botulinum toxin was configured so the "pressure and heat generated would probably destroy 99.9 percent of the biological material inside," said Richard Spertzel, a former U.S. Army bioweapons expert who studied the Iraqi munitions. Like the aflatoxin, in other words, Saddam's botulinum bomb was close to useless.

Spraying an aerosol mist, as a crop duster sprays a field, is usually a far more efficient way to spread biological agents. But Saddam's scientists struggled to optimize the tank pressure, set the nozzles for exact droplet size and concentrations, calibrate aircraft altitude and speed, and so on. Despite experiments with small planes and a MiG-21 jet before the 1991 war, Iraqi scientists did not master sprayer technology and looked years away from doing so.

In the summer of 1996, U.N. engineers dynamited and bulldozed the germ factory at Al Hakam, as well as equipment hauled in from three other sites. The rest of the U.N. investigation into Iraq's germ weapons was hitting dead ends, however. Taha, the British-trained microbiologist, parroted Kamil's line. She insisted that they had destroyed all the evidence. They had poured formaldehyde into each munition to kill the living payload. They then crushed the shells, burned the remains, and blew up the debris. They similarly killed off the stored biological material and poured the glop into a patch of windswept desert. Finally, they burned all the records. There was nothing left, she swore. How could she prove a negative?

She couldn't. But soil tests at the disposal sites proved inconclusive. Maybe the residue degraded. Maybe Taha led the inspectors to the wrong sites. Maybe she fed them lies. She still could not account for seventeen tons of missing growth media, enough to brew four times more anthrax than Iraq had admitted. The unresolved questions and mounting suspicions drove the investigations forward.

Then a disturbing new theory found fertile ground at the CIA.

It did not matter if the U.N. dynamited Al Hakam or if Taha destroyed all her old bombs. Saddam, the thinking went, was hiding another biowarfare program using the missing growth media. The specifics weren't clear, but the logic, or at least the bias, was. It grew more entrenched after British and American air strikes pulverised Iraq for four days in December 1998. When the all clear sounded, Saddam refused to let the U.N. experts return.

Their departure was a disaster for the CIA. The agency had infiltrated spies into the U.N. teams, and the inspectors became the CIA's eyes and ears in Iraq. Now they might as well scribble the Latin *hic sunt dracones* on the map: Here be dragons. The Americans had failed to recruit a single Iraqi agent, not one, who was close to Saddam's illicit weapons programs. Despite years of effort, it controlled only a handful of Iraqi assets overall. The CIA's biggest secret was how dysfunctional it had become.

"In 1998, when inspectors left Iraq, we were at the bottom," said John McLaughlin, the CIA's second-ranking official at the time. "We were almost in Chapter 11 in terms of our human intelligence collection, meaning bankrupt."

Curveball's arrival in Munich a year later helped fill that intelligence void. His hands-on account, rich with vivid details, provided a crucial missing piece of the WMD puzzle. German intelligence shared their debriefing reports with their closest partners: U.S., British, and Israeli spy services.

They all agreed. Not only was Saddam again striving to spread biblical plagues of infectious agents and deadly toxins. He had found a diabolical new way to do it.

CHAPTER 8

Saddam would use trucks.

It was Kamil's idea, Curveball said. Saddam's son-in-law had realized that U.N. inspectors would soon discover and destroy Al Hakam and the other fixed germ factories. He sought a backup plan. So in May 1995, three months before Kamil defected to Jordan, he ordered the Chemical Engineering and Design Center to build a more secure system to replace them.

Once again they would pretend to help Iraqi farmers. This time they would use seed purification as the cover story. Curveball assured the Germans that the boss of the program was Dr. Germ herself.

I worked for Dr. Taha. I met with her often.

For Schumann and Meiner, the news was electrifying. This was huge, a fabulous break. No other Iraqi informant enjoyed that kind of stellar access. The CIA didn't have anyone remotely close to Dr. Germ or directly involved with WMD. The Germans did. Curveball's account grew more important by the day. "We knew what he told us was a political nuclear bomb," Kappel said.

More engaged than ever, Curveball outlined the system in a frenzy. He waved and chopped his arms like semaphore signals, speaking far too rapidly for the beleaguered translator. The Germans scribbled notes as best they could to interpret his descriptions. They understood immediately what he was saying. The Iraqis were building a giant, secret armada of rolling germ factories.

"It was his conclusion that these were to be used for weapons of mass destruction," said Hans Pieper, who was Meiner's boss on the case. "He was very convincing on the subject."

It was brilliant. According to Curveball, Saddam secretly put his entire biowarfare program on the road to evade discovery. He shifted apocalyptic germ weapons and sinister production facilities up and around Iraq like a con man's shell game. The trucks produced no clear emissions that Western spy satellites or U.N. sensors could detect. The menacing fleet of monster rigs would blend in with countless other eighteen-wheelers, refrigerator trucks, and other large vans that rumble down Iraq's highways and weave through its jostling city streets.

If U.N. inspectors started nosing around the area, the germ trucks could just drive away, disappearing into the traffic. Other convoys could act as decoys. Or technicians could convert the lab equipment to civilian needs when it wasn't needed. They could pour in Dettol, a disinfectant, to sterilize the pipes and tanks. They could destroy the evidence.

According to the BND reports, Curveball's design called for connecting three commercial tractor-trailer trucks into a single efficient bioweapons production unit. The first trailer would carry one or two stainless steel fermentors. A fermentor vessel is cylindrical in shape, but with a rounded bottom, so it rests on a stand. Piping, gauges, and ports poke from the sides and top. Before they were dynamited, the massive Al Hakam fermentors stood about nine feet high and half as wide. Those on the trucks would be much smaller in size.

As an engineer, Curveball knew a great deal about the trucks. He knew far less about biology. So the BND analysts helped him. "We filled in gaps," Kappel said. "You're always filling gaps in intelligence."

To multiply anthrax bacteria, scientists start with a reference strain of dried spores. They plant the seed stock in a vial of yeast extract or other warm nutrients. As it grows, they move the material to a flask, then a one-liter beaker, then five, then ten. The process requires at least ten steps and up to a week before the inoculum, as it's called, is ready.

Technicians next pour more growth media into the fermentor. They then add the inoculum. While the material ferments, they check acidity, oxygen, and temperature inside the tank using a control panel. They take samples to count bacteria under a microscope. A mechanical paddle stirs the brew. Anthrax bacteria require oxygen so a compressor pumps in filtered air, as in an aquarium. For anaerobic agents like botulinum, tanks of compressed nitrogen are used.

Fermentation normally takes about seventy-two hours for anthrax, a little longer for botulinum. Scientists then add chemicals to precipitate out solids. The foaming solution is allowed to settle for a day or two.

The result is a frothy, warm solution with a musty smell, like mushrooms. The yellow-brown soup is called slurry.

The second truck would carry mixing tanks to treat the slurry with chemical stabilizers and other additives. The third vehicle would store and prepare the solution for filling bombs and other munitions. As a special protection against discovery, Curveball said the bio-trucks only operated on Fridays, a legal and religious holiday in Iraq, because U.N. weapons inspectors naively conducted fewer raids on Fridays.

Curveball's design was plausible. The U.S. government had built similar germ trucks at the start of the Cold War. William Patrick III had directed the project for the Pentagon's then secret biowarfare program. Patrick was probably America's most experienced bioweaponeer.

Patrick and his colleagues had sought an emergency backup in case Soviet missiles took out America's chief bioweapons factory in southeast Arkansas. They installed fermentors and other equipment on a semi-trailer and ran tests with a simulant, rather than real germs. The data showed they could cook up enough dried anthrax to wipe out a major city.

"We got all our equipment into a standard trailer, an eighteen-wheeler," Patrick recalled. "They make very good units. You can produce your agent as you move along. The Soviets did the same thing."

President Richard Nixon ordered the Pentagon to abandon offensive biowarfare in November 1969. Patrick's team dismantled their eighteen-wheeler and other mobile systems hidden on ships. They destroyed huge stockpiles of anthrax, tularemia, Q fever, and other deadly pathogens. But Patrick never forgot his germ-brewing rigs.

"If you want to have a surreptitious biowarfare program, I can't think of a better way than to use a trailer," he said. "You just move the damn thing around."

The American trucks were self-contained, designed to brew and harvest anthrax spores while driving down the highway if necessary. But the Iraqis planned to use docking stations. It seemed both simpler and safer.

As Curveball described it, the trucks would pull into a warehouse, secure from the optical sensors and radar imaging of spy satellites, and line up side by side. Crews would plug in power and pressurized hoses for water and waste, like hooking up a recreational vehicle at a campsite. After a successful production run, the Iraqis could pump the germ-laced slurry into special freezers onsite or directly into munitions.

But Iraq's slurry was weak and had almost no shelf life. Slurry starts to aggregate into clumps as proteins congeal. It loses virulence rapidly. Saddam's military needed munitions with fresh slurry, and needed to use them in a few weeks to a few months. Otherwise, they risked firing rockets or dropping bombs filled with harmless sludge.

The solution was to dry the slurry and grind the clumps to the proper size. A pharmaceutical spray drier with the proper setting can mill a powder so fine, so carefully calibrated, that it is precisely the correct microscopic size for inhalation, like the contents of an asthma inhaler. It mixes special additives so the particles don't stick together and drop to the ground. The refined product, odorless and virtually invisible in the air, is said to be one hundred times more concentrated in potency, weight, and volume than liquid slurry. Plus it is far more durable. Dried botulinum lasts about a year. Dried anthrax spores may survive for decades.

Taha and her aides insisted they never succeeded in large-scale drying and milling of slurry. For one thing, the drying dramatically raised the risk of deadly leakage. Containment systems must be totally secure. U.N. sanctions barred any imports of the drying machines and no Iraqi company could fabricate one. No evidence or witness emerged to contradict Taha's fervent denials. Until Curveball.

Curveball indicated one afternoon that his trucks carried sophisticated spray drying and mixing equipment.

It appears he only mentioned it once, and without much detail or apparent conviction, because the reference only generated a single *Hortensia* 2 report. But the claim raced like a virus through classified intelligence channels in Washington and London.

A convoy of tractor-trailers cooking up fragile, short-lived slurry was one thing. Bio-trucks operating industrial spray driers changed the equation. It meant Saddam had drastically upgraded the lethality and efficiency of his biological weapons. Iraqi scientists could optimize anthrax and other bio-particles to the precise size and weight to float on the wind and lodge in the lungs. Saddam's germ trucks now were the stuff of nightmares.

The Germans shared dozens of *Hortensia* 2 reports on Curveball that first year, but that sole report on spray driers generated more high-level concern and classified chatter than any other. Curveball's help to the Germans was drawing notice.

Pentagon officials worried that in event of war, bombing or shelling a truck loaded with dried anthrax risked a release of spores into the air. CIA and MI6 officials considered the terrorist threat. Someone could hijack one of these trucks and offload the contents into a car headed for Paris, a ship steaming to Tokyo, a jet flying to New York. In theory, a fistful or two of dried, refined anthrax spores dropped in the subway or in a ventilation duct could kill tens of thousands, overwhelm a city's hospitals and emergency services, and terrify millions. The doomsday possibilities were too numerous, and too frightening, to count.

Curveball initially appeared abashed, almost ashamed, as he recounted his involvement to Schumann and Meiner, they reported later. He certainly seemed distraught. He paced around the room, twitching nervously and sucking down his Cokes. He stubbed out one butt and lit another, his worried gaze darting from face to face. He pleaded for them to understand his predicament and his suffering.

I could not say no. They would kill me if I refused. I had no choice. No choice. What could I do?

I had to help them.

CHAPTER 9

In the summer of 1995, Curveball told the Germans, he began to visit a mobile production center that Taha's team had code-named "313."

After scrutinizing high-resolution satellite imagery of the area he had described, the Germans pinpointed a cluster of tin-roofed warehouses and cement-block sheds near the east bank of the Diyala River, a tributary of the Tigris. It was about fourteen miles southeast of Baghdad.

Shown the pictures, Curveball confirmed the location. The area was called Djerf al Nadaf.

The compound was oddly shaped, like a twisted trapezoid. Out back and on the sides lay ragged flat fields. Drainage or irrigation ditches suggested they were farmed once, but now scrawny goats picked their way through scrub thorn and sharp-edged gravel. Just out front ran a two-lane tarred road lined with brick kilns and smoky foundries. Djerf al Nadaf "looked like every other light industrial site in Iraq," one visitor would recall later.

A few miles away, massive earthen berms, high as a ten-story building, surrounded and concealed the Tuwaitha Nuclear Complex, Iraq's largest nuclear facility. Allied warplanes and missiles obliterated most of the nuclear workshops, laboratories, and reactors during the 1991 war. U.N. nuclear inspectors later searched and sifted the rubble to remove any radioactive or other hazardous materials.

Curveball said that he helped draw up detailed plans for the germ trucks at his desk in the fermentation unit at the Chemical Engineering and Design Center downtown. But now he started to work on matching and assembling the pieces on the cement floor inside the largest warehouse at Djerf al Nadaf. The warehouse would be the first docking station and he was in charge, he said. He was the project manager.

He said it took two years of grueling desk and field work to design, test, and install the various module parts. They had to order stainless steel components from government-run factories, and machine-tool airtight pipes and fittings. He admitted that the technical challenge nearly overwhelmed him and drove him to despair. He knew the fierce Taha wouldn't hear of failure. Scientists had been dragged off to prison in Iraq for less.

The engineers especially struggled with the fermentors' cooling system, Curveball said. Fermentation creates heat, so water is pumped into an inner lining, called a jacket, to cool it down. Even a few degrees too hot can kill the bacteria brewing inside. Curveball said his fermentors kept overheating, especially during the brutal summer months. The detail was important mostly because the Germans could confirm his basic knowledge of the equipment.

"He knew the correct temperature ranges at different stages," said Pieper, the BND biowarfare expert who was Meiner's supervisor. "He was responsible for the gauges and pipes. He constructed, developed, and designed the equipment. He was the boss of screwing this together. He said he made it."

Curveball and his resourceful colleagues finally succeeded. They built Iraq's first working mobile biological factory inside three gray metal trailers in the summer of 1997, he said. He seemed proud of his handiwork. Each trailer looked like a standard ribbed-steel cargo container, the kind stacked on ships and then loaded onto trucks or trains. Iraq had thousands of them. No one would ever spot the germ trailers.

They also grappled with setting up the docking stations. The warehouse had insufficient power and water. So they installed and wired a generator and transmission station in a nearby shed to provide electricity. They hooked up a series of high-pressure pumps in another shed for water, steam, and waste materials, and ran the hoses through a side door of the warehouse.

To support the official cover story, Curveball and his colleagues worked side by side with seed purification employees at Djerf al Nadaf. Local farmers trucked in bushels of yellow corn, wheat, and other seeds. They fed it into an array of clanking mixers and threshers that stood two stories high in a raised bay at the north end of the main warehouse. They piled the filled bags in a heap nearby, and stored loose corn in waist-high mounds. The operation coughed out choking dust, made a hell of a racket, and drew rats and vermin. But the tart-tongued Taha would brook no complaints. She insisted that they keep to the deception.

The warehouse had to be modified. The trucks entered through a large garage-style door at the southeast end of the building, according to Curveball. But the huge rigs couldn't turn around inside or back out again because of a sharp angle. They had to drive out the other end of the warehouse. The clanking tower of seed machinery blocked the obvious way out. At first the problem stumped them.

But they found an ingenious solution. They built a special door. The tractor-trailers could swing left around the machinery and exit out through the corner.

Curveball explained that a two-story section of the northwest corner of the building opened dramatically on a huge hinge, like the swinging bow door of a seagoing auto ferry, or the corner of a child's dollhouse. Hardworking Iraqi farmers, carting their heavy bags of seed in and out, would stare in amazement when the sharply angled door suddenly creaked open. Who had ever seen a door built into a corner? Curveball seemed especially pleased with the side-swinging corner door, as if it were an architectural treasure as well as an engineering feat.

The odd setup—multiple hoses and lines snaking in from outside, stacked sacks and piles of yellow corn, and now a weird swinging corner door—seemed a bit haphazard to the Germans. But they knew the Iraqis jury-rigged lots of things in their weapons programs.

Tell us more, they urged.

Curveball was fastidious about his work. He regularly checked for pressure leaks or loose fittings in the fermentors, hoses, and other gear. Careful testing and painstaking calibration were part of his job. And the equipment all worked, he said proudly.

Meiner and the team of BND experts that he consulted tended to agree. Curveball clearly understood proper engineering procedures. As best they could tell, he provided accurate calculations and dimensions for the fermentors and other equipment. He struggled with some details and appeared equivocal or even evasive at times. But he was a nuts-and-bolts guy, a chemical engineer, not a microbiologist or weapons expert. No one expected him to know everything. And nothing he told them sounded impossible or clearly incorrect. The mobile fermentation and docking system he had described was technically feasible.

After they built the first working design in mid-1997, Curveball's office at the Chemical Engineering and Design Center handed off the seed purification project to the Mesopotamia State Company for Seeds, also known as the Al Nahrayn Company, which was part of the government's Ministry of Agriculture. It strengthened the cover story in case U.N. inspectors got suspicious and came knocking. No one ever did.

Curveball and his colleagues next worked to improve the efficiency of the three-truck system. By May 1998, he said, they managed to cram everything onto two flatbed military transport trucks, like those used to carry tanks and other tracked vehicles. These had reinforced nickel plate flooring and hydraulic support legs for the extra weight. Since they were military trucks, heavy brown canvas hung from a steel skeleton on the sides and top, not the hard shells of the original shipping containers.

The team added other cost-effective improvements. In the first design, they used eighteen separate pumps just to move water, air, steam, and all the rest. Now they reduced the number of pumps to four. They also replaced troublesome paddles in the fermentors with a system that mixed the material with forced air or gas bubbles.

Curveball said he and his colleagues built seven mobile biological production systems in all. Three were fully functional when he left Iraq in March 1999, he told the Germans. His working unit was still parked at Djerf al Nadaf, as far as he knew, but the others were scattered at seed purification and industrial sites across the country. He identified five locations in addition to Djerf al Nadaf: a state company for heavy engineering equipment in Dawrah; the Al Ahrar seed facility at Numaniyah; a crop protection complex near Suwayrah; a seed warehouse at Huwayjah; and a municipal workshop in Tikrit. The Tikrit facility housed two mobile units, he said.

The German handlers pressed him hard about these other sites. They were skeptical whenever any fast-talking Iraqi claimed to visit Saddam's hidden weapons facilities. U.N. inspectors and every Western intelligence agency had scoured Iraq for them. No midlevel engineer could just waltz into Saddam's most secret sites, whatever his ties to Dr. Germ.

But Curveball quickly revised his account. They had misunderstood him, he said. He only worked at Djerf al Nadaf. "All the others, he heard about," said Pieper, the senior BND analyst.

Pieper and his colleagues were convinced the Iraqi was telling the truth.

"Perhaps he is overestimating his own role," Pieper said. "Perhaps he is only a minor guy, not so important. Perhaps he is filling a few gaps to paint a more complete picture. That is normal. Most people love to be admired, to be seen as a big shot. What is important is the story was plausible."

Curveball indicated that scientists arranged quality testing of the trucks' microbial brew at the Amiriyah Serum and Vaccine Institute near Baghdad. The news came as no surprise to the Germans. Before the 1991 war, Amiriyah produced vaccine supplies to fight polio, measles, and other diseases. But scientists there also had secretly worked for Taha's anthrax and other bioweapons program, according to U.N. reports.

German companies had played a role in Iraq's quality testing of chemical and biological weapons back then. Iraqi scientists had caged monkeys, dogs, and other animals inside aerosol exposure chambers at the German-built chemical weapons complex called Al Muthanna, and then pumped in blister and nerve gases to observe the effects. They also sprayed deadly germs and toxins onto animals cowering inside another German-built aerosol chamber at Salman Pak, a factory that predated Al Hakam, the U.N. inspectors had found.

Curveball struck a matter-of-fact tone as he described his work at Djerf al Nadaf. But as he recited his achievements, he started to beam with pride, the German handlers noted. He was an engineer, and successful engineers build things. Big, important things. That's why they are given impressive titles and fancy cars. Morality and ethics aren't part of the equation. No longer embarrassed, he began to boast.

His bio-trailers, Curveball bragged, were first-class, top-of-the-line, state-of-the-art. Technicians could adjust flow rates and temperature and other variables in the fermentation unit at least five ways, he said. That meant they could produce five different biological agents.

The Germans fired off another *Hortensia 2* report based on this claim. It raised sharp new concerns in Washington and London. Bioweapons hunters especially fear what they call the Big Five: anthrax, botulinum, plague, smallpox, and Ebola. The peril, it appeared, was growing by the day.

In follow-up meetings, hale Schumann and paunchy Meiner pushed Curveball for more information about where he worked and what he knew. Meiner, in particular, exhorted Curveball to think hard, to reach back, and tell them everything he had seen and heard.

They prompted him for more details about the German-manufactured equipment in Tikrit. German companies had legally sold thousands of supply and transport vehicles to Republican Guard and Special Republican Guard military and security forces. Did they use German trucks for the mobile program? Did they use German-built aerosol chambers at Amiriyah?

The defector answered emphatically at times, as best he could at others, blowing thick clouds of smoke as he spoke.

He took a lined notepad and dutifully wrote down the names and titles of more than two dozen engineers and senior officials at his office in the Chemical Engineering and Design Center. Almost every name on the list, the Germans quickly determined, had worked on the single-cell protein project, the phony cover story that U.N. inspectors had uncovered at Al Hakam. He also named scientists, technicians, and other people who helped design, construct, and operate the bio-trucks.

He outlined how each office was organized and told them whose nameplate adorned which door. He disclosed who sat where and who ran which scams. He described who directed staff meetings, who made decisions, and who carried them out. He told them who ordered supplies and who delivered them.

Curveball said they had ordered fermentors and other components from an Iraqi military supplier called the Al Nasr Al Azim State Company in Baghdad. This too fit in with what the Germans knew. Earlier reports by U.N. inspectors showed that the same factory, then known by another name, had built stainless steel fermentors, heat exchangers, and other vital pieces of equipment for the germ weapons factory at Al Hakam.

He told them even more about the docking facility at Djerf al Nadaf. The main warehouse was shaped like an L with the right angle pointing due north. They stored seed-handling supplies inside two rooms built into a corner. But they hid the biological materials in an underground chamber accessible to only a few. And he described again his inventiveness in designing his wondrous corner door.

But even in the early meetings, Curveball's brow furrowed when his handlers interrupted too often or prodded him with too many follow-up questions. His machine-gun chatter suddenly went quiet and his supple hands shuddered to a pause. Even his feet, which usually clattered like a sewing machine, braked to an awkward silence.

And when he answered, he spoke with rueful sighs.

I am an engineer. I am not a biologist. I don't know these things.

Schumann and Meiner puzzled over his behavior. Perhaps they were being too aggressive, too confrontational. A new source normally felt apprehensive under pressure. He had to partition his past and rechannel his emotions. A new defector usually was a stranger to himself. He certainly was still a stranger to them, a blur. In time, they figured, he would come into focus.

Curveball's account begged obvious questions, they knew.

Would Taha really brew pestilential poisons in a rat-infested grain warehouse that doubled as a truck garage? If the truck carried canvas sides, how did they keep road dust and desert grit from contaminating the product? What about driving on Iraq's bumpy roads? The vibrations would shake up the slurry, knock out sensitive instrumentation.

Most important, if the trucks collided or rolled over in an accident, they would leave a trail of dead people and animals along the road. The risk was insane. Taha knew the dangers involved. The handlers pressed Curveball for answers. How did they prevent leaks from vessels and hoses? Did they use sealed glove boxes or special safety cabinets? Did they wear full-body, biohazard space suits and respirators? Did they work behind airlocks? Where was the containment system?

Curveball's bio-trucks featured none of those precautions.

He measured his answers carefully, an engineer searching for solutions.

Maybe Taha doesn't care about leaks and people living downwind, he suggested. Maybe it doesn't matter because most of the docking stations are tucked away in the desert anyway, away from major cities.

He picked up a stray notion and offered it for their consideration. Maybe Taha hopes that Djerf al Nadaf and the other germ truck depots are so obviously inappropriate for biological science that foreign intelligence agencies will dismiss the whole idea as preposterous.

I don't know these things.

But then, to the Germans' intense relief, he would get another burst of energy and go full bore again, his rapid-fire voice sweeping them along, his body aquiver, his fluttering hands in flight.

Curveball helped build a small, scale model of Djerf al Nadaf with pieces of foam and wood. They gave him sheets of graph paper and colored markers, and he blocked out the main warehouse and sketched its interior, drawing lines and writing labels. He showed a line of glassless windows up under the eaves to let in light and air. He showed the underground chamber, the two storage rooms, and the two-story tower of seed-sorting equipment.

He diagrammed two long warehouses that sat perpendicular to the main building, and another shed nearby that held the power generator. He added three more storage facilities in an adjoining compound and a dozen or so small outbuildings. He colored in the two-lane access road, boundary fences, a farmer's house across the field, and the drainage ditches along the edges, estimating distances as best he could.

Curveball also drew engineering-style diagrams for the trailers. He outlined each piece of equipment and drew in the hoses they used to connect the fermentors, mixing vats, controllers, and other gear. One couldn't reverse-engineer his drawings to brew anthrax or build a bio-lab in a garage, one official said later. But they were plausible.

Curveball steadily drew his German handlers into his world as easily as he sketched vats and roads, pipes and trucks on paper.

His drawings and models were consistent on one issue. They all showed how eighteen-wheelers entered the warehouse at Djerf al Nadaf through a garage door at one end and exited out the other through the side-swinging door of which he was so proud.

Curveball's elaborate models and diagrams showed "without a doubt," one official noted, that Saddam's rolling germ factories could move in and out of the docking station without hindrance of any kind. It seemed a minor detail at the time.

CHAPTER 10

Alex Steiner picked up most of the *Hortensia 2* reports from Pullach.

Tall and beefy, with a trim gray mustache and goatee, Steiner was head of operations at Munich House and was the DIA's local liaison to the BND. He worked from an airy upstairs office with a bird's-eye view of Shakespeare Platz, the neighborhood park. When he needed a break, he could head across the street to smoke an expensive cigar. Puffing away, he would wander under broad elms and leafy maples, past a small playground and a pair of well-tended flower beds. The gravel paths led to a life-sized statue of a bare-breasted river maiden, her robes draped around her hips. There was nothing like it at the Pentagon.

Steiner also was a rarity. With family on both sides of the Atlantic, he had shuttled between homes in Germany and America as a child and grew up speaking both tongues without a trace of a foreign accent. He conversed in German and its guttural Bavarian dialect so flawlessly, so effortlessly, that he invariably passed for a local. Indeed the BND often demanded that he do so. He usually posed as a German intelligence officer when he took part in a joint interview with a new defector or other BND source. The pretense always worked.

But the Germans refused to let Steiner or anyone else at Munich House meet Curveball. That was okay with him. The case was a royal pain. Steiner was looking forward to retirement. He wanted to sell real estate. Curveball was what he called a "very hot potato" and he didn't get drawn into the details. He barely asked about it in his regular meetings with BND officials at Pullach.

"I'm not the nitty-gritty guy," he would say. "Others do that. I dealt at a higher level." Still, he was duly impressed by the *Hortensia 2* reports he saw, and the way his BND contacts promoted their new celebrity informant. "Of one thousand sources, you may get ten like him."

The figure was about on target. The BND secretly funneled around one thousand classified reports a year to U.S. intelligence, mostly through the DIA, on Iraq, Iran, and other topics of mutual interest. Steiner and his Munich House colleagues struggled to keep up with the unrelenting paperwork. Like any bureaucracy, intelligence agencies tried to reduce everything to a tidy flow of paper. Spying has its own dynamic: you can break the law as long as you file the proper forms.

In the case of a new defector, like Curveball, they first filled out a "knowledgeability brief," or KB. It read like a curriculum vitae. It listed Curveball's education, religion, where and when he first showed up, his degree of access to sensitive information, his familiarity with regime officials, and so on. It omitted his name, address, and other crucial details because the Germans did not share those.

A DIA officer normally evaluated a new source and issued a grade. The scoring matrix ran from 1 to 6 and A to F. A confidential informant marked A-1 ranked as a superstar, a known source with proven access to valuable information. An A-1 meant clean bona fides, demonstrated entrée, and a record of reliable reporting. On the other end of the spectrum, an F-6 rating flashed danger. An F-6 meant an unknown source with unknown credibility.

Curveball's DIA paperwork carried no grade of any kind. Since Steiner's team at Munich House could not meet him to evaluate him, they offered no guidance on whether or not to trust him.

Munich House sent the Curveball brief via an encrypted internal computer network called SAFE to the regional DIA headquarters at the U.S. military European Command base in Vaihingen, outside Stuttgart. Vaihingen approved the report and forwarded it to about two dozen other military and intelligence addresses. A copy went to the Iraq operations chief and his deputies at Defense HUMINT headquarters in Clarendon. Another copy was forwarded to DIA analysts based at Bolling Air Force Base, along the Potomac River a few miles south of the White House.

Still another copy went to the CIA nonproliferation center. After the Cold War, the CIA still ran three competing in-house weapons groups. But George Tenet, the CIA director, had combined the rival units. The new group was named WINPAC, which stood for Weapons

Intelligence, Nonproliferation, and Arms Control. It reported to the analysis side of the CIA, not to the operations side, where spies worked.

WINPAC was supposed to streamline CIA reporting and analysis of weapons-related threats. But it quickly bloated in size. Up to seven hundred analysts soon spread along four corridors on three floors at Langley. The vast majority focused on supporting strategic arms control agreements and tracking the illicit trade in nuclear technology and ballistic missiles. The CIA's strongest suit during the Cold War was tracking big, tangible things like missiles, tanks, and submarines, and the new weapons center saw little reason to change.

Partly for that reason, despite the huge staffing, no more than six WINPAC analysts specialized in the murky world of microscopic germs and viruses. The tiny unit focused on suspected biowarfare programs in Libya, Syria, North Korea, and other nations as well as Iraq. But biowarfare was still considered a low-level threat and the bioweapons experts labored in relative obscurity, largely sidelined and often ridiculed even inside the CIA.

"These guys are really your basic mad scientist," a senior CIA officer said, laughing. "They're the geek squad. They're monomaniacal. They're a breed apart."

In early 2000, as the first Curveball reports began to flow in from Munich House, the WINPAC geek squad added the case to their busy portfolio. They discussed the bio-trucks intensely and excitedly among themselves, and began pushing reports up to higher levels, pleased that they now had a stake in battling the Iraqi threat. It gave them credibility. The geek squad would help drive the Curveball case in Washington.

Politics, paperwork, and language also drove the case. The BND handlers almost always interviewed Curveball using an Arabic translator. But the translator struggled to provide the necessary precision and nuance as he asked Meiner's highly technical questions and then interpreted the twists and turns of Curveball's often rambling replies. Classical written Arabic is the same everywhere, but spoken Arabic has numerous dialects and the Iraqi idioms are especially troublesome to outsiders. Back in Baghdad, Iraqi government officials sometimes spent an hour arguing with a U.N. interpreter over the meaning of a single word.

Curveball tried to help. He mixed in what Kappel, the senior BND official, called "bad conversational English" and a confusing array of technical terminology and jargon that he had learned in engineering school. "But a case officer wants to speak directly to his source," Kappel said. "Curveball also began to learn German and thus there was a big mix that went on."

After each interview, Meiner and other members of the BND team prepared a brief written summary and analysis, in German, of the most important points. The BND reports usually consisted of one to five pages even if the interview lasted late into the night, as at least one session did. They passed these summaries, not the transcripts, in the *Hortensia 2* reports to Munich House.

Depending on the demands of work, Steiner's team at Munich House translated the *Hortensia 2* reports into English. Other times, the translation unit at the regional DIA office at Vaihingen helped out. They dreaded the reports on Curveball because the German handlers laced them with obscure technical and biological terminology, as if they were showing off. "We always had to look in dictionaries," griped one translator.

Once the linguists were done, the material was arranged into numbered paragraphs. These were pasted into a DIA format called an Intelligence Information Report, or IIR. Everything in an IIR appeared in capital letters, a throwback to the era of telex cables, with thick coding at the top and tail. (The CIA similarly referred to internal e-mail as cables.) Most of the DIA intelligence information reports on Curveball were surprisingly concise, only one or two pages, even shorter than the BND summaries.

By the time the Munich House reports reached Washington, Curveball's original words thus had passed through multiple layers. His answers were translated from Arabic to German to English. They were interpreted, summarized, reformatted, and analyzed at every stage. The final version was the processed product of a bureaucratic intelligence mill. But it still wasn't confirmed.

Defense HUMINT figured it wasn't their job. They saw themselves as just a postman. Steiner's team provided the conduit to pass the translated German reports back to Washington. He did not have the resources, the staff, or the time to investigate the background or vet the reliability of a defector he had not met. The Germans controlled the Iraqi and paid his freight, he figured. Let them do it. Or let the CIA do it. They were the pros.

Anyway, Steiner believed that the CIA and DIA weapons analysts back home must have validated the Iraqi and confirmed his information.

Why else would they respond so enthusiastically? His job was to help them, not cause problems. It was their case, not his. Hell, the Curveball paperwork and follow-up were taking far too much of his time anyway. The BND issued a new *Hortensia* 2 report on Curveball every week on average. So the jaded DIA liaison and his team at Munich House just passed them on.

"They made absolutely no effort to look at it, read it, or see if it made any sense," a CIA investigator said later. "They just stuck a number on it and zapped it off to Washington. They said they had no responsibility at all to try to figure out if what he was saying was true or false or whatever. We called it a case of immaculate reception."

The DIA stamped "NOFORN" on its intelligence information reports on Curveball, a clunky classification that bars release to "foreign nationals," including the Germans. The DIA also classified the reports Secret. Under U.S. law, it meant unauthorized disclosure could cause serious damage to national security.

Secret holds a surprisingly low rank on the U.S. government's classification scale. An estimated three million Americans hold security clearances and Secret is among the most common. CIA field reports are classified Top Secret or higher, restricting circulation to a much smaller group. (To restrict access further, the CIA once developed paper that couldn't be photocopied. "They put black writing on red paper," recalled a U.S. official. "The problem was nobody could read it.")

Separate coding limited the Curveball reports only to Americans cleared to read liaison service reports on weapons of mass destruction in Iraq. Bernie Mueller, a U.S. intelligence operative based in Munich, was among them. He was thick around the waist, with curly gray hair framing a round florid face, like a cherub gone to seed. Born in Germany, he had served as an operative in Germany for most of his adult life. He had adjusted from the clarity of the Cold War, when spying focused on Soviet tank maneuvers and Stasi espionage, to the more fragmented world of ethnic cleansing and Islamic jihadists. He followed clandestine postings from Munich to Frankfurt to Berlin and back again.

Mueller enjoyed all things German—the heavy operas, the foamy steins of local lager, even the resurgent saber dueling clubs. The American was so bilingual that he spelled his name both ways. His business card read Bernie Mueller on one side and Bernhardt Müller on the other. It didn't list his employer.

One morning in early 2000, Mueller was sipping his coffee at a government desk behind a thick steel door with a combination lock. He tapped in a few keyboard commands on his computer and called up a list of the latest intelligence information reports from DIA bases in Germany and elsewhere in Europe. He stopped scrolling when he saw the Munich House coding. He pointed his cursor, clicked the mouse, and opened the first Curveball IIR.

He read it carefully. He read it again. Something seemed odd. Because of his position, he also could access a copy of the original *Hortensia* 2 report in German. He carefully compared the two. What he saw made him mad as hell.

Mueller printed them out, rose from his desk, and angrily marched over to a colleague. He threw the two documents on his desk.

Most of the translation was accurate. But a key paragraph had been altered. The original German warned that the accuracy of the information and the reliability of the source "cannot be verified." But the Munich House version simply noted that it "could not be determined."

The change might seem insignificant to a layman, a minor blip in translation. To a professional, the rewrite signaled a shift in tone and substance. The BND warning suggested at least the possibility of a toxic F-6 source, the opposite of an A-1. Defense HUMINT basically abstained. To Mueller, it looked like someone was exaggerating the value of the report. Someone was trying to look good back home.

Mueller had seen it often. In his experience, intelligence officers in the field always sent up the sexiest reports possible. Everyone wants to be noticed at headquarters, especially if they work halfway around the world. Hyping reports seemed pervasive at DIA and Defense HUMINT, where bonuses and awards often cited how many reports someone filed, not what they contained. The military was all about making numbers. So people shoved everything over the transom.

During the spring and summer of 2000, Mueller tracked about twenty Munich House reports on Curveball. They all carried weaker warnings than the original German. When no correction appeared, he concluded that Munich House watered down the caveat to ensure the reports were not ignored. He also noticed something else.

The BND handlers appeared to give Curveball far too much latitude. They asked leading questions about Dr. Germ and mobile production, about fermentors and spray driers. They signaled the issues that concerned them most—and Curveball provided the answers they wanted.

"Curveball gave very specific answers to specific questions. They would ask, 'What do you know about this facility?' And he would answer, 'Oh yes, that facility is very important.' He told them what they wanted to hear."

In the end, he said, "the debriefers fell in love with the source."

Mueller didn't share his concerns with supervisors in Washington because Curveball wasn't his case. None of the post-war investigations would highlight the translation issues that so bothered Mueller. They focused on other, more glaring, errors.

Another U.S. intelligence officer, a doctor, also was starting to wonder.

Curveball had told his German handlers about an accident at Djerf al Nadaf in late 1998 that, he said, had killed a dozen technicians. The details were vague but the disclosure in a Munich House report energized CIA and DIA biowarfare experts. Forensic evidence from the mishap could provide insights into how well Taha had mastered the spray driers and other technical challenges. The mishap even earned a laugh at one meeting. Perhaps the germ trailers had a silver lining, someone suggested. Maybe they would kill all of Saddam's weapons experts.

In any case, the biological accident provided proof, if any still were needed, that Saddam was churning out microbial poisons.

"From the beginning, that was a key dramatic point—that he had seen people die," said a senior CIA official. "That really impressed people. Everyone always talked about it. He saw people die."

Still, no one seemed certain of precisely what he saw. Did people die on the scene? Did something explode? Did a fermentor leak? The translated German reports provided no answers.

Some CIA analysts suspected Curveball witnessed an accidental leak of anthrax spores. One way to test the theory was to check his blood. Presence of antibodies might show if he was given a live-agent vaccine. Iraq had no need to immunize people for anthrax unless they worked with it. The antibodies also might show if Curveball was exposed during a release.

Schumann arranged for Curveball to be tested at the German army hospital at Neubiberg, outside Munich, according to a colleague.

But the doctors couldn't detect clear signs of an anthrax vaccine or exposure.

At that point, the BND handlers agreed to let the Americans try. One of the U.S. national defense laboratories could conduct more sensitive tests. But lab protocols required a strict chain of custody to ensure no one tampered with samples they analyzed. So in May 2000, a middle-aged American physician flew to Munich. A BND contact escorted him to meet Curveball on a busy German military base on a balmy Saturday morning.

Les, the doctor, officially worked for the Defense Department. But he was on loan to a clandestine CIA operations unit that focused on tracking weapons of mass destruction. He concealed his nationality and credentials when he met Curveball, however. The BND handlers had issued Les a severe warning before he entered the room. Since he barely knew any German, they ordered him not to say a word.

Curveball spoke no English, Les was told, and absolutely hated Americans. No one knew why. But if the Iraqi thought Les was an American, they would all catch hell.

They introduced Les as a German doctor. He nodded politely but otherwise stayed silent. It was tough because Les normally was loud and garrulous, a practical jokester back at the CIA. He also was a dedicated physician. And Curveball looked ill, Les thought.

The Iraqi's dark bloodshot eyes blinked painfully in the light. His skin was sallow and sweaty. His clothes were disheveled, as if he had been out all night. He clearly was suffering from a painful hangover. But Curveball also seemed upset, arguing angrily with the Germans about something.

While others in the room distracted the patient, Les drew the blood sample. He attached a vial to the back of the needle and when that was full, he swapped another in its place. When he was done, he discarded his syringe, labeled the vials, and secured them in his bag. It didn't last long, but Les was bothered by the meeting.

The Iraqi appeared "clearly high-strung" and "very emotional, very excitable," he wrote later. Les also worried about why Curveball showed up for an important set of medical tests with such a blistering hangover.

"It was early in the morning, he was hung over and he smelled like booze," Les complained to a colleague after he got back to Langley. He wondered if Curveball might be an alcoholic. That wouldn't disqualify him as an intelligence source. Lots of sources were drunks. But still, Les wondered why the defector was so important. The medical tests had resolved nothing, not even if Curveball was vaccinated. The lab results didn't prove or disprove the accident at Djerf al Nadaf.

Les had other concerns too, and later, much later, he would issue a frantic warning about Curveball. But he let it go for now. The inconclusive medical report was added to the CIA file, but nothing in it indicated that an American had ever laid eyes on Curveball. Apparently the meeting was arranged outside normal channels in Germany as well. Senior BND officials only learned of his visit much later.

It wouldn't have mattered. By mid-2000, the weapons analysts back at the CIA and at the DIA were enamored with Curveball's gripping account, his direct access to Taha, his detailed designs, and meticulous memory. No one doubted that Saddam was building germ weapons. Curveball was only giving them the proof.

For one thing, his claims reinforced the analysts' own convictions. Taha had claimed to help Iraqi farmers as the cover story to hide her germ weapons program at Al Hakam. Now she was doing it again. The parallels were uncanny. Kamil, Dr. Germ, the Chemical Engineering and Design Center, Amiriyah, it all fit together. Jamie Miscik, chief of the CIA analysts, liked to compare their job to assembling a one-thousand-piece jigsaw puzzle, but with only two hundred pieces and no picture on the cover of the box. Thanks to Curveball, the pieces were falling into place. The picture was taking shape.

Curveball's reporting "demonstrates a knowledge of and access to personalities, organizations, procurement, and technology related to Iraq's BW program," a Defense HUMINT analyst wrote. CIA analysts praised his drawings and his command of engineering details. He was "a project engineer involved in the design and production of . . . biological production facilities in Iraq," one concluded. Nothing was "obviously wrong" with his information.

Even the timing fit precisely. If Taha ordered up a secret fleet of mobile germ factories in May 1995, as Curveball said, it explained why the Iraqis surrendered their previous bioweapons program at Al Hakam to U.N. inspectors later that summer.

The CIA analysts found support for this in old reports from U.N. inspectors and their own files. A CIA report from December 1996 had noted that a U.N. team had discovered two handwritten notes, on the letterhead of Hussein Kamil's Military Industrialization Commission, indicating the Iraqis were "considering" mobile germ weapons labs. The analysts took this as corroboration even though the notes were undated and unsigned.

Other U.N. reports showed that Taha's team had tried to buy fermentors in Russia in the summer of 1995. Five Iraqis visited Moscow, including two from the Chemical Engineering and Design Center and three from Al Hakam. U.N. inspectors blocked the sale. And the massive fermentors, each ten thousand liters in volume, were far too large for Curveball's trucks.

The CIA analysts added this report as well to the file as corroborating evidence for Curveball's claims. Then they turned to America's constellation of spy satellites.

In early 2000, they asked the National Imagery and Mapping Agency, which analyzed overhead imagery for U.S. intelligence, to check the Amiriyah institute, where Curveball said they ran quality tests on the bio-brew. The analysts pored over their computers and light tables, magnifying everything they could. They compared current pictures to those from a year ago. There was definitely increased activity and construction, no doubt about it.

But the analysts had no idea what it meant. Spy satellites can't see inside closed buildings. Iraq ran large-scale vaccination campaigns all that year against polio and foot-and-mouth disease. Maybe the activity at the Amiriyah vaccine institute was related. Maybe not. At best, the analysts cautiously concluded, "more than pharmaceutical production or distribution is taking place."

These notes also got added to the file as corroboration.

The imagery analysts identified Djerf al Nadaf and the five other docking stations that Curveball had named. The digital images showed no actual bio-trucks or other illicit activity—just warehouses and other large buildings where they might be hidden. These too were added to the file. It "looked like more corroboration to us at the time," a CIA biowarfare analyst said later.

CIA analysts accepted the Curveball reports without skepticism or doubt as summer turned to fall in 2000. Over at the DIA, thanks to Munich House, Curveball was seen as a rising star.

DIA officials in Washington can rate an incoming field report as "No Value," "Of Value," "High Value," or in the very best cases, "Major Significance," which was known internally as "Major Sig." From the start, "Major Sig" was stamped on the Munich House reports. Like Schumann and Meiner at the BND, Steiner's team at Munich House was garnering praise and basking in reflected glory.

Senior officials in Washington were increasingly interested. Among them was Vice Adm. Thomas R. Wilson, director of the DIA. The thirty-three-year Navy veteran began seeing the Curveball reports, and was briefed on the details, all through 2000. "It was considered high-priority," he recalled.

"The mobile labs certainly fit into the intelligence we had that the Iraqis were trying to defeat U.N. inspections," Wilson said. "In the context of what it appeared they were doing to build weapons of mass destruction, there was every reason to think this was legitimate."

The view grew stronger as time passed. "Everybody's mind-set was we're going to see the WMD," Wilson added. "I don't know anybody who didn't believe it was there."

CHAPTER 11

Curveball was hardly the only Iraqi informant in Germany.

German police regularly stopped suspected undocumented visitors at train stations, bus depots, and elsewhere and demanded to inspect their identity papers. Everyone over the age of sixteen in Germany was issued an official identity card called a *Personalausweis*, and the police called their mini-raids an *Ausweis* check.

In the summer of 2001, police running a spot check netted a major from Iraq's Special Security Organization as he prepared to board a train near Munich. Western intelligence long hoped for inside access to the SSO, the most powerful agency in Saddam's security apparatus. Before his defection, Kamil used the SSO to move and conceal the weapons of mass destruction and to spy on U.N. inspectors. Later Saddam's younger son and heir apparent, Qusay, took over and used the secret police agency to protect his father and enforce his edicts. The SSO held crucial regime secrets.

The police handed the SSO major to Germany's internal security authorities, who held a quick closed-door hearing and then passed him off to the BND. At first, the bull-necked military officer angrily refused to talk.

"I am not a traitor," he said, flushed with defiance.

That was not relevant, his captors pointed out. He had no diplomatic immunity. Once news of his detention reached Baghdad, Qusay's henchmen would assume he had cooperated. If the Germans deported him back to Iraq, the regime would kill him. They also would torture and kill his wife and children.

"Help us," the Germans promised, "and we'll get your family out of Iraq."

It took a while but the Iraqi gave in. He began to talk, reluctantly at first, then more openly. He had personally directed Saddam's security operations in the region north of Baghdad, especially around the city of Mosul, he admitted. He denied any knowledge of secret germ production trucks or any other weapons of mass destruction. Still, he provided a trove of information about other sensitive facilities.

Two DIA interrogators soon got the call and joined the debriefings in a local hotel room. One worked for the DIA's Human Factors Analysis unit, which tried to understand the psychology of informants. The couple had to pretend they worked for the BND, using false names and speaking only German through an Arabic translator.

They grilled the Iraqi for six to eight hours a day for a week. The Iraqi still was mulish, still loath to give away too much. So, early in the process, one of the DIA debriefers handed him a pencil and drafting pad and asked him to sketch one of the Iraqi intelligence monitoring facilities he had described in Mosul.

The Iraqi scribbled away and handed over a crude drawing.

Then the American reached into his briefcase and pulled out a detailed map of Mosul from the Pentagon mapping agency. He carefully spread it across the table, smoothing it flat with his hands. He asked the major to pinpoint the street where the intelligence building stood. The Iraqi leaned over and studied the paper for a moment, then circled the site with a black marker.

The DIA officer reached down into his briefcase again. This time he pulled out a sheaf of spy satellite pictures. He spread these across the table. They were not the grainy images available on the Internet, full of blurry buildings and cars as tiny dots. These were highly classified, high-resolution images from the U.S. spy satellites that orbited almost every hour over Iraq. The billion-dollar craft can see a basketball on a cloudless day, or stream data to generate three-dimensional radar images of buildings and terrain.

The man's face grew pale as he leafed through the images. One showed a crystal-sharp overhead image of the intelligence facility that he had just marked on the map. He stared at it in disbelief. Other images highlighted other obscure sites he had described. He held each picture up, nodding wordlessly. Finally, he slumped back in his chair to steady himself. He seemed astonished.

"Did the Americans really have Predators over us?" he asked after a moment's hesitation.

The Pentagon only possessed a few Predators at that point. But they had pumped stories into the media that suggested drone aircraft carrying infrared video cameras and other surveillance gear swarmed like mosquitoes overhead.

"No, these aren't drones," the DIA officer replied. "These are American satellites. We can see everything in Iraq now."

He smiled broadly as he gathered up his pictures and maps and stuffed them back in the case.

"You don't want to show the unclassified stuff to a guy like that," he explained later. "You want to show your best stuff. You want to impress him. You want him to think that you already know everything and he's just there to confirm it. That way, in his own mind, he's not really telling you something new. He's just confirming a few details."

The gambit worked. The reluctant Iraqi officer began to speak much more freely about important military targets in Iraq. It turned out he had an extraordinary memory. He identified secret Iraqi intelligence and security buildings, Ba'ath political party offices, telecommunications and energy facilities, military barracks and gun emplacements, as well as safe houses and underground bunkers where Saddam met his advisors or slept. He also helped identify schools, hospitals, and religious sites that should not be attacked.

"He was stunning, among the best we ever had," said the American. "He was a major, which was perfect. He had enough access to what we wanted. But he wasn't so high up that he couldn't get out of Iraq."

The Americans ultimately helped smuggle the major's family out of Iraq through Turkey, and settled them together in Germany.

Another Iraqi defector to Germany had served as a personal driver for Saddam and his two sons. He helped the DIA pinpoint key targets in Baghdad. The DIA brought only a handful of Iraqi informants to the United States in the intelligence community's equivalent of the Witness Protection Program, but Saddam's chauffeur was among them. They set him up with a new name, a comfortable home, and a job as a car mechanic in southern California.

The CIA also brought two other Iraqis to America: a senior official from Iraq's intelligence service and another officer from the Special Security Organization. He escaped to Jordan and made his way to Germany in 1998. He later was flown to Washington and became the chief source of intelligence data for regime targets in the British and American air strikes that December.

The crop of defectors proved invaluable in helping the Pentagon select military targets in Iraq for the 2003 invasion as well. "It is difficult to overestimate the importance of our sources in Germany," said the DIA official, who helped debrief about fifty Iraqis in the six months before the war. "The German defectors were phenomenal. If we did not have these sources in Germany, I assure you the war in Iraq would have been very different."

Perhaps the most unlikely informant was a gray-haired, stoop-shouldered Iraqi in his seventies who spent nearly two decades mopping marble floors, replacing light bulbs, and moving gilt-edged furniture. He was the chief janitor of the main presidential palace in Baghdad. Like Curveball, he had arrived in Germany on his own, and applied for political asylum.

After getting the call from the BND, a DIA team interviewed him four to five hours a day for five days straight.

"These guys were better than any general," the DIA official said. "You don't want the head of the program. He almost always will lie. Because he has blood on his hands, and he's going to lie about what he did. Or he is going to boost his importance for a better deal. He was 'Saddam's best friend.' Or he 'knows where all the WMD are.' And 90 percent of what he tells you is crap.

"You want the driver. Or the guy who was the janitor in the president's palace. He's everywhere. He has the keys to everything. He can go anywhere. He knows the layout of all the buildings. No one questions him. He's observant. He knows who works there. He knows where people sleep. He knows how supplies are delivered. He knows when people come and when they go. He knows all the timetables.

"What time do they meet? Which conference room do they use? How often? Who has a bodyguard? Does someone have a double? He knew where Saddam's bodyguards lived, and where the Special Security Organization was based. He knew how the place functions. A janitor is a gold mine. He's not trained to lie or to resist interrogators. He has everything to gain by cooperating."

Although DIA files listed each source with a color and number, the debriefing teams chose more personal nicknames for nonofficial communications. The aging palace custodian was dubbed "The Janitor." The chauffeur was "The Driver." And a defector known for his gagging body odor inevitably was known as "Stinky."

The DIA had only one real source inside Iraq before the 2003 war. He lived near Baghdad's Al Hamra Hotel, a yellowing high rise heap notable for barely edible food, moldy carpets, and a surly staff riddled with informants for Iraqi intelligence. The DIA spy was a British-educated trader who was allowed to travel to Jordan occasionally to conduct his business. The DIA met him in Amman, hustled him onto a military plane under cover of darkness, and flew him back to the United States for quick debriefings and lavish meals at stylish restaurants in Washington, San Francisco, and Los Angeles, the DIA official recalled.

"His son ran an Internet café. The computer network attack people liked to talk to him. . . . They gave him tiny cameras and he would bring pictures out. Or he would go on a trip, write up his notes, then take pictures of the notes and burn the notes. It was mostly atmospherics, and it wasn't really very useful. But it was the only Iraqi agent we had, so people treated his information as important."

CHAPTER 12

One American already had spent years searching for Saddam's germ trucks.

Scott Ritter Jr. had joined UNSCOM, the U.N. disarmament effort in Iraq, shortly after the 1991 war. He created a special intelligence unit, apparently a first at the U.N. The CIA and other spy services quickly recognized the advantages of using U.N. teams to collect intelligence inside Iraq, and they began working closely with him.

Ritter, a former Marine, was strong and tall, with square-jawed good looks. His tousled brown hair poked out beneath a light blue U.N. baseball cap. But he was self-righteous and abrasive, and showed no qualms about bruising egos and making enemies. He was an inspector, he figured, not a diplomat. Anyway, he enjoyed his bad boy reputation. "I went through Iraq like Attila the Hun," he boasted later. Members of the Clinton White House called him Darth Vader. Others compared him to Colonel Oliver North, the gung ho Marine at the center of the Iran-contra scandal in the Reagan White House.

Ritter especially took delight in provoking Saddam's regime. He deliberately drove his white U.N. vehicle close to a walled compound called Dora Farms, along the Tigris in south Baghdad. Saddam's wife and three daughters lived inside, and the dictator's yacht tied up at the dock. Each time a car drove too close, Iraqi military rapid reaction teams exploded out the gate, weapons at the ready. Ritter liked to drive by there three or four times a day just to piss them off.

He summed up his approach in a pep talk that he gave each new U.N. team as they prepared for a mission. He sounded as tenderhearted as an Army drill sergeant.

"Look, when we go into Iraq, they're going to try to intimidate you," Ritter warned. "To them, fear is like blood around a shark. They smell fear. They're going to come at you. They're going to come at you hard. And they're going to try and make you lose focus on what you want to do. They're going to bring out guns. They're going to yell. They're going to posture.

"It isn't going to work with this team. Because there's only going to be one alpha dog in country, and that's me. When the Iraqis come up with their tail up, my tail goes higher. When they growl, I growl louder. When they bark, I jump on them and I kick them to the ground because I'm in charge and you work for me. So when the situation goes to hell in a hand basket, I don't want you running around with fear in your eyes. I want you looking at me. As long as I'm standing there, proud, in charge, in control, you don't have to worry about a thing."

Before joining the U.N., Ritter had taken part in a Pentagon-run arms control mission to the former Soviet Union. He came away appalled that Moscow had concealed an extraordinary biological warfare empire during the Cold War. They had fifty laboratories, sixty thousand people, and the CIA had missed the whole thing. Ritter felt similarly outraged after his first year in Iraq, convinced that Iraqi officials were hiding germ weapons and factories. Ritter felt not just thwarted. He took it as a personal affront.

In late 1992, after a year in Iraq, Ritter wrote a memo to Rolf Ekeus, the chief U.N. weapons inspector, in New York. Baghdad could build germ factories on trucks, Ritter advised. He had no proof. But he laid out the logic for what he called "mobile capabilities." We can't locate Saddam's germ factories so either they don't exist—or they are hidden. If they're on trucks, how would the Iraqis provide security? How would they communicate? How can we find them?

Ekeus was persuaded by Ritter's hypothesis. CIA officials also were convinced. Washington lent a high-altitude U-2 spy plane to UNSCOM and imagery analysts began searching for the presumed "signature" of a mobile germ factory. They looked for two or three large trucks, parked beside one another, with communications gear, water, and power sources. Security forces and emergency decontamination vehicles would be nearby.

In the spring of 1995, as Curveball reported to his new job at the Chemical Engineering and Design Center in Baghdad, Israel's Aman military intelligence passed an urgent tip to Ritter's unit. Iraq, they said, was hauling and producing biological weapons inside disguised commercial vehicles.

The Iraqis, according to the intelligence, churned out biological agents inside red and white, candy-cane-striped refrigerator trucks marked "Tip Top Ice Cream." It seemed no wackier than many things in Iraq. U.N. inspectors soon located several trucks. Excited, they ripped open the doors and peered inside. The compartments carried ice cream.

Another Israeli tip suggested that the Iraqis hid fermentation units inside green moving vans marked "Sajida Transport," named for Sajida Talfa, Saddam's first wife. Dutch intelligence, citing information from a source code-named Fulcrum, sent the inspectors tracking trucks with sequentially numbered blue and white license plates. Despite an extensive search, Ritter's team never found any evidence and some inspectors began calling the hunt a waste of time. They argued that mobile germ factories would be complicated to build, dangerous to operate, and difficult to hide.

Ritter refused to back down. He launched raid after raid. "It was my baby," he recalled later. He wasn't discouraged by the failure to find any hard proof. "If you get there, and there's nothing there, well, it's on wheels," he reasoned. "They moved it."

His theory gained credence in September 1995, shortly after Curveball first went to Djerf al Nadaf.

Lt. Gen. Amir Hammudi Hasan Saadi sat down in Baghdad with four senior U.N. inspectors. Saadi wore a neatly combed coif of silver hair and carried an air of cultivation. He spoke fluent English and German after obtaining his master's degree from Oxford University and a doctorate at the University of Munich. He had been Kamil's chief deputy in the secret weapons program. Now he was Saddam's senior scientific advisor.

The four U.N. inspectors—Hamish Killip and David Kelly of the United Kingdom, Rod Barton of Australia, and Richard Spertzel of the United States—were determined to solve the bioweapons mystery. Colleagues dubbed them the "Gang of Four" for their close collaboration. They were still collecting the clues, still trying to understand why the Iraqis bought so much growth media, and Saadi was running them in circles. Almost on a whim, Killip asked if the Iraqis ever considered building germ trucks.

"Oh yes," Saadi said proudly. "That was my idea."

Killip and the other inspectors were dumbfounded.

Saadi said he got the idea when Kamil ordered him to start

bioweapons production before the 1991 war. The old laboratories at Salman Pak, where Taha had tested germs on animals, were too well known to U.S. intelligence. A secret program needed a secret factory. Saadi said he summoned Taha in and ordered her to find a secure production site.

But then he ventured a more radical idea.

Why not try mobile platforms? Like Curveball, Saadi was a civil engineer, a problem solver, a doer. He outlined his concept to Taha. She could use three flatbed trucks, he said. Put her fermentors on the first, downstream processing on the second, and holding tanks on the third. They drive into a warehouse. Plug in water, power, whatever they needed. Run a batch off in a few days. Then move to the next location and do it again. Fantastic!

All she needed, Saadi continued enthusiastically, was to adapt multiple vehicles and then design modular production units, full-on containment systems, clandestine supply depots and docking stations, munitions-filling teams . . .

"It would be simple," he concluded.

Taha politely listened to her boss. Then she shot it down as absurdly impractical.

"Forget it," Taha told him. "It's far too complicated. I'm a microbiologist, not an engineer. There's no way I can do that."

Saadi smiled at the four U.N. inspectors. End of story, he told them.

Killip, the British army biowarfare expert, looked skeptical.

"That's it?" he asked.

"That's it." Saadi shrugged. "We never built them."

The U.N. team pressed for more details. But they finally dropped the subject. Saadi was doing his usual thing of just flinging ideas around, Killip thought. To Spertzel, it sounded like a flight of fancy, nothing more. Barton figured maybe Saadi heard about the Soviet biotrucks. They didn't ask Saadi where he got the idea, or if he discussed it with anyone other than Taha. Saadi didn't give them any drawings, blueprints, or documents, and they didn't pursue it. Too many other issues demanded attention. They agreed with Taha. Mobile germ factories sounded awfully complicated.

But CIA analysts took Saadi's comments far more seriously. Subsequent U.S. intelligence reports would treat Saadi's offhand remarks as confirmation, if not a virtual confession. The search continued.

In March 1997, an American U-2 spy plane photographed three or four large box-type trucks parked at a construction site outside a garage used by Iraq's intelligence service. Ritter got an urgent message. This was it, the big break. He grabbed a team and they raced to the scene. Leaping from their cars, the inspectors yanked open the double doors on each trailer. They were loaded with construction material.

Ritter had another brainstorm. He asked UNSCOM headquarters for permission to conduct random roadblocks. He proposed that U.N. teams arbitrarily stop and search any vehicle that aroused suspicion. He also asked for hot pursuit authority, with a fleet of fast cars and helicopters capable of spraying slippery foam on the roads, in case they had to chase a fleeing germ truck. Supervisors quickly rejected both proposals.

"We were told that was insane," Ritter conceded later. "And they were right."

He began having second thoughts about his hypothesis and the actual risk of Saddam's bioweapons. "All they had were dumb bombs filled with liquid agent," he said. "The only way one would kill you would be if it hit you on the head."

But Ritter did not give up. In the fall of 1997, a U.S. State Department officer assigned to UNSCOM in New York arranged for Ritter to contact Ahmed Chalabi, an Iraqi exile leader, in London.

Chalabi was smart, charismatic, and exceedingly ambitious. The CIA had approached the former banker in London after the 1991 war to help corral fractious Iraqi émigré groups into a coalition to oppose Saddam. The new Iraqi National Congress soon began funneling low-ranking military and intelligence walk-ins and defectors to the CIA. The group also recruited an armed militia in Kurdish-controlled areas of northern Iraq.

Under the code name DB Achilles, the CIA threw its support behind a Chalabi-led military coup against Saddam. But Iraqi intelligence agents, taking advantage of bitter infighting among the exiles, easily penetrated the plot. On the eve of the planned attack in March 1995, the CIA sent a frantic warning to Chalabi that "the action you have planned for this weekend has been totally compromised" and "we believe there is a high risk of failure." But the exile leader refused to abort, and armed Iraqi troops overwhelmed the rebels. Irate CIA officials blamed Chalabi for the bloodshed.

To hedge its bets, the CIA took operational control of a rival

London-based exile group, the Iraqi National Accord, the INA, from British intelligence. They scheduled another coup in June 1996. But Iraqi intelligence infiltrated this as well. Determined to crush the CIA-sponsored rebels for good, Baghdad sent thousands of troops into northern Iraq. They executed several hundred suspected coup sympathizers and imprisoned two thousand others. The CIA frantically evacuated about 650 Iraqis on its payroll and resettled them in the United States.

Recriminations erupted inside the CIA. Chalabi's critics accused him of exposing the INA plot, while he blamed the CIA for pulling the plug on his group and backing his rival. The split seemed final. Agency leaders viewed Chalabi as ineffective, self-aggrandizing, and probably corrupt. "There was a breakdown in trust and we never wanted to have anything to do with him anymore," CIA director Tenet said later. In February 1997, the CIA cut off Chalabi's funding and formally severed its relationship with his organization.

Ritter knew some of the details, but following orders, he and a British intelligence operative on his team flew to London and took a taxi to a townhouse in posh Mayfair in January 1998. The Iraqi émigré introduced them to his intelligence chief. The four men sat for three hours as Arab servants silently served a light dinner and tea.

"Chalabi outlined what he could do for us," Ritter recalled. "His intelligence guy outlined their sources and said he had people inside the government. They told us they had the run of Iraq. Just tell them what we needed. So we outlined the gaps in our understanding of the Iraqi program, including the mobile bio-weapons labs. Basically, we gave them a shopping list."

During their meeting, Ritter handed Chalabi a fifty-page report on how Iraq concealed evidence and hardware. He also handed over computer encryption software so they could exchange secure e-mail and attachments.

"They began feeding us information," Ritter said. "We got hand-drawn maps, handwritten statements, and other stuff flowing in. At first blush, it looked good. But nothing panned out. Most of it just regurgitated what we'd given them. It was crap. Total crap."

CHAPTER 13

Schumann and Meiner were disheartened as well.

As the interrogations dragged into a second year, as 2000 eased into 2001, and as a harsh winter settled in, Curveball's easy charm and candor ebbed away. His confiding smile turned brittle and his earnest gaze iced over. He grew despondent and bad-tempered.

I already told you everything I know, he said irritably.

But what did he know? Schumann and Meiner wearily struggled to pin down what he really saw and did, as opposed to what he only heard from friends or office workers. They badgered the exhausted Arabic translator to parse his language for possible clues. They tried in vain to walk the defector through his story yet again, detail by detail. They felt less and less confident about their star source.

Even in the beginning, he spoke in a disjointed fashion, terse one minute and expansive the next. He served up a mix of office gossip and technical jargon. He meandered from year to year, place to place. He could never get the chronology straight. But now his recall began to falter even more. He confused places and names. He changed aspects of his account or, worse, denied what he previously seemed to have said. Sometimes in the next session, he supplied fresh answers, new specifics, and more names, as if he had recharged his memory.

"He is saying one thing in the morning and another at night," Meiner whined to a supervisor. "It's hard to understand how he thinks."

"This guy is driving me nuts," Schumann echoed in dismay. "He changes his mind from one second to the next."

Sharp contradictions—official reports called them inconsistencies and discrepancies—suddenly shredded an account that previously looked impregnable. At first, Curveball said he was a senior engineer. Now it appeared he was just a trainee. He installed fermentors. No, he just helped design them. He supervised construction and testing. He didn't. He oversaw production. He produced nothing. It seemed some days that he didn't care what he said.

The more the Germans grilled Curveball, the more confused they became. His information had seemed so solid, so unassailable. Now it was turning to tatters. Everything was maybe, could be, probably. He seemed adrift, pulled by unseen forces, lost in an inner world they could not pierce. Their hard intelligence grew softer, like crumbling clay in their hands.

The initial BND reports indicated Curveball had managed the project at Djerf al Nadaf. Now he vehemently denied that. Cursing in anger, he accused the translator of misinterpreting his Arabic and the handlers of putting words in his mouth. Gone was his contention that the trucks prepared deadly germs. He knew only that he worked on a "secret" project; no one ever told him what it was. The technicians did not disclose what they brewed in the fermentors, he declared. They used code letters, speaking only of Agent A, Agent B, Agent C, and so on.

"He didn't know what he was producing, whether it was anthrax or not," Kappel said. "He did not know what they wanted to produce. He did not know what these vehicles were designed to produce."

Gone too now was any talk of industrial spray driers or dried anthrax spores. He knew nothing about them, he insisted. Even the slurry was unsuitable for munitions. "It was not necessarily transformable into weapons," said Pieper, the BND analyst. "It was not weapons-grade material."

Next Curveball conceded that he left Djerf al Nadaf before any production actually commenced. He wasn't certain if the trailer-based systems really operated at all. He only heard about it from others.

"He could not say if they functioned, if they worked," Kappel added. "He did not know if this was a production facility for biological weapons."

Curveball lastly conceded that maybe technicians really brewed fungicide or bio-pesticides on the trailers to spray on seeds to improve agriculture. Perhaps the cover story was true. He didn't rule it out. The Germans struggled for answers.

I am telling the truth, he muttered furiously.

Even in the classified files, clarity comes and goes like fog from the train, mist on a mirror. It becomes difficult to decipher precisely what

Curveball said and what others understood, concluded, or projected. His account was all reflections anyway, translated, interpreted, and analyzed by others. The Germans saw one reality, the Americans another, the British yet another.

Still, it was strange. Most defectors inflate their roles to gain favor with the spy services that take them in. They exaggerate details as they retell their stories, riding a rising tide of lies. But Curveball's account was shrinking, not growing.

Frustrated, the BND officers on the case convened a series of uneasy meetings. What the hell was going on? Was he lying now, or was he lying before? Was he scamming them?

Pieper, Meiner's boss, argued that Curveball's original information was so exquisitely detailed, so utterly persuasive, that it had to be true.

Curveball was young and inexperienced, just out of school, and he knew little about biological programs or unconventional weapons, Pieper pointed out. He couldn't make those details up. No impostor could withstand such intensive questioning. If Curveball were older, in his forties, or if he claimed vast expertise with germ weapons or direct involvement with other secret programs, it "would be easier to assume he was lying," Pieper said.

"Do you think a twenty-something guy makes a plan like this?" he asked. "'I will go to Germany. I don't speak the language. I know nothing about the country. But I will make up a story and even though I am a chemical engineer, I will make up a story about biological weapons. And I will trick them all.' Is this logical? No."

Given Curveball's erratic behavior, Schumann and the other BND officers no longer trusted him entirely. But they trusted their instincts. He had told the truth during his first debriefings a year earlier, they agreed. They knew that memories are fungible, constantly changing. Under stress, or over time, clarity of recall can evaporate or reformulate in unexpected ways. So they ignored his denials, his backsliding and memory lapses.

Some BMD colleagues questioned Schumann's judgment. "It's clear the source became more important because the Americans kept asking about him," one said. "So the reports became more detailed, more embellished. And the case officer's status became more important."

As far as the German intelligence agency was concerned, Curveball's monstrous germ trucks probably were brewing pestilence and death that very day in the dusty warehouse with the weird swinging door at Djerf al Nadaf. The seeds of Curveball's initial story had taken root.

"We were convinced it was aimed for bioweapons production," Pieper said.

The *Hortensia 2* reports would show no dramatic change, no clear indication of the tectonic shifts in Curveball's account. Curveball was still a star in the BND firmament. The BND handlers suddenly had more urgent concerns.

CHAPTER 14

Curveball was becoming a nervous wreck.

He carped about his life. His apartment was cramped and wretched. He felt trapped and abandoned, like a prisoner in a cell, a castaway on an islet. He telephoned Schumann at night, at home, on weekends, at all hours, just to moan. The constant pealing of church bells drove him crazy. The motorcycles outside roared too loudly. The damp cold made his teeth ache. He needed a dentist. A doctor. He needed more Coke.

Mostly, he pestered his handler about his future in Germany, and that of his poor wife and parents still stuck in Iraq. Why was it taking so long to get him a job, to get them out of Baghdad, to get his asylum? He worried constantly, his anxiety rising by the day.

Schumann allowed Curveball to phone his mother so she would know he was well. But be brief and be careful, the German cautioned; Saddam's eavesdroppers surely will listen. The warnings pushed Curveball's despondency to panic. Who would protect them? Who would protect him? Saddam's spies were everywhere, even in Germany. The more he met with the BND, the more likely someone would spot and expose him. Saddam would kill them all in their beds.

In the next breath, he threatened to go back to Iraq on his own.

"This guy is driving me nuts," Schumann groused to his supervisor again.

To be fair, the Germans were driving Curveball nuts. The BND could have arranged political asylum at the outset. It instead requested Bavarian state authorities to issue him a temporary permit, similar to a visa, to stay in the country. He had to reapply, with BND help, for an extension every six months. The BND figured short-term permits gave them leverage. It pressured defectors to keep collaborating.

The tactic backfired with Curveball. He bitterly resented it. He had fulfilled his part of the bargain, he shouted. He had told them everything he knew. Why didn't they give him asylum? Where was his big house, his Mercedes? Why were they tormenting him? So they pushed the asylum paperwork through but it made no difference. If anything, the Iraqi became more petulant, less cooperative.

"He knew he was important," said Kappel. "He was not an idiot."

Curveball was spending more time in the Internet cafés, endlessly patrolling the Internet for information. He had grown more obsessed with Mercedes-Benz sedans, or saloons as they are called in Germany. One can imagine him dreamily poring over the automaker's rich Web site. One model offered "sculpted contours set off by the taut lines of its lower bodywork." It sounded like the soft porn on his TV.

He begged his handlers to find him a high-paying engineering job. Schumann repeatedly explained that a University of Baghdad undergraduate degree in chemical engineering was all but useless in Munich. No German company would hire him until he passed local engineering boards and exams. How could he study, how could he take the test, how could he work in an office, when he still didn't speak German?

Schumann had arranged private language lessons. But no matter how many German classes Curveball took, how many tutors they hired, he forgot the vocabulary, confused his genders, and mangled the grammar. He battled with syntax and tenses, gagged over his pronunciation. He was hopeless. Schumann was disappointed but supportive, like a tolerant father with an erring son.

His drinking worsened. He'd get weepy and sloppy, his eyes struggling to focus. He wasn't a mean drunk, but he was tactless and opinionated, loud enough to draw unwanted attention that unnerved his handlers. They did not believe Curveball was an alcoholic, unlike the CIA doctor who grumbled because the Iraqi suffered a hangover during a blood test early on a Saturday morning. This was Bavaria, home of the world's best beers. Everyone drank on Friday night.

But they worried as his behavior grew more unpredictable.

By early 2001, a year after his first debriefing, Curveball appeared to be losing his grip on reality. He is acting "emotionally unbalanced" and "psychologically unstable," his worried handlers told superiors. He is "not completely normal." He is "cursing, yelling and crying."

The Germans thought he suffered from depression. He lost weight and grew consumptive in appearance. His parched face took on a hollow, haunted look, his cheeks etched with fatigue. He forgot to shave and stubble rode up his face like a stain. His eyes looked glazed, glassy, like he was in a trance. He suffered wild mood swings, what Schumann called "roller-coaster emotions."

He chatted cheerfully one minute and then plummeted into morose silence. He is "sometimes cooperative, sometimes very aggressive" and "sometimes dreaming, sometimes scared to death," Schumann reported. Curveball "lives in two worlds." He heaped bilious insults on them and then broke down and begged forgiveness, his face contorted in contrition. It was impossible to have a normal conversation.

"One minute he is high up, laughing, very euphoric, jolly, telling jokes," Kappel said. "Everything is fine. Maybe he will end up running a big business in Argentina or somewhere. The next he is deep down and shouting, 'Fuck you, asshole! You don't understand.'"

The BND did not assign a psychiatrist to study the cause of Curveball's emotional ordeal or to prescribe medication. Perhaps they tried and he refused; that's unclear. Schumann simply reported that the Iraqi had suffered a nervous breakdown and needed time to rest. "No one was very sure what was going on," said Kappel.

His desperation now reached fever pitch. Curveball refused to meet his handlers. Or he postponed appointments at the last minute. Then he simply vanished. It happened more than once. He failed to show up for yet another round of questions, sparking anxious alarms and frantic searches. They couldn't find him and they couldn't contact him. He didn't answer his phone or respond to urgent messages. They checked his apartment and found only the stench of stale smoke and old food. Curveball had disappeared.

It was worse than embarrassing. The nation's spy service couldn't find a crucial informant in its own backyard. Jumpy sources require endless patience, even endurance. But this was maddening. Curveball had run away.

"We lost contact," Kappel winced. "Normally we don't expect people to disappear. He depends on us."

Perhaps he just wandered the winding streets, partaking of the brothels, the beer gardens, the Mercedes showrooms. Maybe he fled in panic. No clear record has emerged. Some suspect he boarded a bus or train and left Germany at least once. He visited England. Or France. A girlfriend perhaps. One intelligence report indicated he was hiding in Austria. The CIA heard he toured Switzerland or a coastal resort in Spain.

When he showed up again on his own after a few days or weeks, Curveball greeted them sullenly, like a spoiled teenager. During the next meeting—please, Meiner would say, we need to go over this again—he smoked ferociously and incessantly, an insolent face shrouded in billows of gray. He chewed his nails and his fingertips looked red and raw. He paced in dark anger. He trusted no one.

"He was fed up with us, fed up about his situation, fed up with the questions," said Schneider, Schumann's supervisor. "He was difficult to integrate into local society. And he was afraid."

It seems more likely that Curveball was terrified. What if someone fingered him as the source? What if word got back to Baghdad?

"He must have been scared out of his mind," said a British intelligence officer. "He was desperate to stay there. He was very emotional, very high-strung. He's trying to run this game on the Germans. It's working, but not quite. And the stress is tremendous."

Signs of paranoia set in. Hard, unblinking eyes followed him everywhere, he told his handlers. He heard footsteps clatter outside his window, muffled footfalls sweep up the steps. The phone held telltale clicks. Saddam's legions of thugs, or assassins from an Iraqi exile group, were closing in, Curveball whimpered. They would slaughter him and butcher his family like sheep.

It was possible. The Iraqi intelligence service kept close tabs on the growing Iraqi émigré community in Germany. Saddam's agents routinely blackmailed visiting Iraqi students, businessmen, and scientists to become regime informants, forcing them to spy on one another to protect their families back home from harm. No evidence suggests Iraqi agents ever assassinated political opponents or dissidents in Germany. But the threat of vicious reprisals back in Iraq was constant and real.

Or was someone else tracking him?

British intelligence had obtained Curveball's true name. Unlike the CIA, British intelligence officers worked closely and well with the Germans. The BND denied slipping the name to MI6, and the British wouldn't say if their spies or eavesdroppers stole it. But it soon became apparent that the British were running a side deal of some kind directly with the BND.

Outsiders assume U.S. and British spy services work seamlessly together. The early CIA modeled itself after MI6, adopting its structure and systems. Officially, neither service spies on the other. In fact, both sides do and the relationship sometimes is tense and rife with suspicion. This was one of those times.

"People were really pissed off that the Brits were talking to the Germans about the case and they didn't share it all with us," a senior CIA officer said.

The Brits finally passed the name to the CIA London station, which filed it to the operations desk back at Langley. Soon after, a team of operatives studied telephone directories, anything they could find, for an address around Munich to match the name. But it was a common name, like Ahmed Mohammed, and the covert search party turned to farce.

"It was like a Keystone Kops episode," David Kay, America's chief weapons hunter in Iraq, said later. "Two men showed up and pounded on the wrong door. They started asking some guy about biological weapons. He got scared and called the police. It caused a neighborhood ruckus. The Germans were incensed. It caused a real stink."

Even before the call, BND surveillance teams had tracked the hapless search party. The Germans didn't interfere because the hunters never came close to their quarry. "We saw people wandering in places they should not be, strolling around talking to families," Kappel said. An unauthorized operation by a foreign spy service on German soil violated domestic law. "I know the Americans tried to find Curveball, and this was illegal," he added.

Some U.S. officials suspected that the BND deliberately furnished the wrong name to MI6 to mislead the CIA. "People raised questions about whether it was legend or real, put out by the Germans to confuse us when we were looking for him," Kay said.

But the senior CIA officer swore that the agency never tried to find Curveball. "The Germans really believe it, but it's not true," he said. "They asked us about it later. Look, I admit there were people here who wanted us to, who pushed for independent meetings. There are always people in Washington who have this brainstorm and they say, 'Hey, why don't you just see this guy? Just knock on his door.'

"But we knew they were watching him. I mean, they were with him all the time. They were all over him. It would have been walking into a trap. It would be committing suicide to go in. I guarantee you, if anyone tried to see him, if they were posted to Germany, they would have been expelled. And if they came from outside, they probably would be arrested. The Germans were really serious about it. So no, we did not try."

He added, "The Brits are very aggressive. Maybe they did it. It would not be unusual for them."

What is clear is the BND believed Curveball faced potential peril and they moved him at least twice on short notice for his protection. "He came to them and said, 'I'm in danger,'" said the same CIA official. "They react to that."

CHAPTER 15

August Hanning, the president of the BND, viewed the threat seriously enough that he approved Curveball for insertion into a special resettlement program, similar to the FBI's witness protection system.

The BND may have taken him up into the Peissenberg, in the foothills of the Alps, a few hours from Pullach.

Hidden behind a tall fence was an elegant stone manor called *Torfmoos*, named for the spongelike sphagnum moss that covered nearby bogs. It nestled in the corner of a military base, at the end of a narrow road. Armed patrols and hidden video cameras watched for intruders in the woods. Security was assured.

They may have set him up in a modest pension-style hotel that a former BND operative ran on a back street in Munich, or in an apartment in Augsburg. Further north, they could use an old Prussian hunting lodge near Potsdam. They had access to dowdy safe houses and snug flats near the docks in Hamburg and commercial areas in Frankfurt. The Germans used them all to hide or debrief Iraqis and other defectors in the past.

The BND rarely used the option after the Cold War. Resettlement is expensive and difficult to arrange under Germany's legal system. Except for marriage, courts rarely permit Germans to change their names. Once an informant joins the protection system, however, the BND issues a false name and various legal papers—a passport, driver's license, credit report, and so on—attesting to the defector's new identity. They provide a sizable stipend, comfortable housing, full health insurance, and a retirement account. They may set up a battery of counseling services and, in some cases, round-the-clock bodyguards and surveillance. They arrange job training, language lessons, employment options, medical care, and more.

"Curveball got the whole package," said an intelligence official.

The relocation program carried a hidden cost, however. The BND now assumed the obligation of taking care of Curveball. The service called it an unwritten code. They were his guarantors, his protectors. They had vouched for his value to national security. Put simply, they were stuck with him.

"Sometimes you have to support these defectors the rest of their lives," the official added. "You have to deal with their problems. You have to help their families. If he is sick, you get a doctor. If he runs someone over with his car, you arrange the lawyer. You are responsible. You own them."

But Curveball now owned them as well. The BND could not just forsake their legal and moral commitment to him. They had vowed to protect him, and had spent a fortune on his upkeep. They could not repudiate him without risking scandal. The last thing any spy service wants is an informant to go public and complain. No one would trust them again.

At the start, the BND handlers explicitly warned Curveball not to disclose his former work, or his collaboration with German intelligence, to anyone else. He would put his own life, and that of his family back in Iraq, at risk if Saddam found out. The Germans cranked up the pressure once the defector entered the relocation program. Now they threatened to strip him of his salary, housing, and security if he talked to the press or if he exposed the BND role.

"We told him, 'If you talk to anyone on the outside then you cross the line,'" Kappel said. "'You are out and you get no more help from us. It is over. Nothing. There is also no return.'"

Some defectors and agents resettled abroad. They opted to build new lives in neighboring Austria, and the BND arranged permission and assistance in Vienna from the BVT, the Federal Agency for Protection of the Constitution and Counterterrorism. Or they relocated to the sunny Mediterranean coast of Spain with help from the CNI, the National Intelligence Center in Madrid.

The BND repeatedly pushed Curveball to leave Germany, to start a new life. Supervisors viewed it as the ideal solution. He had become a full-time job and a full-time headache. They were tired of his mercurial emotions and battery of complaints.

"We tried like hell to get rid of him," said Kappel. "We didn't want to be social worker and financial backer for the rest of his life."

Curveball had traveled in Turkey and the BND ran a sizable intelligence network there. Schumann pleaded with Curveball to let the BND relocate him to a new life in Turkey. He would feel more comfortable in a nation that was overwhelmingly Muslim, mostly Sunnis like himself.

And he would feel safer. A dark-skinned, Arabic-speaking Iraqi would not stand out or draw attention, as in Germany. The BND would arrange his protection in Ankara with the MIT, the Turkish National Intelligence Organization. His wife could join him. Everything cost less there so his BND stipend would go much further. Plus good food, great beaches, belly dancing, anything he needed. He would be happy.

Curveball adamantly, absolutely refused to consider the idea.

"He is afraid that we will not allow him back to Germany if he leaves," Schumann reported. "I told him of course he can come back. But he just wants to stay here."

Schumann was deeply disappointed but he defended Curveball's decision. After helping the desperate Iraqi through one personal crisis after another, he felt responsible for him. Curveball was like an orphan, lonely and vulnerable. He had betrayed his country and abandoned his family. He was confused and afraid. They had to help him.

"Medically, I would say he is very unstable," Schumann said at a BND meeting called to discuss the case. "As an operations officer, I would say he is an asshole. But he's important. And he's mine."

But Curveball turned viciously on his case officer, accusing him of shortchanging or cheating him. Now he demanded payments for every interview, every meeting. Soon he refused to meet or talk again unless they paid him more. He began to haggle with his handlers like they were facing off in a Baghdad souk.

"He tries to bargain all the time," Schumann said in annoyance.

Curveball already received a large monthly allowance. After he entered the defector relocation program, they raised the stipend again so he didn't have to work. But the perks, and additional surveillance, cost money. The BND was spending more than a million dollars a year on Curveball's upkeep and protection, chump change for the CIA but a big tab for German intelligence.

Schumann refused to pay Curveball any more.

"He is irresponsible with money," the case officer told his superiors. "He is overall irresponsible."

The defector threw tantrums in response. He accused his handlers of abusing him. They had tricked and lied to him, he snarled. They were pathetic and unworthy.

"Curveball would say, 'I want to travel. I need a home. I need more insurance. I need a new car. I need a job. I need more money.' The case officer had to say yes or no, mostly no. There were a lot of no's. And Curveball did not like it," Kappel said.

So Curveball pivoted and turned to Meiner for help. He switched on his fawning charm and high-watt smile. Schumann refused to pay more money, to get him a job, to buy him his Mercedes, he complained. Curveball successfully played his BND handlers against each other. The analyst and the operator began to bicker and squabble, adding new tension to the case.

In mid-2001, the BND asked the American, British, and Israeli intelligence agencies for any help in verifying Curveball's story.

"I won't say we were begging," Kappel said. "But we looked desperately for other information. Unfortunately there was none. Our problem was we had a guy. And nobody else."

The Germans were in a bind. BND operatives in Baghdad could not just bang on the front gate at Djerf al Nadaf and ask to see secret germ trucks or to look for strange, movable doors. Nor could they barge into Curveball's old neighborhood to chat with his parents and friends. Iraqi security agents kept the BND officers under close surveillance, and surely would haul in anyone they met.

Curveball's problems came to a head in the late summer of 2001. He was alone in his dumpy room when the telephone rang. It was his brother. They had not spoken in years.

The brother had fled Baghdad in 1992 and joined Ahmed Chalabi's entourage as a junior bodyguard and hanger-on. He had steadily assumed more responsibility in the security apparatus and, he said, now held a senior position. He apparently obtained Curveball's phone number during a conversation with his mother in Baghdad.

Speaking in Arabic, the older man quickly came to the point over the phone line, as he recalled it later.

I'm calling on behalf of the Iraqi National Congress. Dr. Chalabi is looking for information about Saddam he can give his friends in Washington.

I know you worked at the Chemical Engineering and Design Center in Baghdad. Did you work on any sensitive projects? Do you know anything about Saddam's weapons of mass destruction? Do you have anything for us?

Curveball answered abruptly, anger in his voice.

I don't want to help you.

Then he hung up the phone. He didn't tell his brother about his dealings with the BND. And he didn't disclose to the Germans that his brother worked for Chalabi. The CIA would tell them two years later.

The unexpected communication traumatized Curveball. His worst fears had come true. In his eyes, he was a marked man now. A dead man probably. The exile groups were riddled with Saddam's spies. Now they had tracked him down. He grew frantic with fear.

The BND was ready to pull the plug anyway. Most debriefings of defectors last a few weeks at most. Curveball's interviews and interrogations had consumed hundreds of hours and dragged on for twenty-one grueling months. Yet they still couldn't confirm crucial parts of his account. They still didn't know for certain if he had told the truth about Saddam's weapons of mass destruction.

His memory of names, places, and events was several years old and not getting any fresher. Plus he seemed less rational and less cooperative by the day. He barely spoke to them except to complain. They never could pin Curveball down about his travels, his disappearances, and countless other things. He had led them down one strange path after another, but nothing led to clarity. He could not, or would not, answer them directly. His handlers were exhausted and annoyed.

The BND finally closed the Curveball file in early September 2001. The decision to terminate was not related to the terrorist attacks in America later that month. But after September 11, the case jumped in a startling new direction.

WASHINGTON
2002-2003

CHAPTER 16

Tyler Drumheller occupied prime real estate inside the CIA.

As chief of the European Division in the clandestine service, he supervised spying and covert operations in Western Europe. It entitled him to a spacious fifth-floor corner office with a row of windows in the old headquarters building at Langley. Looking out, he could see the thick forest that swaddles the 250-acre campus. His deputies' desks lay outside his door, while various group and country offices were arrayed around and beneath him, lining three long corridors on the fourth and fifth floors.

Drumheller ran guerrilla wars in Africa and secret agents in Europe for more than two decades before he was named Chief/EUR, as it appeared on cables, in July 2001. He got promoted to SIS-4, a Senior Intelligence Service rank equal in pay and perks to an Army four-star general or a senior ambassador in the diplomatic service. Like the rest of government, the CIA enforces a pecking order and Drumheller stood near the top. He liked the extra money and status. He especially liked that his office looked larger—even his conference table was bigger, he boasted— than that of his boss, James L. Pavitt, who headed the Directorate of Operations. Pavitt worked in the nosebleed section up on the seventh floor, halfway down the hall from George Tenet's corner suite.

Drumheller's office featured a lumpy, government-issued sofa of indeterminate color and age, with a matching pair of easy chairs around a coffee table. He inherited a large battered desk with two phones—one for encrypted calls, the other for normal conversations— and two computers—one linked only to the CIA's classified internal network, the other to the Internet. As a rule, agency security officers viewed computer technology as more of a threat than a boon. Personal computers, handheld palm devices, portable hard drives—anything that conceivably could sneak digital secrets out the door—were strictly forbidden in the building.

Drumheller's office showed few personal touches. After a lifetime of living undercover, of a career based on lies, he felt uncomfortable displaying family photos or private mementos. So he hung a photograph of New York, an Austrian watercolor or two, and a large whiteboard with felt-tip markers inside a dark wooden case. But visitors usually peered at the huge maps tacked to the walls. One thing seemed obvious. The CIA was stuck in the past. It still divided the world along Cold War lines.

The European Division's responsibilities stopped at the German border. Everything to the east—including new NATO members like Poland, Hungary, the Czech Republic, and other post-communist states—might as well have stayed in the Warsaw Pact. They fell under the CIA's Central Eurasia Division, which used to be called SEE, for Soviet East Europe. To confuse matters further, the European Division also included Turkey, which lies mostly in Asia Minor. It also included Canada because, as best Drumheller could determine, someone had to deal with it.

In all, Drumheller and his deputies supervised several hundred desk jockeys at headquarters, and hundreds more case officers and other operatives scattered at several dozen CIA stations and bases overseas. He proudly called them the "pointy end of the stick." Most of his field officers worked abroad under official cover. It meant they got posted to U.S. embassies and consulates, foreign trade missions and international organizations, where they enjoyed diplomatic immunity if they were caught spying. The CIA also deployed a far smaller group of so-called NOCs, spies with "non-official cover." They posed as academics, businessmen, and other professionals, and carried no diplomatic protection. They were the high-wire acts of spying, trapeze artists without a net.

Drumheller hardly fit the popular image of a secret agent. He was a bear of a man, massive and bull-necked. He favored loud sports jackets and usually wore his tie askew or none at all. He was balding but for shaggy strands of brown hair that drooped over his ears and collar. He was, one friend said, the "un–James Bond," so prodigious in size, so conspicuous in appearance, that he was the last person one might expect to be a spy.

He thus was perfectly suited for the job. Hearty and affable, he spoke with a soothing lilt that suggested easy self-confidence. He chuckled with a deep rumble, and his broad grin and outgoing nature won instant friends. His blue-gray eyes showed the only hint of a predatory nature. They aimed intently on each face, registering the details. One could imagine him snapping a mental picture and filing it away each time he blinked.

The son of an Air Force chaplain, Drumheller spent most of his youth on U.S. military bases in West Germany. He had a keen ear for languages: he learned four fluently and could get by in several others. He liked living abroad, and liked living by his wits even more. He had a taste for disaster and an unerring instinct for being in the wrong place at the right time. The CIA obliged, assigning him as a foot soldier, and later a commander, to some of the nastiest front lines of the Cold War.

The CIA taught him Chinese first, but not for a posting in China. They sent him instead to Zambia, in southern Africa. In the early 1970s, Beijing sent more than ten thousand workers to build a modern railway between Zambia's rich copper mines and Tanzania's port of Dar es Salaam, nearly 1,200 miles away. Drumheller was supposed to watch the Chinese.

"It was like building the Union Pacific Railroad all over again," he recalled. "Except this was Africa. The Chinese were fighting lions. They disappeared into the swamps. Elephants crushed the tracks. Thousands of Chinese suddenly were roaming around southern Africa."

The Chinese officials who ran the railway pegged the amiable, shambling American as a spy almost from the start. "They figured no one other than an intelligence officer bothered to learn their language," he added. "They were probably right."

The CIA posted Drumheller to South Africa in the early 1980s. The country was roiling under the racist laws of apartheid. Shortly after he arrived, the white supremacist rulers in Pretoria declared a state of emergency. Township violence boiled over as police and military troops bulldozed neighborhoods, imprisoned thousands of people, and killed or tortured others. Drumheller, under diplomatic cover as a U.S. embassy political officer, spied on government death squads, and ran a covey of agents who stole sensitive secrets from deep inside the regime's nuclear weapons program. He also collected intelligence on the African National Congress and other banned resistance groups.

After a brief stint back at Langley, Drumheller studied Portuguese to help run two related conflicts on South Africa's borders. Civil strife had raged in Angola and Mozambique since independence from Portugal in 1975. But they quickly became bitter proxy wars, waged from distant shadows, for Washington and Moscow.

Working from Lisbon, Drumheller helped direct a covert CIA supply line of shoulder-launched Stinger missiles and other weapons to UNITA rebels in Angola in the west. He also secretly funneled arms and ammunition to RENAMO insurgents in Mozambique in the east. In both countries, the CIA-supported factions fought rivals armed by the Soviet Union and backed by Cuban troops.

The stealthy CIA conflicts in southern Africa drew little attention in America. Few outsiders noticed as the rival factions slaughtered civilians and committed atrocities, destroyed railroads and bridges, and laid waste to towns and farmlands. No one knows how many died, but estimates usually top one million. The bloodletting didn't end until 1992 in Mozambique and a full decade later in Angola, long after the Cold War.

By then, Drumheller was spying in Europe. In the early 1990s, the CIA posted him to Berlin, again as an embassy political officer. In 1998, he was promoted to CIA chief of station in Vienna. While there, he heard that the BND had begun to debrief an important Iraqi defector about Saddam's germ weapons. But it wasn't his case and it meant nothing at the time.

Curveball didn't appear on his radar until the fall of 2002, when he already was running the European Division back at Langley. He knew the White House was training its gunsights on Iraq, of course. On August 26, Vice President Dick Cheney put the nation on alert when he delivered a stark warning to a veterans convention in Nashville.

"Simply stated, there is no doubt that Saddam Hussein now has weapons of mass destruction," Cheney announced. "There is no doubt he is amassing them to use against our friends, against our allies, and against us." He added, "Many of us are convinced that [Saddam] will acquire nuclear weapons fairly soon."

The proposed return of U.N. inspectors to Iraq, Cheney warned, offered no solution. Indeed, the U.N. experts posed a "great danger" because they would "provide false comfort" that the Saddam threat had eased. Without naming Curveball, Cheney praised Iraqi defectors as a more reliable source of information. "We often learned more as the result of defections" than from U.N. inspectors, he said.

Tenet was surprised when he read about the speech. Cheney's staff had not cleared his address with the CIA, as is normal for remarks based on intelligence. The speech "went well beyond what our analysts could support," at least on nuclear weapons, the CIA chief later wrote. Agency experts believed that Saddam, if left unchecked, was nearly a decade away from nuclear capability. But Tenet said nothing to Cheney. "I should have told the vice president privately that the Nashville speech went too far," he admitted. "I should not have let silence imply agreement." Under pressure to go along, the usually forceful Tenet would not challenge his superiors when they were wrong.

Cheney's bellicose talk, and Tenet's silent acquiescence, set the pattern for the coming months. Bush, Cheney, and Condoleezza Rice, the national security advisor, repeatedly exaggerated what intelligence agencies believed or could confirm. In speeches and papers, they hyped Saddam's supposed attempt to obtain low-enriched uranium in Africa and to purchase aluminum tubes for nuclear enrichment. The evidence in both cases already was in sharp dispute and soon would collapse. More important, the White House repeatedly linked Saddam to the 9/11 attacks and the Al Qaeda terrorist network despite strong doubts inside the CIA. Those inflammatory charges far overshadowed Curveball's claims at the time.

Drumheller still was focused almost obsessively on the 9/11 attacks. He raided his overseas stations to support the CIA-led ground war in Afghanistan. And he commuted again and again to European capitals to improve relations with local spy services, to get them all working together. The major French intelligence agency, the General Directorate for External Security or DGSE, as well as internal security services, immediately responded and provided extensive help on counterterror operations.

But on the last Thursday afternoon in September 2002, Drumheller lumbered down the harshly lit hall from his office, climbed into the elevator, and rode up to the seventh floor. Pavitt held biweekly meetings with each of his division chiefs, and today was Europe's turn. A moment later, he entered Pavitt's office. They were old friends from the mid-1980s, when they both were desk officers in the Africa Division. They greeted each other warmly. Hugh Turner, the associate deputy for operations, joined them.

They made an odd mix. Drumheller swept in like a tornado, a garrulous giant. Turner, a Green Beret in Vietnam, sat trim and stiff, the classic gray man in intelligence, the fellow you never noticed at a cocktail party who turns out to be the guy who stole the silverware. And

Pavitt, their boss, was a bit of a dandy. He eschewed the lumpy-sofa look for his office, instead importing expensive art deco furniture and a sleek glass desk, under framed European opera posters and African art. His full head of snow white hair matched his crisply starched shirts.

Pavitt had joined the CIA in 1973 after a tour in Berlin and was posted to Austria, Germany, Malaysia, and finally as station chief in Luxembourg, relatively cushy overseas assignments. He dined and lived well, colleagues said enviously and perhaps unfairly, while they dodged bullets and dysentery in Third World horror shows. He returned to Langley in the late 1980s and rose quickly in the ranks. But the agency was struggling. The end of the Cold War meant deep budget cuts, shedding of staff, and plummeting morale. Tenet named him chief of operations (the official title was deputy director of operations) and head of the clandestine service in August 1999. He appeared in a TV documentary soon after, but the producers protected his undercover status by obscuring his face with a digital white splotch. His kids teased him mercilessly after the show. They called him "Mr. Q-Tip."

Pavitt's spies were caught flatfooted on 9/11 but he rose to the challenge. Six days after the attacks, he appeared on closed-circuit TV screens at Langley. He was bringing hundreds of employees in from other parts of the CIA to assist in counterterrorism, he announced. Celebrated case officers of yore, he said, had volunteered to return from retirement to join the fight.

By early 2002, Pavitt boasted, he had "more spies stealing more secrets than at any time in the history of the CIA."

Pavitt reckoned he had the greatest job in the world. "Every morning I am briefed on an astounding array of incredible secret operations," he explained. "I'm briefed on agent meetings, recruitments of new agents, placement of technical devices, captures of terrorists, near misses and harrowing escapes clandestine service officers have carried out in a 24-hour period. Every morning, my day starts that way."

But the clandestine service, the secret agents at the heart of the CIA, was being maligned unfairly, he griped. "My officers have been described as gun-slinging cowboys on the one hand and risk averse on the other, and worse yet, just plain incompetent." Most people, he said, "do not have the first idea of what a spy, an agent, really is."

Espionage is "not James Bond or Jason Bourne or other fictional spies," he said. The work "demands a balance of delicacy, poise, timing and getting to know an agent or potential agent as well as he or she knows a member of his or her family. The officer must learn the motivations, the emotions, the loyalties, the vulnerabilities and limits that drive this most unique of human beings. It requires professional detachment that allows the officer to see the truth from the half truth, the nuance of act, the coloration of bias."

When Drumheller walked into Pavitt's office in September 2002, the CIA had fulfilled none of those goals with Curveball. Not one CIA operations officer had debriefed the defector. They knew nothing about his motivations, emotions, loyalties, or limits. They didn't know anything about his vulnerabilities or what drove him. The Germans still refused to tell them his name, or to allow direct access.

Two veteran DIA analysts based at Bolling Air Force Base had just flown to Munich with a detailed list of questions for Curveball. The DIA had sought a meeting ever since the first DIA team had been turned away in early 2000. The Germans finally gave the okay. It's not clear why. The BND had not formally interviewed the defector in a year.

When the pair came back, they went to see their division chief.

"We never actually did talk to the guy," the lead analyst complained. "The Germans kept him secure. They wouldn't let us see him. We asked them a question, the Germans asked him for us, and then the Germans gave us the answer. They didn't ask all our questions, and they couldn't accept any follow-ups. Everything was secondhand. It was very frustrating."

The DIA put a report out and Pavitt heard of the concerns.

Meeting that Thursday afternoon, Drumheller updated his superior on counterterrorism operations in Europe. They were certain more terrorists were hiding and plotting and would strike again soon. He handed over orders for Pavitt's signature, and they discussed new assignments and plans. They didn't have a long agenda, and they talked regularly anyway. They swiftly moved on to gossip and personnel issues—who was sick, who was divorcing, and who was retiring.

Finally, as Drumheller gathered his papers to leave, he mentioned that he planned to have lunch the next day with the BND resident agent from the German embassy in Washington.

"I'm going to see the German guy tomorrow," he said. "Is there anything you want me to ask him?"

Pavitt looked up. It appeared that he had just remembered something.

"Yeah," he replied. "As long as you're meeting him, ask him if we can get access to that Iraqi defector. I can't remember the crypt. The WMD defector the Germans got in Munich."

Drumheller was too skilled a bureaucrat to admit he didn't have a clue what his supervisor was talking about.

"Sure. No problem, boss," he said cheerfully and sauntered out.

Back in his office, he phoned Margaret, one of four group chiefs under his command. She handled Germany and several nearby nations in Central Europe.

Drumheller told her about Pavitt's request.

"What the hell is Jim talking about?" he asked. "Who is this defector?"

Several minutes later, Margaret marched into his office. As usual, she was energetic. She launched into a chair.

"It must be Curveball," she told him. "He's the mobile lab guy."

She sketched out the details.

"The Germans can't validate his story," she told him. "And they won't give us access."

But a handful of weapons analysts have latched on to his story of biological weapons, she added. Somebody found the Curveball reports in a safe after 9/11 and now WINPAC thinks he came down from fucking heaven. They figure the mobile weapons labs are their ticket to glory. They're like a cult down there. It's crazy.

Drumheller thanked her. He punched in Pavitt's phone number at his desk.

"Jim," he said. "The defector you're talking about, that's Curveball, right?"

"Curveball. Right."

"I'll get on it."

Drumheller puzzled over Pavitt's request.

Most defectors he knew were compulsive liars. In his experience, U.S. embassies drew scam artists and con men like flies and, sooner or later, the regional security officer or a consular officer called the station chief: Hey, we got a weird guy down here you should talk to . . . And the guy would warn of a coup or assassination threat, or offer some other juicy tidbit and ask for a passport to Disneyland.

Usually it was garbage. But Drumheller always listened, always erred on the side of caution. Sometimes even a crazy guy turns out to be right, he knew. Sometimes even liars can be honest. Hell, he figured, the best liars always tell some truth. That's why people believe them.

The challenge was how to handle the information. He wouldn't just stick unfiltered crap in his report to Langley. He added every caveat possible. He wrote, "I don't know this" and "I don't know that." He never just wrote, "The guy said this," and let headquarters sort it out. Sending unconfirmed intelligence like that up the pipeline was just begging for trouble.

Because if the information was scary, he knew, it looked a lot scarier when it hit Washington. People there think it's real. Sometimes raw intelligence gets to a policy maker without any evaluation as to whether it's right, or why it's wrong, and everything goes to hell, he thought. It takes on life and becomes impossible to kill.

Still, Drumheller was perplexed by Pavitt's request. Curveball must be important if Pavitt is asking for access. The CIA would never let a foreign service meet one of its important sources. Especially the BND. Everyone knew their terrible reputation. He wondered what was up.

CHAPTER 17

Shortly after noon the next day, a CIA driver picked Drumheller up in a black town car and took him down the George Washington Memorial Parkway, across the Potomac and into the cobblestone streets of trendy Georgetown.

As usual, the BND officer had booked a table at Sea Catch, a little-known restaurant in an old shipping warehouse converted to boutiques and galleries. It was a short cab ride to the German embassy complex and it was his favorite place for lunch meetings.

Pushing open the door, Drumheller entered a long, low-ceilinged room of rough-hewn wood, ballast stone, and polished brass, like the belly of an old schooner. Directly in front, he could see a long raw bar carved from white marble and loaded with fresh oysters and clams. The dim light of an overcast sky slanted through narrow windows along one wall.

Drumheller spotted his companion, a small, swarthy Bavarian who used the BND cover name Gradl. He perched stiffly at a table beside the hearth at the far end of the restaurant. Smoky fires once blackened the granite slabs, but only a thin gas-fed flame flickered now.

The CIA officer stole a glance at his watch. As usual, he was fifteen minutes late.

Gradl was on time, of course. He served in the German air force as well as in the BND, and he was always punctual. After a stint as head of counter-proliferation and special projects, he was sent to Washington and promoted to brigadier general in the mid-1990s. Gradl was highly regarded but not very popular. Colleagues called him pompous and officious, whatever his rank. He waited impatiently by the logless fire.

Drumheller did not regularly lunch with other foreign spy service chiefs in town. But his predecessor started these monthly meetings with Gradl and it would be awkward to just cut them off. He hoped the back channel would help defuse tensions with the BND. Plus he liked escaping the office cage to relax for an hour or two.

If Drumheller was effusive and disheveled, Gradl was prim and proper. A full head shorter than the American, he was whippet-thin and elegantly groomed. He wore a narrow, Errol Flynn mustache, and cut his hair short and tight in military style. He exercised regularly and appeared fit as a fighter pilot.

They greeted each other politely and when the waiter came, each ordered the catch of the day and a glass of wine. Gradl's English was flawless, even better than Drumheller's fluent German, from years of service at joint NATO military commands in Europe. They discussed the bitter German political campaign that had just ended and caught up on who was headed to Germany from U.S. intelligence, and who was arriving in Washington from Pullach or Berlin. The deputy BND director planned a round of high-level meetings at CIA headquarters the next month and Gradl fussed about the visit. He seemed preoccupied with protocol. Were they supposed to meet him inside the door or outside? he asked. Who would be there?

"This is important," he said sternly. "Let's go over the details again."

Drumheller was amused. Gradl acted the typical uptight German, he thought, fretting over nothing and everything. The CIA officer ran through the arrangements again and reassured Gradl that he had everything under control. Gradl calmed down. They reserved sensitive, classified topics for more formal meetings in a secure BND room deep inside the embassy compound, or back in a CIA bubble filled with acoustic damping material that seemed to suck up any sound.

Drumheller finally popped Pavitt's question near the end of the ninety-minute meal. He waited for the waiter to move away. He tried to keep it low-key. He saw no point in letting on that the CIA needed something.

"Oh, by the way," he said. "Pavitt asked me to ask you about the Iraqi defector. Can we meet him?"

"Curveball?"

"Yeah."

The German general looked up in surprise. His eyes sought Drumheller's, probing. He knew all about the case. He paused to collect his thoughts.

"Don't ask," he advised. "First off, they're never going to let you see him."

"Why not? What's the problem?"

"He hates Americans."

"No problem," Drumheller responded. "I'll send someone who speaks native German." He flashed a wide grin. "He's Iraqi. He'll never know the difference."

The two spies shared a raw laugh. But after a moment, Gradl spoke again, the humor drained away. His voice grated with a hard, military edge.

"Second, it would be a waste of time because he's crazy," he cautioned. "He has all sorts of problems. He's very erratic. We think he had a nervous breakdown."

He briefly recounted Curveball's history to Drumheller. They had resettled him but were forced to move him twice to protect him, he said. They desperately tried to relocate him to Turkey to get him out of their hair. But he refused to go. Now he was driving them all nuts.

Drumheller nodded sympathetically. Most defectors were trouble, he agreed.

"Look, we can't validate what the guy said because we don't have any other sources," Gradl went on. "There are a lot of questions about the reporting. And given all the complications, we, I, personally think the guy may be a fabricator."

Drumheller was careful not to betray his sudden alarm. He kept his broad face blank of emotion, free of distress. But he understood Gradl's warning. An important source of intelligence may be a fabricator. A fraud. A liar. A disaster.

"If you ask to see him, it's going to cause a problem," Gradl continued. "Because it will put us under pressure. We will never admit Curveball is not credible. And we don't like to say no to requests from Washington. But we will. You're going to put us in the position of having to say no."

Drumheller stared at the German general but said nothing.

"It's not really worth asking to see him," Gradl concluded, almost as an afterthought. He amended that to make certain no doubts remained. "It's not going to happen."

"Okay," Drumheller replied evenly. "I'll take care of it."

They paid separate checks so no one later could accuse either spy of trying to recruit the other.

CHAPTER 18

Drumheller gamed out the problem as he rode back to Langley.

If Curveball really was a fabricator, he thought, the BND oversold their source. His story probably sounded too good to check. But they built in an escape hatch. They just say they can't verify his information. If they don't say he is correct, they don't have to say he's wrong. They're covering their asses that way.

But from what? What were they hiding?

Drumheller reviewed his long lunch conversation as the car sped north through the rainy afternoon traffic. *We will never admit Curveball is not credible.* That's what Gradl said. Then it clicked.

Of course they won't. It would bring scandal.

If Curveball was found to be a liar, a phony, they would have to kick him out of the defector resettlement program. They had vouched for him, spent a fortune, changed his name, and moved him twice. German law was very strict, he knew. Someone would be held accountable. BND officers had been fired or worse for protecting phony agents. Careers and pensions were at stake. The state prosecutor would ask embarrassing questions. How long did you know your source was a fraud? Who else knew this?

Like any good intelligence officer, Drumheller then challenged his own thesis. Maybe the opposite was true, he thought. Maybe the BND was denying access for another reason. Gerhard Schroeder now headed the most left-wing government in postwar Germany. He won reelection by bashing Bush and vowing to oppose war in Iraq, or least keep out of it. Germans of all ages were marching and protesting in the streets. Maybe Schroeder's people feared Curveball looked too convincing, too explosive, too good.

Maybe they sent Gradl out to see me today because they're trying to throw us off the scent, Drumheller mused. Maybe they are trying to deliberately low-ball Curveball to deflect our attention from him. Maybe he is so damned good the Germans are getting cold feet and are afraid they'll give the White House a pretext for war. They don't want to be blamed. They probably figure Bush has enough ammunition without them. They heard Cheney's speech. They know the White House is trying to link Saddam to 9/11 and nuclear bombs.

Either way, Drumheller assumed Ernst Uhrlau, Schroeder's national coordinator for intelligence, was involved. The BND would brief him on a case this big, especially if the CIA was banging on the door. Drumheller didn't like Uhrlau. After the 9/11 attacks, he had flown to Berlin and angrily demanded that the Germans help more on counterterrorism. Uhrlau lost his temper and nearly threw the burly CIA officer out of his office.

The Bush administration had publicly blamed the tragedy, in part, on the ineptitude of German authorities. Three of the four 9/11 pilots, including Mohammed Atta, the ringleader, had lived up to nine years in Hamburg. They studied at technical colleges and formed an Al Qaeda cell. Why didn't the Germans stop them?

Uhrlau was outraged by the criticism. The Americans were fingering him, the former Hamburg police chief, for their own staggering screw-ups, he fumed. The Americans had totally bungled the case. Now they were trying to bully him in his own office. He couldn't believe it. They demanded access to German sources and raw intelligence. But they refused to share any of theirs. They acted like the BND was still a CIA puppet.

Worse, they wanted him to shred German privacy laws and civil liberties. They wanted him to wiretap phones, monitor bank transactions, and eavesdrop on e-mail. They wanted to use polygraphs, and detain people with little or no evidence. The CIA had begun kidnapping people. Operatives in ski masks had begun to snatch terror suspects off the street and fly them off to secret prisons, drugged, diapered, blindfolded, spread-eagled and chained down, away from prying eyes and bleeding hearts. Drumheller had been briefed on renditions in Europe.

"We were told the CIA was taking the gloves off," recalled a German intelligence official. "They said, 'If anyone gets in the way, we'll blow him away.'" Uhrlau, the career cop, was horrified. He feared the unchecked abuses of an extremist government far more than terrorist bombs and cells. Germany had experienced both. Uhrlau grabbed the moral high ground. He would not stand for kidnapping, torture, and other cowboy tactics. He believed in the rule of law. The CIA officers, in his eyes, were acting like criminals.

Riding back to Langley a year after his battle with Uhrlau, after his lunch with Gradl, Drumheller suspected that Uhrlau was keeping Curveball under wraps out of spite. *He still hates us because we blamed the Hamburg cell for 9/11,* the CIA officer thought. *He wants us to beg him for access. This is about pride of service. He's holding an important source and he's lording it over us. He's making us dance and he's enjoying every minute of it. It makes him feel important.*

Drumheller sifted the evidence again. The problem was bigger than Uhrlau, he decided. The German human source reporting was awful, dreadful, always had been. *If Curveball said ten things, they'd hype five and hide the rest. They probably inflated the shit out of Curveball,* he thought. *They're afraid we'll get in there with their source, sit down with him for ten minutes, and decide, "Jesus, this is all bullshit. This guy is crazy." Or that they totally screwed up and hyped the reports. They'll be embarrassed. That's their real fear. They don't want to be embarrassed.*

Back in his corner office, Drumheller telephoned Pavitt to report on the lunch with Gradl.

"No dice," Drumheller told him. "They won't do a meeting. It's too complicated. He said Curveball had a nervous breakdown and might be a fabricator."

"Okay," Pavitt replied. "That goes along with some other stuff we've got. Stay on top of this, will you? And let WINPAC know."

"Sure," Drumheller replied. Pavitt's calm response struck him as odd. He didn't sound surprised at the German warning.

Drumheller briefed his executive assistant and asked him to e-mail a note to Alan Foley, a former Soviet expert who now headed WINPAC, the CIA weapons center. Drumheller knew Foley from Austria and liked him. He used to show up at regular intervals to check on an undercover CIA weapons office there. It spied on the International Atomic Energy Agency, the U.N. nuclear watchdog group, which was based in Vienna.

Drumheller didn't think much of WINPAC, however. Field operatives tend to look down at analysts and he was no exception. To his jaundiced eye, analysts acted like petty academics. They fought over obscure theories and who got credit for a footnote. They tied themselves in knots over reports that no one read, as if their careers were at stake. Plus they weren't all geniuses even though they acted that way. Most times they couldn't give you a straight answer. Their reports skidded all over the place, with qualifiers coming and going, so they could always claim they had predicted precisely whatever eventually transpired. Most of them, he figured, couldn't cut it in operations.

Later the same day, Drumheller called his executive assistant and Margaret, the group chief who first told him about Curveball, into his office. They took seats around his battered coffee table. They were directly responsible for CIA operations inside Germany. It was Drumheller's old stomping ground. Yet they knew almost nothing about a major human intelligence case taking place there.

Drumheller recounted the warning from Gradl and his own doubts and questions. If the defector's stuff was unverified, he asked, why was WINPAC so interested? If he was crazy and a fabricator, why was the case even alive? It didn't make sense. He was passing messages between Pavitt and Foley. Maybe, he surmised, there was some other high-level interest. They all knew that Cheney had been visiting the CIA to ask about intelligence on Iraq.

"I have a funny feeling about this Curveball case," he declared.

Drumheller told them to start snooping around and report back to him. If he was going to stay on top of the case, as Pavitt ordered, he needed to know more. And if Gradl's warning was accurate, they needed to kill the information before it could do any damage. After all, he reminded them, Germany was their turf.

"Let's find out all we can about Curveball because we're in the middle of it now," he urged.

CHAPTER 19

The CIA was beating the bushes for sources on Iraq in the fall of 2002.

Lindsay Moran, an energetic case officer with shoulder-length dark hair, was studying Russian for her next posting when she abruptly got orders to join the Iraq operations element at Langley. It was created to provide intelligence support in event of war and now invasion planning had begun. One afternoon, Moran was rushing down a corridor at headquarters and ran into a friend from her previous post in the Balkans. He headed the unit she was about to join.

"Hey, I'll be working with you," Moran greeted him. "I just got surged over to Iraq."

Her friend smiled and pulled her aside to speak in private.

"You know, the big secret is we don't have any Iraqi agents or assets," he confided when they were alone. "We're starved for reliable information."

She didn't know what to say, so they both chuckled and went on their way. She considered it the usual "esprit de cynicism" in the CIA, nothing to worry about. But once she started her new job, she was astonished to read the classified cables pouring in from CIA stations. Everyone had been tasked to recruit Iraqis. From what she could see, case officers with no knowledge of the language, culture, or even basic psychology of their targets were making a last-ditch effort to recruit Iraqis at any cost.

In one cable, a CIA case officer vividly described his failed attempt to convince an Iraqi diplomat to accept a briefcase filled with cash. It would be comical if it weren't so woefully sad, Moran thought. "The Iraqi was running down the street in his pajamas with the CIA officer in hot pursuit, threatening the Iraqi with repercussions if he didn't accept the pitch to come work for the CIA," she recalled. "And all the while, the Iraqi is shouting, 'This man is a CIA spy!' to all and sundry in the street."

Defectors, and especially the exile groups that helped them, were only too happy to help. "They were adept at feeding us what we wanted to hear," said a former DIA official. "Most of it was garbage."

The defectors became "a cottage industry," said a former CIA operations officer. "There were maniacal, urgent requirements coming from Washington. The world out there understands exactly what we're looking for because we send the word out to all the stations and it has a frantic element to it. And these guys, the Iraqis, are really smart. They drop something on the British, the Americans, maybe the Germans, and everyone has a 'third party rule' that says we can't tell each other where we got it to protect the source, and it all becomes an echo chamber for the same bad intelligence."

Ahmed Chalabi's organization had the biggest impact. Partly due to his lobbying, Congress had passed the Iraq Liberation Act in 1998 to make "regime change" an official goal of the U.S. government. Under the new law, the State Department gave the Iraqi National Congress $33 million to further its political opposition to Saddam.

A month after the September 11 attacks, Chalabi's group reported to U.S. officials that it was collecting "sensitive information that reveal Iraq's link with 9/11 aftermath and anthrax exposures in USA." Someone had mailed letters laced with anthrax spores. The bioterror attack killed five people and sickened seventeen others. The INC claimed it was also "successfully chasing after Iraq intelligence activities in both Europe and USA," and was "contacting defected Iraqi officers . . . for better coordination."

In early 2002, Chalabi's aides handed over three hundred pages of supposedly critical intelligence. An interagency group called the National Intelligence Council, based at the CIA, agreed to translate and assess the material. Their judgment was brutal. The INC documents contained "little of current intelligence value." Information on the Iraqi military was "out of date and no longer useful." A report on the Special Security Organization "contained numerous errors." "None of the documents, except press clippings, had sourcing or attribution that can be verified or traced." That May, the State Department followed the CIA lead and cut off Chalabi's funding.

This time, the White House stepped in. The National Security Council transferred support for Chalabi's organization to the Pentagon.

Paul Wolfowitz, the deputy defense secretary, ordered the DIA to take over. The Pentagon began paying about $335,000 a month to Chalabi's group. The Iraqi National Congress agreed in a letter to debrief "Iraqi citizens worldwide" to provide "a continuous flow of tactical and strategic information regarding Iraq, in general, and the Saddam Hussein regime, in particular."

The flow carried more garbage. Defectors and other informants from the Iraqi National Congress—the DIA filed reports from at least twenty—provided unreliable or false information so regularly that case officers stamped a special disclaimer on anything from Chalabi's group. "The INC guys we met were all liars and provocateurs," said the former DIA official. "We were under pressure to meet them. But we always caveated the INC sources. They were the worst."

Before one debriefing, an INC official was overheard coaching an Iraqi defector to "deliver the act of a lifetime." But he failed the test. The self-described nuclear physicist knew little of advanced mathematics or physics. He described nuclear reactors that do not exist. He also asked to use the toilet frequently, the DIA team noted later, "particularly when he appeared to be flustered by a line of questioning, suddenly remembering a new piece of information upon his return. During one such incident, [the source] appeared to be reviewing notes." The debriefers wrote him off as a fabricator.

Another Iraqi who escaped to Jordan in mid-2002 seemed more promising. A DIA officer who questioned the defector, using an Iraqi National Congress official as translator, got such sensational answers that the agency flew the Iraqi to Washington for more debriefings and formal resettlement in America. "The CIA then interviewed the source with an agency translator and got a completely different story," said a CIA official. "It became clear the INC translator had dramatically altered the defector's account."

Three Iraqi informants had provided corroboration for Curveball's account by late 2002. The most significant came from Chalabi's group.

In February that year, Iraqi National Congress representatives in Washington had arranged for the DIA to meet Major Mohammed Harith, a defector from the Iraqi intelligence service, in Jordan. Harith, also known by the name al-Asaaf in CIA files, boasted that he personally had hatched the idea to build mobile biological labs during a meeting with Taha in the summer of 1996, just as Al Hakam was being dynamited.

"We learnt our lesson from the U.N. inspections," he said in an interview that the INC videotaped and provided to British journalists. "Houses and factories can be searched. So I had the idea to use trucks. If we disguised them as milk and yogurt trucks, who would suspect they are carrying anything suspicious?"

Harith said he arranged the purchase of seven Renault flatbed trucks and installed incubators for bacteria, microscopes, and air-conditioning. They crisscrossed the Euphrates River valley between Hilla and Kut. By 1998, the vehicles "were stored in the Republican Palace garage when not in use," he said. He later gave far more detailed versions of his story to CBS's 60 *Minutes* and *Vanity Fair* magazine.

The CIA, already distrustful of Chalabi, was skeptical of Harith's extravagant account. Despite his midlevel rank, he claimed to have phenomenal access to the most secret parts of Saddam's weapons programs. "We question the source's credibility," the agency warned. A DIA officer agreed after debriefing Harith four times in Jordan. The Iraqi "may have been coached" and apparently had embellished information, he wrote.

But Harith passed a DIA polygraph test with flying colors, and that overcame the gnawing doubts about him. In early March 2002, the DIA issued an intelligence information report citing Harith's claim to have purchased seven Renault flatbed trucks for mobile labs. It was added to the files as evidence supporting Curveball.

The second informant, an Iraqi civil engineer seeking asylum, told Defense HUMINT agents in June 2001 that technicians had filled biological warheads from trailers parked in underground bunkers at an armaments factory near Karbala. Workers wore special protective gear and anyone with "open sores was strictly forbidden access to these facilities," he said. "Warheads with biological agents were stockpiled on the site."

Spy satellite imagery of the Karbala factory and other sites the engineer named showed no sign of suspicious activity. But CIA analysts wrote that off to Iraq's attempts to hide evidence from satellites. A report of the engineer's account was added to the file.

The third source was an Iraqi official who secretly spied for British intelligence under the code name Red River. Traveling outside Iraq in September 2002, he told his MI6 case officer that Iraq had developed fermentors for trucks or railway cars. He said the systems could produce single-cell proteins for animal feed. It was the same cover story the Iraqis had used at Al Hakam.

Red River admitted, however, that he was quoting a "new sub-source" with links to opposition groups. "The informant was suspicious about the true nature of the systems, although he did not connect them with biological warfare," MI6 reported. The British wouldn't let the CIA meet their source and the case become a sore point between the two services. Still, a single report from Red River also was inserted into CIA files as corroboration of Curveball's account.

The information from the three Iraqis contradicted or differed from Curveball's account in numerous ways. Their reports would sit in the CIA files like time bombs.

CHAPTER 20

After 9/11, it was as if Curveball suddenly drove his hellish trucks straight into the front lobby of CIA headquarters.

Prior to the terror attacks, the CIA ladled cautions and caveats into classified assessments of Iraq's suspected biowarfare program. The destruction of the Al Hakam factory kept the small band of bioweapons experts, the so-called geek squad, in check. In late 1997, they concluded that Saddam's regime "would likely wait" to restart the germ program until sanctions ended or U.N. inspectors left. A CIA report the next autumn noted that the program still appeared on hold.

The uncertainty continued after U.N. teams were forced out in December 1998. The following August, a National Intelligence Estimate entitled *Worldwide Biological Warfare Programs: Trends and Prospects* judged that Iraq was "probably continuing work" on developing biowarfare agents and "could" restart production in six months.

The language began to harden after Curveball began talking.

In December 2000, after a year of *Hortensia 2* reports to Munich House, the analysts advised that "new intelligence" had caused them to "adjust our assessment upward." The evidence now "suggests that Baghdad has expanded" its program by establishing "a large scale, redundant and concealed BW agent production capability."

Curveball also took center stage for the first time in a separate report that same month.

"Credible reporting from a single source suggests" the regime is rebuilding its biowarfare arsenal "on a large scale and has developed a clandestine production capability," warned a report called an Intelligence Community Assessment. It cautioned, however, that analysts "cannot confirm whether Iraq has produced . . . biological agents."

All such caution, all such doubt, disappeared after 9/11 and the anthrax letters attack that followed. The WINPAC geek squad led the charge. The biowarfare analysts reported in October 2001 without any hedging or qualification that Iraq "continues to produce at least . . . three BW agents" and that Iraq's mobile germ factories provide "capabilities surpassing the pre–Gulf War era."

The calculation was implausible, if not absurd. The fermentors that Curveball had described each had about a five-hundred-liter capacity. Assuming every component on the trailer worked flawlessly, assuming the crews ignored Friday holidays and worked non-stop, and assuming every state of every batch was perfect, each mobile unit would need a week to brew enough slurry to fill a single R-400 aerial bomb. The munitions would have burned off the contents anyway.

The fermentors at Al Hakam alone were five to ten times larger than those on the trailers, and their failure rate was pathetically high. They were far too heavy to operate on a truck in any case. To meet the CIA claim, Iraq needed dozens more mobile weapons factories and a success rate it had never come close to achieving. It was what the CIA called a WAG, a wild-ass guess.

But the frightening new assessments dramatically raised Curveball's profile, as well as those of the CIA analysts who wrote them. In the summer of 2002, Tenet went to the Oval Office to brief President Bush and Vice President Cheney about the mobile program and to show them illustrations of the trailers prepared by CIA artists. Tenet also showed the drawings to congressional leaders in closed-door sessions.

"We know Iraq has developed a redundant capability to produce biological warfare agents using mobile production units," he told the Senate intelligence and armed services committees in early September 2002, citing a "credible defector who worked in the program." They had "the potential to turn out several hundred tons of unconcentrated BW agent per year."

Saddam had built a terrible arsenal before 1991, and the CIA now was certain he had amassed another even worse. Like medieval clerics tracking witchcraft, CIA analysts saw evidence everywhere they looked. If years of fruitless searches had found no hard proof of the mobile weapons labs, it only proved how well the Iraqis had concealed them. The absence of evidence became proof of their existence.

In the early fall of 2002, Curveball still played a minor role in the administration's public case against Iraq. White House charges that

Saddam was aggressively pursuing nuclear weapons and had an established relationship with Al Qaeda packed a far more potent punch. On
September 8, both Vice President Cheney and Condoleezza Rice took
to the Sunday TV talk shows to highlight the nuclear danger. "We don't
want the smoking gun to be a mushroom cloud," Rice warned. Two
weeks later, President Bush told reporters, "[You] can't distinguish
between Al Qaeda and Saddam when you talk about the war on terror."

As the rhetoric rose in intensity, the White House pushed Congress
to authorize use of force if Saddam did not disarm. Anxious Democrats
asked to see the current intelligence estimate on Iraq. There was none.
The White House had begun gearing for war without any strategic-level
intelligence assessments on any aspect of Iraq.

The next day, officials from the six agencies that collect foreign
intelligence gathered at the National Intelligence Council office, at the
other end of the hall from Tenet's suite at Langley. A National
Intelligence Estimate represents the best collective judgment of the
entire intelligence community. Preparation of an NIE, as it's known,
normally requires six to ten months of drafts, debates, and more drafts.
The deliberative process is designed to weed out bias and produce
unvarnished assessments, regardless of whether they conform to U.S.
policy. No other intelligence document is considered more important.

The council cranked out the Iraq NIE in nineteen days flat.

Those writing the document were given clear marching orders.
"The going-in assumption was we were going to war so this NIE was to
be written with that in mind," said an analyst who helped draft the
estimate. "That was what was said to us. 'We're going to war.'"

Entitled *Iraq's Continuing Programs for Weapons of Mass
Destruction*, the NIE ran ninety-two pages, each stamped "Top Secret"
on the top and bottom. The sections on Saddam's nuclear program and
ties to terrorists carried numerous qualifiers. For the first time, biological weapons took the lead. The section labeled "Biological Warfare
Program—Larger Than Before" contained the NIE's most assertive and
alarming language. And virtually every paragraph derived from
Curveball's information.

U.S. intelligence now judges with "high confidence" that Iraq "has
biological weapons," it read. "We assess that all key aspects—research
and development, production and weaponization—of Iraq's offensive
BW program are active and that most elements are larger and more
advanced than they were before the Gulf War."

According to a "credible source," meaning Curveball, Iraq uses mobile factories to produce germs and toxins and "may have other mobile units for researching" and other vehicles to fill bombs and warheads. It has mastered "the ability to produce dried agent." A new calculus appeared. Within three to six months, the NIE claimed, the mobile units could "produce an amount of agent equal to the total" that Iraq produced before 1991.

A declassified version, quickly released to the public by the CIA, went much further. It warned that Saddam could deliver biological weapons "potentially against the US homeland," a terrifying phrase that did not appear in the classified version.

The October 2002 NIE also declared with "high confidence" that Baghdad had chemical weapons and "has renewed production" of blister and nerve gases, including mustard, sarin, cyclosarin and VX. Saddam, the report judged, probably was hiding one hundred to five hundred metric tons of chemical warfare agents, "much of it added in the last year." It was the strongest judgment in the NIE after biological weapons.

Curveball was partly to blame.

The WINPAC chemical weapons experts were "drifting" toward concluding that Iraq had an insignificant program, a senior CIA analyst later explained. They did not feel confident in the evidence. But they got nervous when they saw the increasingly strong assertions from the germ weapons team. The biowarfare reporting, based almost exclusively on Curveball, "pushed [us] the other way," the senior analyst admitted.

They knew that Saddam's pre-1991 chemical weapons production was larger and more advanced than his biowarfare program. If the geek squad was so certain about Iraq's germ weapons now, the senior analyst reasoned, Saddam must be churning out even more chemical poisons. So the chemical warfare experts shed their doubts and revised their analyses sharply upward.

"Curveball made the chemical guys more confident," explained a U.S. official who investigated preparation of the NIE. "And they wrote much stronger reports. They didn't want anyone to think they were missing anything. So they just ramped up the conclusions."

The British government was following a similar tack. The Joint Intelligence Committee, or JIC, which assesses intelligence for the prime minister and his government, took the lead.

In April 2000, after seeing the first BND reports on Curveball, the committee reported that Iraq "seems to be exploring the use of mobile facilities." A year later, they cautioned that "our picture of Iraq's BW programme is unclear" other than "good intelligence of one facility that could be used to support BW production," meaning Curveball's worksite at Djerf al Nadaf.

The picture cleared dramatically after 9/11. In March 2002, the British committee judged Iraq "self-sufficient in the production of biological weapons." Four biowarfare agents could be produced within days, if they were not already stockpiled: anthrax spores, botulinum toxin, aflatoxin, and possible plague.

In September 2002, Blair's government released a public dossier that warned Iraq has "developed mobile laboratories for military use" and "specifically envisages" the use of biological weapons. Blair told the House of Commons that "Iraq was trying to acquire mobile biological weapons facilities, which of course are easier to conceal. Present intelligence confirms that it has got such facilities."

Like Congress, Parliament voted to support armed force to disarm Saddam. In the debates and in news accounts, the possibility of a sneak biological attack on British allies and British military bases in Cyprus provoked the greatest emotion and ultimately influenced the outcome.

In London as well as Washington, more and more now hung on Curveball.

CHAPTER 21

Margaret, the group chief for Germany, rushed into Drumheller's office.

"You're not going to believe this," she said with a grin.

It was the middle of October 2002 and Drumheller's group chief and his executive assistant had just spent two weeks nosing around the CIA. Both were veteran clandestine officers who had survived war zones and grueling foreign assignments. But snooping on home turf proved nerve-wracking. They flopped down on the misshapen couch in the corner. Out the window, they could see a few red maple or bigtooth aspen, maybe a grove of sweet gum, suddenly ablaze with autumn color.

"The Curveball case is really a mess," Margaret began.

She was embroiled in a huge fuss with the geek squad at WINPAC, she explained. The bioweapons analysts had gotten really mad because she was asking too many questions about Curveball. They had staked their credibility on the Iraqi. His mobile weapons labs formed a key part of the National Intelligence Estimate.

"They're really pissed at us," she added cheerfully.

Margaret said the chief WINPAC analyst on the case, Beth, seemed to take every question about Curveball's reliability as a direct attack on her own integrity. The other BW analysts seemed just as fanatic. After years of getting no respect, this was their biggest case by far, their moment in the sun. They had bonded over Curveball. Three of them had sent outraged e-mails to Margaret, telling her to butt out.

"They basically took the position, 'How dare you do this? We're shocked that [operations people] would question our judgment,'" Margaret told Drumheller.

Then she burst into a loud, delighted laugh.

During the early e-mail skirmishes, the analysts screwed up. They forgot to remove Margaret's e-mail address from the messages flying back and forth between the CIA analysts and their DIA colleagues. Margaret didn't hack in and she certainly had the security clearance for the back-channel gossip. But the dunderheads didn't notice that they left her name in the address bar and, well, now she was reading all their private e-mails about Curveball—and about herself. She had printed out dozens of them.

"It's really nasty stuff," she gloated.

She gleefully recounted the highlights: Drumheller and his staff are idiots. They're morons. They're not scientists, they're not engineers, and they're not analysts. They're field hands. They wouldn't know a mobile weapons lab if it ran them over and sprayed them with anthrax. They're trying to sabotage us. They're trying to undercut our reporting. "We'll fight this to the death," one melodramatic message vowed.

Drumheller roared with laughter.

WINPAC reported to the Directorate of Intelligence, or DI. Drumheller's team worked for the Directorate of Operations, known as the DO. The rivalry between the desk-based puzzle solvers and the gun-slinging field operatives was legendary. They had opposing cultures and skills. But passing spiteful notes back and forth, like high school cliques, seemed especially petty, Drumheller thought.

Margaret wasn't finished. She had attended several meetings with the geek squad after she secretly read their invective and abuse, mostly aimed at her. She couldn't resist baiting the analysts across the conference table, she recounted.

"Look, I know you guys don't like the DO and our questions," she had said sweetly, blurting the story out between gales of laughter.

"And they'd say, 'Oh no, we're all professionals here. We understand.'

"And I'd say, 'Oh no, I know you really feel that way.'

"And they'd all deny it. They didn't have a clue."

Margaret erupted in buzz-saw laughter and Drumheller and his deputy joined in. Margaret was a piece of work. A little strident, perhaps, but a talented manager and a wizard in the field. After a moment, they grew serious.

The important thing, the truly amazing thing, Margaret told them, was Beth and the other WINPAC analysts blew off her doubts. They totally ignored her questions about whether Curveball might be a fabricator. It was infuriating.

"They've done nothing to verify the reporting," she said in disbelief. "They've done nothing to validate his reliability."

The analysts had ignored several BND warnings about Curveball, she added. Gradl's warning wasn't the first. Margaret recounted all sorts of cable traffic from the Germans from 2000 and 2001, when the Germans were debriefing the defector.

"They can't vouch for what he's reporting," she said.

The CIA files also showed caution signs. In early 2001, when Curveball was starting to fall apart, the CIA's Berlin station chief had sent a cable to the counter-proliferation division at headquarters. The Iraqi was "out of control" and "could not be located," he wrote, quoting a BND official. A copy of the cable went to WINPAC.

Another warning had come in March 2001. The BND had informed the CIA that Curveball "had changed some of his stories." In another report that spring, a DIA bioweapons analyst had cautioned that Curveball's material is "presently compromised by reporting inconsistencies."

There was more. In April 2002, British intelligence officials had warned the CIA that they had begun "to have doubts about Curveball's reliability," according to a cable. MI6 was "not convinced that Curveball is a wholly reliable source" and "elements of [his] behavior strike us as typical of individuals we would normally assess as fabricators." The British still believed in Curveball, however, because of his mastery of technical details.

Other concerns had appeared. British and Israeli photo analysts had reviewed several years' worth of satellite imagery of Djerf al Nadaf. They notified the CIA weapons center that a large, dun-colored wall flanked three sides of the main warehouse. It had first appeared in May 1997—two years before Curveball left for Germany. The wall stood about six feet high and only four or five feet from the building.

The wall clearly blocked trucks from entering or exiting the warehouse at opposite ends, as Curveball had described. If trucks couldn't get in or out, the building couldn't be a docking station. If it wasn't a docking station, what the hell was going on?

The bioweapons experts at WINPAC had ignored the earlier warning cables. Now they ignored the wall.

Analysts "set that information aside" because it contradicted Curveball's information, one explained later. Anyway, they could think of plenty of explanations for the wall. The Iraqis built a temporary wall to deceive spy satellites. Or they used a hidden gate in the wall. Or they broke down and rebuilt the wall each time the trucks visited.

Whatever the wall was, it didn't prove Curveball's story was wrong, the analysts insisted.

Drumheller was baffled as the discussion wore on.

Everyone in CIA operations knew that HUMINT intelligence could be second-rate. He had told Pavitt, his boss, that Curveball might be a fabricator. He had messaged Alan Foley, head of WINPAC, about the warning from Gradl. Margaret was trading scathing e-mails with the analysts working the case. Now all this stuff was turning up in the files.

Drumheller didn't know if Curveball was a liar or not. And every intelligence case had inconsistencies, dubious sources, missing pieces of the puzzle. Maybe the analysts were right, he thought. But they at least needed to check Curveball out. Was he a scam artist or wasn't he?

Drumheller instructed Margaret to keep pushing, to find out more.

"For God's sakes," he said. "We don't want to rubber-stamp something that could help start a war."

CHAPTER 22

Iraq dominated the news in the final weeks of 2002.

Under intense international pressure, Saddam finally allowed the United Nations Monitoring, Verification and Inspection Commission, or UNMOVIC, to send inspectors to Iraq as the successor to the now defunct UNSCOM. The new U.N. teams launched their first raid on November 27 after nearly four years' absence.

In early December, Iraq handed over a twelve-thousand-page "currently accurate, full and complete declaration" that supposedly detailed its weapons programs. The documents revealed little new about biological weapons, however. They largely repackaged Baghdad's last formal declaration from 1997, and included not one word about mobile weapons labs.

Drumheller was shuttling to Turkey and elsewhere to line up support for the coming war from other spy services. Paris and Berlin kept embassies in Baghdad, and both the French and German services planned to leave a skeleton staff of operatives in place if the bombs fell. He forgot about Curveball for several weeks.

But the case re-erupted inside the CIA the week before Christmas.

Tenet's chief deputy was John McLaughlin, a balding, elfin figure who rose through the ranks as an analyst. He looked the part, with wire-rim glasses, suspenders, and an erudite mien. He and his boss were exceedingly close. McLaughlin called himself Tenet's "alter ego" while Tenet routinely introduced his deputy as "the smartest man in America." Others nicknamed him Merlin for his skills as an amateur magician. McLaughlin excelled in sleight of hand, pulling coins out of someone's ear or turning a dollar bill into a twenty. He hung an original program from a Harry Houdini show in a place of honor on his office wall. Magic, he believed, provided a perfect metaphor for intelligence work. You can't always believe what you see.

In his thirty years at the CIA, McLaughlin had briefed five presidents, starting with Jimmy Carter, and he hung a line of grip-and-grin pictures on his wall to prove it. He also framed a slogan: "Subvert the Dominant Paradigm." Challenge the conventional wisdom. Except that on Iraq's WMD, McLaughlin felt, the conventional wisdom was more than ingrained. It was cast in concrete.

Even if he had doubts, which he didn't, the evidence seemed overwhelming. Given what hundreds of CIA papers, U.N. reports, other spy services, and think tanks had concluded, he would have to prove everyone else wrong if he suddenly were to decide that Iraq was free of WMD and posed no danger. He would be laughed out of town.

McLaughlin knew there were growing questions about Curveball. But no one was beating drums outside his door. He assumed that Defense HUMINT had vetted the defector's reliability before they disseminated so many reports. The Iraqi was their case, after all. At the CIA, the Operations Directorate always checked bona fides of sources before analysts assessed the information. That's how the system works, and he believed in the system. Collectors validate sources while analysts evaluate data. The idea that a CIA weapons analyst needed to validate the reliability of a DIA source in Germany made no sense to him. Still, he knew there were questions.

On the wintry morning of December 18, McLaughlin's executive assistant, a veteran clandestine service officer named Steve, telephoned Drumheller. Could he come upstairs to talk about Curveball?

When they met, McLaughlin's aide had a request. The White House wanted to use Curveball's information in public, he said. German intelligence had to give permission because they controlled the source. Could the European Division please check with the BND?

That afternoon, Drumheller had Margaret shoot a priority cable to the chief of the CIA station in Berlin. Ask the BND if the White House can use the Curveball material, she instructed. Go right to the top, to August Hanning, the BND president. While you're at it, she added, tell him we need to debrief their source. Tell him this is critical.

The next day, Steve organized a second, more formal meeting. He wanted to sort out any discrepancies or doubts about Curveball, he said. McLaughlin understood that the germ trucks were crucial to CIA claims given to Congress, the White House, and the public. He didn't want anything to blow up in their faces later.

Steve had heard about the bickering between Drumheller's staff and the geek squad analysts. Hoping to mediate a truce, he typed an invitation to meet in McLaughlin's conference room that afternoon, December 19. He titled it "Meeting to Review Bidding on Curveball" and explained that he hoped to "resolve precisely how we judge Curveball's reporting on mobile BW labs." He would "summarize the conclusions" in a note for McLaughlin, he added.

He sent the e-mail to Drumheller's aide, Margaret, Beth from the Curveball team at WINPAC, and a clandestine operations officer from the counter-proliferation division.

Shortly before the meeting started, Margaret outlined her concerns in an e-mail to several colleagues in operations. She forwarded a copy to Stephen Kappes, a former Marine officer who had replaced Turner as Pavitt's chief deputy. Margaret wrote her e-mails the same brash way she talked. She opened this one in bold type:

Although no one asked, it is my assessment that Curveball . . . was more forthcoming and cooperative when he needed resettlement assistance; now that he does not need it, he is less helpful, possibly because when he was being helpful, he was embellishing a bit. The [BND] has developed some doubts about him. We have been unable to vet him operationally and know very little about him.

Margaret took the same presumptuous, no-one-asked-me-but-I'm-telling-you-anyway attitude at the meeting that afternoon. Accounts vary as to precisely what was said, but not to the venomous, vindictive tone of the exchange.

Margaret went in full throttle, ripping for a fight. They wanted a showdown? That was fine with her.

"Look, nobody has vetted Curveball," she began impatiently. "Nobody has verified his story."

She built her case with a vengeance. Gradl had told Drumheller the Iraqi was crazy and might be a fabricator, she stressed. His story improved when he wanted asylum and went to shit when he got his German green card. The BND still refused the CIA any access and would never polygraph him. The BND couldn't run a goddamn two-car funeral, she reminded the group.

Margaret's temper began to rise. As her tone grew louder, she got personal. The CIA was a man's world and she had learned the hard way that a foul mouth and swagger got her respect. Plus she couldn't help but remember the spiteful e-mails from Beth's team.

Analysts sitting on their asses in Langley didn't understand how Iraqi defectors lie compulsively to get what they want, Margaret told them. The operations side had a whole science devoted to figuring out if a source really had access to information, and if the sources actually believed it. The analysts knew nothing about asset validation. They knew nothing about human behavior.

"That's our job," she said sharply.

She turned and appealed emotionally to Steve. "Don't rely on Curveball," she pleaded. "Don't rely on WINPAC." Too many red flags were waving, she said. The case screamed of a problem.

"He's a disaster," she declared.

Beth fought back just as obstinately. She defended her team and endorsed Curveball tenaciously. She fought like a bulldog, a colleague said later.

The defector knew how fermentors worked, who was important in the program, how they procured stuff, and a lot more, she argued. Everything he said made sense—Kamil and Dr. Germ, the cover story about farmers, the mobile replacement for Al Hakam, everything. His reporting was "highly detailed and technically accurate," she insisted.

"Of course we'd like to talk to him," Beth admitted.

But other reliable sources had confirmed his information, she said. The Brits backed him. So did satellite imagery. So did U.N. reports. That was as good as it got, in her opinion.

She taunted Margaret. Did operations have better sources? Why couldn't the clandestine service recruit any decent spies in Iraq? Why didn't they get off their asses?

Besides, Beth went on, so what if Curveball was a little crazy? No one had ever met a normal defector. The point was he couldn't make all this up. His reporting "was too detailed to be a fabrication," she argued.

Field operatives like Margaret "cannot evaluate his expertise," Beth said smugly. "You are simply not qualified to judge the complicated, technical aspects. That's our job."

Margaret glared back at the analyst.

"Well, you can kiss my ass in Macy's window," she replied acidly. Everyone remembered that line later.

They argued back and forth, tempers exploding, profanities flying.

Steve was appalled. He tried to calm them, or at least to stop their cursing at one another. His effort to negotiate a truce had sparked a knife fight.

Beth didn't give an inch.

"Look, we can validate a lot of what this guy says," she contended at one point.

"Where did you validate it?" Margaret demanded.

"On the Internet."

"Exactly, it's on the Internet," Margaret roared back. "That's where he got it too!"

Margaret sputtered in anger. How could the analysts possibly judge Curveball as credible? Were they as crazy as Curveball? They had no confirmation, no proof. Even the Germans did not vouch for him.

After forty minutes or so, McLaughlin's deputy called a halt to the slugfest. They all retired to their offices—Margaret to the fifth floor, Beth to the fourth, the counter-proliferation guy back to the basement—unsure which way Steve would rule.

Steve was in a tough spot. As a veteran operations officer, he sympathized with Margaret's argument. He knew before the meeting that Curveball was the key source on bioweapons. He also knew that the defector drove the BND nuts, that he drank too much, and that he was mentally unstable. It didn't prove the Iraqi had lied. In his view, it just proved that the BND was too inept to manage a difficult source. But it didn't look good.

On the other hand, Steve understood that the closed-door shouting match was nothing compared to the uproar he would cause if he pulled the plug on Curveball. Backtracking now would send a shock wave through U.S. intelligence. It would mean the CIA leadership no longer stood behind two years of classified reports and threat assessments, or the closed-door briefings Tenet and McLaughlin had given to the White House and Congress. It meant the CIA no longer supported the National Intelligence Estimate, the gold standard of the entire U.S. intelligence community. It meant the CIA didn't back a crucial part of the White House case for war.

McLaughlin, his boss, would be humiliated. Tenet would go bonkers. He'd have to do something he hated—admit a mistake to the president, eat crow on Capitol Hill. Steve hadn't risen in the CIA by forcing his bosses to walk off a cliff.

The Curveball doubters got more support the next day.

An operational cable arrived from the CIA station chief in Berlin. He finally had reaching Hanning. The BND director had sent over a signed, two-page letter in German to Tenet, with an accompanying English translation. The CIA station chief transmitted key portions back to headquarters.

The letter from Hanning was uncharacteristically blunt.

"I want to stress that this is single-source information," he wrote. "It is unconfirmed and untested." Like the Germans, he added, British and Israeli intelligence believed "the information was plausible, but were unable to verify it."

Hanning again refused to let the CIA question the defector. But American authorities could use the information in reports and speeches "with the expectation of source protection," he wrote, meaning they must agree to conceal his identity and BND involvement.

Hanning's aides viewed his offer as a compromise, a minor concession to American pressure. The BND chief was an ardent chess player. Giving way here was like sacrificing a pawn.

Drumheller grew angry when he read the cable. The Germans are trying to play it both ways, he thought. They put out product from Curveball and we got excited. So now they're nervous. They won't give us access because we'll see he's a nutcase and it will embarrass them. It's bullshit.

That afternoon, Steve e-mailed a memo to Beth and asked her to proofread it. He had drafted a summary of the turbulent meeting the previous day, he wrote. He had worked hard to marshal his arguments and had reached his decision. He entitled it, "Reliability of Human Reporting on Iraqi Mobile BW Capability."

Steve's conclusion was clear. "The primary source of this information is an Iraqi émigré. . . . After an exhaustive review, the U.S. Intelligence Community . . . judged him credible."

He was throwing his full support behind the geek squad. Beth and her team had won the argument hands down. The analysts savored the memo, relished every paragraph. Curveball was credible! Margaret could kiss her own sweet ass in Macy's window.

Near the bottom, Steve's memo conceded that the CIA was "handicapped in efforts to resolve legitimate questions" about Curveball's veracity. He also noted that the BND "may now be downgrading its own evaluation of the source's reliability."

But he played down or ignored the objections that Margaret raised with such high-decibel fervor. He viewed Beth as "the master of the case" and he looked to her for answers, he said later.

Steve listed five reasons to support his judgment. They were mostly the old arguments: the technical reporting, the satellite imagery, the old U.N. reports, and so on. But one bullet point read, "Confirmation/replication of the described design by U.S. contractors (it works)."

WINPAC had asked Battelle, a nonprofit research corporation, to study Curveball's descriptions of the bio-trailers. Battelle works closely with the government, especially on classified projects. It manages or co-manages four national defense laboratories, including Oak Ridge and Brookhaven, involved in nuclear weapons and other sensitive programs.

"They took seventy-five or eighty Curveball reports and sent them to the lab, and asked 'Does it work?'" a senior CIA official said. "And the answer came back, 'Yeah. This makes sense. These are workable designs.'"

Still, Drumheller was flabbergasted when he later read Steve's memo. Was he kidding? An exhaustive review? That's what he called Margaret and Beth shouting in a room? Curveball had freak-out episodes. He was out of control. A total flake.

A day or so later, Drumheller launched another attempt to alert higher-ups. He and Margaret took the elevator back up to the seventh floor and met with Pavitt, head of the clandestine service, and Kappes, his deputy.

"Jim, we've got a real problem here," Drumheller said. "We need to do something."

Margaret repeated the arguments, minus the fireworks that marked her blowup with Beth. Stop this train before it wrecks us all, she pleaded. Pavitt had started the clandestine counter-proliferation division. He preached asset validation like religion. Surely he saw the need to intervene.

Pavitt well understood the problem.

"The fact is there was yelling and screaming about this guy," he said later. "My people were saying, 'We think he's a stinker.' They pushed and pushed and pushed. But the other side was saying, 'We still think he's worthwhile.'"

Pavitt wanted no part of it. He refused to get involved. He refused to support his own staff.

Curveball was not their source, he admonished Margaret. The Iraqi was just a refugee. They had not met him and should not interfere. Margaret was "not qualified to make a judgment" about Curveball's story, Pavitt told her. Let the analysts make the call. He was their problem.

"I don't want my people doing analysis," he said. "This isn't our case."

After the meeting, Pavitt sidelined the problem until it dropped from sight. Drumheller and the other skeptics were wasting their time. Pavitt said he never conveyed their doubts to Tenet or McLaughlin. Like Tenet, he wouldn't challenge his superiors. But no one else in the CIA leadership took responsibility either.

Privately, Pavitt figured that one dicey defector wasn't going to stop the war. The buildup had begun in earnest. Tens of thousands of combat troops already were being deployed to the Persian Gulf, secret military and intelligence bases being built in the desert, massive supplies pushed up the pipeline. The White House wouldn't stop now. So Pavitt dismissed the concerns of his staff that Curveball might be a fraud.

"Look, even if they stood on their heads and tap-danced up and down Pennsylvania Avenue, I don't think it would have made any difference," Pavitt argued.

He insisted that he did not know Curveball was "of such import" to the CIA case against Iraq. "Nobody in the DO took this guy seriously," he said. "Nobody knew that so much hung on what this one refugee said," given the other White House charges on Iraq.

"Later, I remember the guffaws by myself and others when we learned what happened. We said, 'How could they have put this much emphasis on this guy?' He wasn't a source. He wasn't worth jack shit in our minds."

CHAPTER 23

The tempo picked up again after the New Year.

The White House wanted to use Curveball's information in President Bush's 2003 State of the Union speech. Every sentence in the annual address to Congress is supposed to be carefully vetted, checked, and double-checked. Steve sent a note down to Drumheller and asked him to make sure that German intelligence cleared the defector's account of the germ trucks. Despite her misgivings, Margaret fired off another cable to the Berlin station chief.

President Bush intended "to refer to the Curveball information" in public, she wrote. Was that okay with the BND? Would they vouch for it?

Margaret also told the station chief to urgently request "transcripts of actual questions asked of, and responses given by, Curveball concerning Iraq's BW program." To her astonishment, she had discovered that the CIA analysts still worked off the DIA versions of the *Hortensia 2* reports. The CIA files were third-hand at best. They had not seen any interview transcripts.

The reply arrived three days later, on January 27, the day before the president's speech. Still no transcripts. And the Germans still would not vouch for their source. They have "not been able to verify his reporting," the Berlin station chief wrote once again. "No one has been able to verify this information."

Then the CIA veteran added an unusual personal note.

"The source himself is problematical," he wrote. "Defer to headquarters but to use information from another liaison service's source whose information cannot be verified on such an important, key topic should take the most serious consideration."

Drumheller picked up the phone and called Margaret after he read the message.

"Okay," he said, relief in his voice. "That will put an end to it."

He called Steve and told him that the BND was still barring access to Curveball and the debriefing transcripts. He had Margaret draft a memo, which Drumheller then sent to McLaughlin's aide to make sure they understood the problem. The e-mail had bullet points for emphasis. It read in part:

- We are not certain that we know where Curve Ball is. . . .
- Curve Ball has a history of being uncooperative. He is seeing the BND soon for more questions. The BND cannot move the meeting up. We have asked.
- The BND has agreed to our using the information publicly, but does not want it sourced back to them. . . . We should be careful to conceal the origin of the information since if Curve Ball is exposed, the family he left in Iraq will be killed.
- The BND cannot vouch for the validity of the information. They are concerned that he may not have had direct access, and that much of what he reported was not secret (per WINPAC, the information they could corroborate was in open source literature or was imagery of locations that may not have been restricted).

After getting the memo, Steve told Drumheller that he would speak to his boss. He apparently did so, because McLaughlin made a point of asking Beth, the chief geek squad analyst for Iraq, about Curveball.

"Are you comfortable with this?" he asked.

"Yes," she replied. "The reporting is credible."

The next night, Bush appeared in the House of Representatives and solemnly addressed both houses of Congress. He devoted much of the speech to readying the nation for war. It would be remembered for a single sentence, Bush's claim that "the British government has learned that Saddam Hussein recently sought significant quantities of uranium in Africa." Later, embarrassed by the fact that some of the evidence had been forged, White House officials conceded they erred by including the line. The controversy would haunt Bush's team.

But another part of Bush's speech also created shock waves.

"From three Iraqi defectors we know that Iraq, in the late 1990s, had several mobile weapons labs," Bush announced. "These are designed to produce germ warfare agents and can be moved from place to place to evade inspectors. Saddam Hussein has not disclosed these facilities. He's given no evidence that he has destroyed them."

In a radio address and White House statement several days later, Bush expanded the charge. "Firsthand witnesses have informed us that Iraq has at least seven mobile factories for the production of biological agents," Bush warned. With these, "Iraq could produce within just months hundreds of pounds of biological poisons." The president's uncompromising comments put Curveball's account before the world for the first time.

Afterward, Gradl picked up the phone and called Drumheller in a state of near panic. "Oh my God, they're going to kill me," the BND officer moaned.

His bosses back in Germany were apoplectic. They felt that Bush had "pinpointed their guy," he complained. Curveball thought so too. He had seen Bush on TV and had gone crazy, frantic with fear.

"Now they are going to have to resettle him again," Gradl wailed.

Drumheller apologized profusely. He didn't know what to say. No one had warned him of what the president would say. The call depressed him.

He already felt overwhelmed by the stress at work. For the first time in his life, he couldn't sleep properly. He was irritable in the office and short-tempered at home. His weight had ballooned.

Bush had asked Secretary of State Colin Powell to make the public case against Iraq at the United Nations Security Council on February 5. Powell and his aides already were scrutinizing the intelligence out at the CIA. Tenet's aides circulated an early draft of Powell's speech and asked senior staff to ensure it did not contain errors or inadvertently disclose sensitive sources and methods.

When Margaret read her copy, she just about flipped. She couldn't believe it. She marched into Drumheller's office and dropped it on his desk. She had highlighted the sections on mobile germ factories with a marker.

"Look at this. There's still all this Curveball shit."

Drumheller quickly read the draft. He was amazed. They had banged this drum now for two months. Why was no one listening?

"I need to see McLaughlin," he said.

Even at his rank, Drumheller needed permission to go outside normal channels. He first called Kappes, Pavitt's deputy, and told him he planned to call McLaughlin's chief aide again.

"I'll tell them we still haven't figured out if Curveball is reliable," Drumheller said.

"I thought it was all resolved," Kappes told him.

"No," Drumheller told him. "It's not."

Drumheller called back upstairs and got another one of McLaughlin's aides, his chief of staff.

"You have to understand," Drumheller said. "There's a real problem with that speech."

They spoke for a while, and McLaughlin's aide told him that the corroboration from the three other sources was paper thin. None of the others had actually seen the mobile bioweapons labs. They had just heard about them.

Curveball was "the only tangible source," McLaughlin's deputy said. He was their "smoking gun."

"You've got to be kidding," Drumheller replied. "You can't be hanging everything on this guy."

"That's it."

"Jesus Christ," Drumheller swore. This is insane, he thought.

There was a pause.

"I'll call you back," he heard. Click.

A few minutes later, McLaughlin's chief of staff was on the line again.

"Come on up," he said. "John wants to talk to you."

Drumheller headed for the elevator. Curveball is our only source, he thought. He may be a fabricator. If so, he is spewing poison into the intelligence stream. The only solution is to recall all the reports.

Putting out a burn notice on a source is humiliating. Drumheller had seen it only three times in his twenty-six-year career—twice in Africa, and once in Europe, all during the Cold War. Each time, the CIA was forced to mop up a fiasco. They tracked down and reeled back every line in a complex web of shoddy reporting, false analyses, and sheer confusion that flowed from a single bogus informant.

Drumheller knew that the Germans would never admit Curveball was a fraud because they never claimed he was right. Hell, they always said it was unconfirmed, he remembered. But the CIA analysts seemed so cocksure about the Iraqi, a defector they had never met, that the president was citing him. It was the strangest damned case he had ever seen.

He entered McLaughlin's office suite, and the chief of staff took him to an adjoining glassed-in conference room. It was about 3:30 in the afternoon, and they had to make it quick because McLaughlin and the other top brass gathered at four for back-to-back meetings and videoconferences on Iraq and other topics that ran until seven. They took seats at a table flanked by hanging plants.

McLaughlin strode into the room a moment later. Tenet's chief deputy bore the brunt of supervising the intelligence for the coming war. He was managing the details, working eighteen-hour days, and the strain showed. He looked bone-tired. He was briefing the president regularly, fending off questions from Cheney, tending to cranky members of Congress, and suffering through Tenet's bullying rants. He didn't need more pressure. He was already getting squeezed from all sides.

"Tyler has real reservations about Secretary Powell's speech," the chief of staff said by way of introduction. "He's worried about the mobile labs."

"Sir, this is a problem," Drumheller began cautiously, as he recalled it, careful not to climb too far out on a limb. "Some of the Germans think this guy may be a fabricator. We don't know he's a fabricator. But there is no validation of this reporting. We need to pursue it further."

McLaughlin visibly sagged. He seemed suddenly stricken, Drumheller observed, almost ill.

"Oh my!" Drumheller heard him say. "I hope that's not true."

Drumheller started to summarize his concerns, from Gradl's warning at lunch to the cautious cables from Berlin station. But McLaughlin cut him off and turned to his chief of staff.

"Let's look into this," he said. "Let's run it down."

The CIA's deputy director looked over to Drumheller.

"Thanks for bringing that up," he said. "We'll take care of it."

Drumheller sighed in relief. It's about time somebody in command listened, he thought. He returned to his office. The meeting had lasted only a few minutes. His executive assistant met him at the door and asked how it went.

"I think I made the point," Drumheller replied. "They realize it's a problem. They're going to look into it. They're not going to just use it. They certainly can't resolve it before the speech."

He asked her to get him a copy of Powell's draft.

"We're going to redact it from the speech," he announced.

He grabbed a pen and they went through it together, carefully crossing out offending sentences or paragraphs, anything linked to Curveball. He told her to send it to the officer tasked with coordinating edits and changes to the speech. Don't even retype, rewrite, or reformat it, he ordered. Just get it there now.

That weekend, news stories focused on the intense preparations for Powell's speech. This is good, Drumheller thought. They're really serious. They won't use any crap.

He called Gradl over at the German embassy. Powell would not cite information from Curveball, he promised the anxious spy. He had personally redacted it from the speech. Gradl could tell his bosses.

"Don't worry," Drumheller said. "I've taken care of it."

After that, he relaxed. He felt happy for the first time in, well, a while. It wouldn't last.

On Monday, February 3, two days before Powell was due to give his speech, Drumheller received another request from the CIA deputy director's office.

McLaughlin wanted him to check with the Berlin station chief again "on the current status/whereabouts" of Curveball, according to a memo from Steve, McLaughlin's executive assistant.

"We want to take every precaution against unwelcome surprises that might emerge concerning the intel case; clearly, public statements by this émigré, press accounts of his reporting or credibility, or even direct press access to him would cause a number of potential concerns," Steve wrote.

McLaughlin "would be grateful" for an update on the likely German reaction, he added.

Drumheller read it again to be sure it was not a joke.

McLaughlin would later deny that Drumheller told him of his concerns about Curveball and that he recommended removing his evidence from Powell's speech. However, Drumheller has always maintained otherwise and so to him, McLaughlin's request illustrated the darkest side of intelligence. It seemed that McLaughlin was more worried that Curveball might embarrass the CIA than whether the Iraqi had conned them all with a fraud. Therefore, under pressure to build the case for war, the CIA chiefs figured they'd get to Baghdad, find warehouses full of WMD, and no one would remember a bogus defector. In the meantime, they were covering their behinds, Drumheller thought.

He didn't know how to reply.

CHAPTER 24

The doctor who drew blood from Curveball in May 2000, and who worried that the Iraqi was an alcoholic, also previewed Powell's speech.

Les worked on a secret task force that Tenet had created in the counter-proliferation division in early 2002 to focus on Iraq's weapons of mass destruction. He was a skeptic, an iconoclast, a pain in the rear who often clashed with other biowarfare experts. The task force worked from the CIA basement, and Les was unaware of the battle Drumheller was waging up on the fifth floor.

But Les faced increasing frustration as the Curveball case took on a life of its own. He had complained directly to supervisors at WINPAC and repeatedly locked horns with Beth, the geek squad chief. But she dismissed his concerns, arguing that she had corroborating sources and information that she couldn't share with him.

Reading the Powell draft, Les resolved to put his concerns on the record even if it was too late to change anyone's mind. On Tuesday, February 4, the day before Powell was to address the Security Council, Les wrote a long, impassioned e-mail to Kevin, his direct supervisor, the deputy chief of the WMD task force.

"I believe I am still the only [U.S. government] person to have had direct access to him," Les wrote. He added, "I do have a concern with the validity of the information," given Curveball's "terrible hangover" on the morning they met. "I agree, it was only a one time interaction, however, he knew he was to have a [meeting] on that particular morning but tied one on anyway." Are there "underlying issues" with this source? How "in depth" has he been vetted by the BND?

Les disclosed that he had asked the BND handlers if U.S. intelligence could debrief Curveball directly. The Germans had flatly refused. But they also had admitted that they "were having major handling issues with him and were attempting to determine, if in fact, Curveball was who he said he was," Les tapped out.

"These issues, in my opinion, warrant further inquiry, before we use the information as the backbone of one of our major findings of the existence of a continuing BW program!"

Les reached another disturbing conclusion.

"It was obvious to me," he wrote, "that his case officer, for lack of better words, had fallen in love with his asset and the asset could do no wrong. I mean the story was 100 percent correct" as far as the BND's chief handler was concerned.

Les expressed similar doubts about the three other Iraqi sources. No one, he noted, had confirmed the information from the civil engineer who had heard of bio-trucks in bunkers near Karbala in June 2001. "We sure didn't give much credence to this report when it came out," Les asked. "Why now?"

The MI6 informant, Red River, had only quoted a hearsay account about fermentation systems that he hadn't seen. Red River didn't even claim the equipment was connected to germ warfare. He "sure didn't corroborate" Curveball's information, Les wrote.

The third source, Les added, Mohammed Harith, the Iraqi intelligence major who was channeled to U.S. intelligence by Ahmed Chalabi's organization, was the worst of all.

"This is the *Vanity Fair* source—who was deemed a fabricator," Les wrote. "Need I say more?"

Amazingly, it was true. Shortly after Harith's report about seven Renault trucks was added to U.S. intelligence databases in March 2002, a foreign spy service had passed word that the Iraqi had approached them in the past. He was "largely unreliable and partially fabricated the information he provided," they warned.

With that ammunition in hand, the DIA had formally cut all contacts with Harith on March 20, 2002. The CIA had followed up in April with two assessments suggesting Harith had mined the Internet for his supposed intelligence. "Much of his information was in the public domain, lacked sufficient detail to verify his access, or was incorrect," the CIA cautioned.

The DIA gave in. In May 2002, the agency issued a classified notice officially branding Harith as a liar. "We have determined that [he] is a fabricator/provocateur," the notice warned. Harith's information "is assessed as unreliable and, in some cases, pure fabrication. We have determined that he had also been coached by the Iraqi National Congress (INC) prior to his meeting with western intelligence services."

The DIA burn notice went to the CIA, and for all practical purposes, it stamped a danger sign on Harith's forehead. Yet here he was again, nine months later, being used to corroborate Curveball's account for Powell's U.N. speech. Les was aghast.

In response, Kevin, the deputy chief of the Iraq WMD task force, invited him to come over to hash it out.

"Let's keep in mind the fact that this war's going to happen regardless of what Curveball said or didn't say, and that the Powers That Be probably aren't terribly interested in whether Curveball knows what he's talking about," Kevin wrote in an e-mail. "However, in the interest of Truth, we owe somebody a sentence or two of warning, if you honestly have reservations."

The two met later that night and discussed it. Kevin urged Les to relax. The speech was "too far along" to complain now, he said. Powell was already in New York. Let it go, Les, he urged.

The deputy chief assumed WINPAC knew the Curveball case best. He figured Les was only joking when he claimed a corroborating source was a fabricator. Or else, the analysts were aware of it and had resolved their doubts. Anyway, Kevin explained later, Les had shared his doubts with everyone in CIA management "and they had heard it and heard it and heard it and were not interested in hearing it again."

Later that same night, the eve of Powell's speech, Drumheller was relaxing and watching the TV news at home in Vienna, Virginia, when the phone rang. His daughter was dating a medical student who usually called between 10 p.m. and midnight because of his crazy schedule at the hospital. So she rushed over and grabbed the phone.

After a moment, she glumly handed it to her father.

"Dad," she said. "It's Mr. Tenet."

Surprised, Drumheller sat up on the couch and greeted his boss. Tenet told him he was in New York City working out last-minute details of the speech with Powell. Sorry to call so late, Tenet apologized, but he needed a favor. Was the line secure? Drumheller asked him to call back in a few minutes. He went to his basement, got a key out of his CIA safe, and hooked up his STU-III, the agency's encrypted, bug-proof telephone.

When Tenet called again, he said he needed MI6 to approve use of a piece of intelligence that Powell planned to cite in his speech the next morning. Tenet wanted to check with Richard Dearlove, the MI6 director in London, but it was before dawn in England. Did Tyler have Dearlove's home number? Drumheller didn't, but gave him the home number of the MI6 chief in Washington.

Drumheller could hear voices and commotion in the background. It sounded like a party. The CIA had set up a command post for Tenet at a hotel near the U.N. Tenet confessed to him that he had not slept in seventy-two hours, or at least it felt that way, and was totally exhausted. Drumheller wished him luck.

Then it struck him. He still didn't know if McLaughlin had deleted the Curveball material from Powell's speech. He would ask. This was his last chance.

But Drumheller froze. Did he really want to criticize McLaughlin? Or Pavitt, his friend and boss? It was so late, and he could hear the fatigue and distraction in Tenet's voice. He could not bring himself to disparage a case that was not officially his. Tenet was director of central intelligence, America's most powerful spy, the man who briefed the president of the United States nearly every morning. So Drumheller spoke obliquely.

"You know, boss, I know you guys are real busy but there are problems with that German case," he ventured. "There are real questions about it."

"Yeah, yeah, yeah," he heard Tenet reply. "I'm exhausted. Don't worry about that. We've looked at all that."

"Okay, good," Drumheller said, and hung up. He had taken it to the top. He had done all he could. He felt relieved.

CHAPTER 25

At precisely 10:30 the next morning, February 5, Powell began to prosecute America's case against Iraq at the United Nations Security Council.

While Drumheller and Les had waged separate campaigns to keep Curveball out of his speech, Powell had spent the week in grueling preparations.

It began when I. Lewis "Scooter" Libby, Vice President Cheney's chief of staff, sent Powell a forty-eight-page, single-spaced draft of a speech filled with incendiary charges, including Saddam's alleged alliance with Al Qaeda. The vice president then buttonholed Powell after a meeting in the Oval Office and urged him to use as much of the terrorism material as possible.

It was far too long, Powell pointed out. Foreign ministers wouldn't sit there for five or six hours. Cheney was unmoved.

"Fine," he declared. "Break it into three parts. Give the speech over three days."

It sounded like an order. "We were having a thin lips moment," Powell said later.

He stared at the vice president in disbelief.

"You don't know the U.N.," he replied evenly. "Even I couldn't listen to me for three days."

As it was, they barely had time to prepare. Tenet had invited Powell and his aides to Langley so the CIA could help vet the intelligence he would use. The State Department group arrived late Thursday and took over a conference room that adjoined the director's seventh-floor office. But the first day was a total loss.

Powell was annoyed at the start when he learned the CIA had not seen Libby's material or checked it for accuracy. McLaughlin and other intelligence officers in the room were just as appalled as they read the draft marked OVP—Office of the Vice President. It featured a laundry list of unconfirmed rumors based on dubious evidence, with little attribution or sourcing.

Powell wasn't the only one sticking his credibility on the line. The CIA was stepping out of the shadows as never before. Even Powell compared it to the Cuban Missile Crisis of 1962, when Adlai Stevenson, the U.S. ambassador to the U.N., stood in the Security Council and confronted the Soviet ambassador with grainy photos of ships carrying missiles to Cuba. But Powell planned to show much more than pictures.

He wanted to declassify intercepted phone calls, satellite and spy plane imagery, information gleaned from defectors, whatever it took to build an airtight indictment of Iraq. The CIA, as well as Powell, needed to ensure the intelligence was rock-solid.

The group reviewed the White House draft charge by charge, line by line, seeking to identify the sources and whether they were valid. As the hours ticked away, Powell's team crossed out one paragraph after another.

"I wouldn't use the oddball stuff with respect to whether the Iraqis were involved with 9/11," Powell said. "I threw that out. No one could ever establish it. It was just wishful thinking."

Next to go were pictures of Iraq's "nuclear mujahideen," when Powell realized the CIA could not identify them. He also jettisoned the charge that Iraq recently sought significant quantities of uranium from Africa. Bush had made the claim in his State of the Union speech a week earlier. But Powell was surprised to learn that the CIA couldn't confirm it. He examined an intelligence chart that supposedly outlined the development of Saddam's nuclear program. It looked like a bowl of spaghetti. That went too.

"They had all kinds of stuff they wanted me to use that I wouldn't use," Powell said. "Like that the Iraqis were trying to send remotely piloted vehicles into the United States. I said, 'Guys, why would they go to all this trouble when all they have to do is go to Hertz?' "

They finally agreed late that afternoon to simply toss the White House draft in the trash. McLaughlin was relieved. He considered most of it garbage. Powell instructed the group to write him a new speech based on real intelligence, not half-baked theories and baseless accusations cooked up by Cheney's aides.

Tenet recommended that they try the National Intelligence

Estimate from the previous October as the template for the speech. The intelligence community already had scrutinized and approved the NIE, so it was the most authoritative material available. Powell agreed but stipulated that he still intended to review the data to weed out potential problems.

"I was culling the material to pull together the best case I could," he said. "Not just the best case. The strongest case. Because I knew it would be assaulted by everyone.

"I was being as careful as I possibly could," he added. "I understood the stakes, and I also understood the world was watching this closely."

McLaughlin and other senior CIA officials later would deny that the October NIE played a major role in the run-up to war because few members of Congress bothered to read it. That was true but irrelevant.

Powell used the estimate as the foundation for his Security Council address. The Bush administration's most cautious and internationally respected figure embraced the National Intelligence Estimate to make America's most persuasive case for war. That was its real significance.

Starting again Saturday morning, a core group of CIA and State Department aides worked all that day, that night, and through Sunday. The lack of sleep took its toll. Powell's chief speechwriter, utterly exhausted, began talking to herself at 2 a.m. A bleary-eyed CIA analyst stumbled and appeared near collapse. Powell came and went during the days, depending on other commitments, but stayed every night for six hours.

Powell believed that much of the intelligence was open to interpretation. They had no "smoking gun," no photographs of secret bombs, no proof of anthrax. Too much seemed circumstantial, he thought. Much of it relied on inferential reasoning and what he called worst-case charting. "If you keep picking the most serious alternative at every junction, if you keep assuming the worst case whenever you hit a doubt, you run yourself into a wall pretty quickly," was how he explained it later.

He scrutinized the satellite photos. Agency experts explained that the Iraqis cleaned out a poison gas plant before U.N. inspectors arrived. Maybe. The pictures hardly seemed conclusive.

The nuclear data looked even weaker. According to the CIA, Iraq's attempts to import thousands of aluminum tubes proved Saddam was building centrifuges to enrich uranium. McLaughlin brought one of the suspect tubes into the conference room and rolled it across the table to Powell.

But Powell's own staff in the State Department's intelligence wing, as well as nuclear experts at the Energy Department, disputed the CIA analysis. Powell agreed to mention the tubes but rejected a suggestion to hold one up as a prop during his speech.

The electronic intercepts of telephone conversations, which the National Security Agency had sucked out of the ether, seemed especially ambiguous. Powell's team listened to tapes of Iraqi army officers speaking in Arabic, and read the translations. CIA analysts said the unidentified soldiers warned one another to hide unidentified incriminating evidence. Powell's aides weren't so sure.

"We brought more Arabic linguists in to translate independent of each other," said Lawrence B. Wilkerson, Powell's longtime chief of staff. "We all listened to the tapes a couple of times. We discussed them for a long time. We said, 'Hey, this could go either way.' This could be an innocent conversation about getting ready for a U.N. inspection."

The CIA's best evidence, those in the room agreed, was for the mobile germ factories. The CIA chiefs and Lawrence Gershwin, the national intelligence officer who handled biowarfare, emphasized the importance of the mysterious fleet as the cornerstone of Iraq's secret biowarfare program. No one mentioned Curveball. Instead, Tenet said the agency had four sources and all were solid and trustworthy.

"He said these were the people who worked on it, the people who designed it," Powell said. Tenet and McLaughlin "were very confident of that. When they tell you, 'We have the people who were actually building it,' you believe them. They sounded very solid in their judgment."

He asked for more details. The CIA officials, Wilkerson recalled, told Powell that "the principal source not only worked in the mobile labs, but had seen an accident that killed twelve people and even been injured in the accident and knew others who were injured. This gave more credibility to it." That would go in the speech.

They also told Powell that the chief source "was able to draw those labs so specifically that everyone said, 'Eureka! This is it.' And we used those drawings to make slides," Wilkerson said. Powell would feature them too.

Graphic artists in a CIA basement studio had prepared schematic illustrations of three tractor-trailers parked side by side. Their canvas tops were pulled back in one illustration and yellow arrows pointed to blue vats identified as fermentors, gray boxes labeled as spray driers, and so on.

Someone brought the drawings up and displayed them to the group. Powell was delighted.

"The CIA had cartoons and diagrams and line drawings on what this was all about," he said. "We spent a lot of time looking at them. I kept pressing on this, because I knew they were very important and very visual, and they were something people could look at and get their brains around."

He asked Tenet repeatedly if the CIA was certain about the germ trucks. Tenet guaranteed him not once, but several times, that it was "totally reliable information," Powell recalled.

No one in the room challenged or corrected the blustering CIA chief. No one warned Powell of the battle between Drumheller's skeptical aides and the WINPAC true believers. No one mentioned Les's lonely one-man crusade to short-circuit the process. No one brought up the BND concerns. Nor did anyone caution Powell that one of the corroborating sources was a known fraud.

A Defense HUMINT division chief who attended Powell's prep sessions for two days knew that the DIA had issued a formal "fabrication notice" about Harith. But the DIA manager didn't say a word to Powell. He didn't realize they were discussing Harith, he explained later. The CIA analyst who coordinated Powell's speech had a different excuse. "We lost the thread of concern . . . as time progressed, I don't think we remembered" that Harith was a known fraud, the analyst said.

Powell began to view the germ trucks as the linchpin not just of Saddam's biological weapons program, but also of the American case against Iraq. The National Intelligence Estimate and various CIA reports had cited the trucks as one of many WMD worries. Powell chose to put them in the public spotlight as never before.

"We pressed as hard as we could on those and the CIA stood by it adamantly," he said. "This is one we really pressed on, really spent a lot of time on. . . . We knew how important it was."

Finally, he was convinced. So was Wilkerson.

Trim and balding, Wilkerson spent thirty-one years in the U.S. Army and considered himself a student of both strategic and tactical intelligence. He flew combat choppers in Vietnam and later taught at both the Naval War College and the Marine Corps War College. Now a retired colonel, he understood that intelligence was not a perfect science, not by a long shot. He'd seen too many mistakes over the years. He was determined to use only "ironclad evidence" in Powell's speech.

"The mobile biological labs were probably the most solid piece of intelligence that Tenet and McLaughlin gave us," he said. "They stood by it 100 percent. All the analysts, all the leadership stood by it. They were convinced that of all the things Powell was going to present, this was the most solid and most incontrovertible."

He added, "No one warned us there was anything bad or suspect about the mobile labs."

On Monday, February 3, Powell's aides flew to New York and took over a conference room on the top floor of the U.S. mission, just across busy First Avenue from the U.N. and the icy East River. They set up chairs and arranged desks to resemble the huge horseshoe table in the Security Council, with name cards to show where each country's chief envoy would sit. After several practice tries, Powell did his first full dress rehearsal of the speech late Tuesday night. At the end, Powell turned to Tenet.

"George, you back up everything, right? One last chance."

"Absolutely, Mr. Secretary," Tenet replied.

"Well, that's good, George, because you're going to be with me tomorrow. You're going to be in the camera with me."

The next morning, Powell deliberately positioned Tenet behind his right shoulder at the Security Council table. The symbolism was unmistakable. The CIA publicly backed the intelligence. TV cameras dutifully focused on America's top spy, grimacing and looking ill at ease. It was, he admitted later, "about the last place I wanted to be."

Germany's foreign minister, Joschka Fischer, a former leftist radical, presided at the top of the U-shaped table as president of the Security Council, a job that rotates from country to country. Fischer brought a large delegation, nearly forty people, including a senior BND expert involved in the Curveball case. Fischer was dead set against the war but it now looked unstoppable. U.S., British, and other coalition troops already were closing the noose around Iraq. At least Powell would explain why.

"We knew our own intelligence was vague," said Jens Ploetner, one of Fischer's aides. "We didn't know what Washington had. We thought maybe they had the smoking gun. The whole world was waiting to see this.

"My gut feeling was the Americans must have so much from reconnaissance planes and satellites, from infrared spotter teams, from Special Forces, and other systems. We thought they must have tons of stuff."

Leaning forward in his chair, behind a nameplate marked "United States," Powell began speaking in a somber tone, as if he were reluctantly diagnosing an incurable disease. He used no hyperbole or fancy rhetorical tricks, just a piling on of facts. The effect was sobering and severe. He promised to provide indisputable proof that Saddam's regime was concealing weapons of mass destruction.

"The material I will present to you comes from a variety of sources," Powell said. "Some are U.S. sources. And some are those of other countries. Some of the sources are technical, such as intercepted telephone conversations and photos taken by satellites. Other sources are people who have risked their lives to let the world know what Saddam Hussein is really up to."

A few moments later, he expanded the pledge.

"My colleagues, every statement I make today is backed up by sources, solid sources. These are not assertions. What we're giving you are facts and conclusions based on solid intelligence. I will cite some examples, and these are from human sources."

Then he got to the meat of his case.

"First, biological weapons," he began.

"One of the most worrisome things that emerges from the thick intelligence file we have on Iraq's biological weapons is the existence of mobile production facilities used to make biological agents," Powell warned.

"Let me take you inside that intelligence file and share with you what we know from eyewitness accounts," he invited.

"We have first-hand descriptions of biological weapons factories on wheels and on rails," Powell said. He deliberately drew out the key words: first . . . hand . . . descriptions.

The huge chamber listened silently, with barely even a rustle of paper. This was raw history and everyone knew it. Virtually every word from Powell now was coming from Curveball, although he wisely didn't mention the odd code name.

The mobile weapons labs are easily moved and designed to evade detection by U.N. inspectors, he said. "In a matter of months, they can produce a quantity of biological poison equal to the entire amount that Iraq claimed to have produced in the years prior to the Gulf War."

The program began in the mid-1990s but U.N. inspectors only had vague hints at the time, he said. Confirmation came later, in the year 2000.

"The source was an eyewitness, an Iraqi chemical engineer who supervised one of these facilities," Powell disclosed. "He actually was present during biological agent production runs. He was also at the site when an accident occurred in 1998. Twelve technicians died from exposure to biological agents."

Powell briefly scanned his notes and then continued.

The eyewitness, he said, reported that Iraq always produced its biological poisons starting on Thursdays at midnight, and finished by Friday night, because U.N. inspectors would not bother them on the Muslim holy day.

"This defector is currently hiding in another country with the certain knowledge that Saddam Hussein will kill him if he finds him," he added.

Powell assured the diplomats that the "eyewitness account" had been "corroborated by three sources." He ticked them off briefly.

The first source had "confirmed the existence" of transportable facilities moving on trailers, he said. By that, he meant the civil engineer's unverified report of bio-trucks at Karbala. Another source, "also in a position to know," had reported production systems on trucks and railcars, he said. That was Red River, the British source with the hearsay account.

Finally, Powell added, an Iraqi major who defected had "confirmed" that Iraq "has" mobile biological research laboratories. Powell had just cited Mohammed Harith, the informant from Chalabi's group who already had been deemed a fabricator.

Their information "is highly detailed and extremely accurate," Powell intoned. "We know what the fermentors look like, we know what the tanks, pumps, compressors and other parts look like. We know how they fit together. We know how they work. And we know a great deal about the platforms on which they are mounted."

As he spoke, the CIA's cartoon drawings and cutaway diagrams of canvas-topped eighteen-wheelers flashed up on two huge screens mounted on the far corners of the Security Council chambers, so everyone could see. They also flickered on TV screens around the world. The trucks seemed sinister precisely because they looked so familiar, as if demonic moving vans suddenly began to spray pestilential poisons in a horror movie.

Iraq has built at least seven mobile germ factories, including a rail-based system, Powell warned, but the six truck systems each had up to three vehicles. Just imagine trying to find those eighteen trucks among the thousands and thousands of trucks that travel Iraq's roads every day, he urged the diplomats.

The trucks were sophisticated facilities, he warned, able to produce enough dry biological material "in a single month to kill thousands upon thousands of people." Dried agent "is the most lethal form for human beings," he added, and Iraq had "perfected drying techniques" and incorporated them in its mobile factories.

That was the single BND report based on Curveball's comment about spray driers. It had never been confirmed.

Powell finished by listing Iraq's research before the 1991 war into potential bioweapons agents, from plague to camelpox. Saddam could even develop smallpox, he added.

"There can be no doubt that Saddam Hussein has biological weapons and the capability to rapidly produce more, many more," he finished up.

Powell's eighty-minute presentation galvanized American opinion in favor of war. Pundits and editorial writers hailed the speech and opinion polls showed an immediate jump in support for Bush's threat to use force. News organizations played up the germ trucks as the centerpiece of Powell's address. Curveball's vehicles assumed a macabre, almost mythic status. They became "Winnebagos of Death," "Germ Caravans," and "Hell on Wheels."

Others were less impressed.

Werner Kappel, the senior BND official, turned on the large TV in his corner office in Berlin and invited members of the Curveball team to join him. They watched in mute shock as Powell highlighted the trucks and cited an "eyewitness" three different times, a defector who was "hiding in a foreign country." Someone cursed under his breath.

Kappel was the first to speak when the speech ended.

"*Mein Gott!* We had always told them it was not proven," he said in dismay. "It was not hard intelligence."

Those in the room knew that Powell grossly mischaracterized the warehouse accident. The Americans apparently had misunderstood or misinterpreted the BND reporting. Curveball had never claimed to the BND that he had witnessed the incident, or even was anywhere near Djerf al Nadaf that day.

"He only heard rumors of an accident," Kappel said. "He heard it thirdhand."

Powell's diagrams of the trucks stunned them as well. They appeared identical to a set that the BND staff had produced, except the CIA illustrations used different colors. "Those are our damn trucks," Kappel complained.

Kappel had expected to see photographs, hard evidence. Powell's illustrations weren't proof. They were hearsay. Kappel couldn't get over it. Powell had used artists' conjectures based on analysts' interpretations of Arabic-to-German-to-English translations of debriefing reports of a manic-depressive defector the Americans had never talked to.

It was ludicrous, insane, Kappel thought. He read secret intelligence reports every day and most of them, he suspected, weren't true. People hear what they want to hear. And the Americans were going to war on this?

After the speech, the BND group sat in uneasy silence.

"What the hell is going on?" Kappel asked his colleagues. No one had an answer.

Ernst Uhrlau, Germany's national coordinator for intelligence, was incredulous as well. Curveball proved nothing, he thought. The Iraqi was a piece of a puzzle, a single source of information. His story was unverified, unconfirmed, unknown.

Uhrlau quickly decided what must have happened. Germany opposed going to war so the Americans were using BND intelligence to justify an invasion. The White House had tried for months to link the 9/11 cell in Hamburg to Saddam. That didn't work. Even the CIA didn't buy it. So they were using Curveball. The CIA was sticking it to the BND again, just like in the past, he concluded.

At Munich House, Alex Steiner, the head of operations, heard from a senior BND operations officer who seemed frantic. "No proof, no proof, no proof," the German kept on repeating. Curveball's information was "not confirmed."

Rolf Ekeus, the former chief of UNSCOM, went to the U.N. to watch. He was not convinced by Powell's presentation. The illustrations of the trucks were "beautifully painted," he said that afternoon. But the Americans should show "real pictures" or it meant nothing.

U.N. inspectors in New York and Baghdad were startled to hear Powell declare that they didn't work on Fridays. Apparently the CIA had not bothered to check. The U.N. teams worked on Fridays precisely because it was an Iraqi holiday. They searched fewer sites since most things were closed. But headquarters in New York had ordered field visits every Friday specifically to curb Iraqi cheating. And Iraq couldn't produce anthrax and botulinum toxin in a single day, Friday or not. No one could. It took at least three or four days, probably a week. So would the inspectors kindly stay away on Saturday, Sunday, and the rest of the week?

Drumheller watched the speech with disbelief on the TV in his CIA office. Jesus, he thought, someone really screwed up.

He called his executive officer and asked about the draft of Powell's speech that they had marked up and sent upstairs, the one in which he had carefully deleted all the material from Curveball.

"Hey, did we send them the wrong thing?" he asked anxiously. "Did we send them the nonredacted copy?"

The aide went back to her desk and checked. She returned a minute later carrying her backup copy. They definitely had submitted the edited version.

"Here's what we sent them," she said, handing it to him. "They didn't listen to you."

"Jesus Christ," Drumheller said, staring at the document. He recalled his phone call with Tenet the previous night. "Well, I guess that shows how much influence I have around here."

That afternoon, Drumheller's phone rang. Gradl sputtered on the line.

"Tyler, what the hell is going on over there? You promised us this wouldn't happen!"

Drumheller apologized again.

"Calm down," he said defensively. "This is way over my head."

On February 11, a week after the speech, Margaret sent an e-mail to a Defense HUMINT division chief at Clarendon asking again why they had not vetted Curveball.

The division chief forwarded the e-mail to an aide with a caustic note attached. He didn't realize that he also copied the message to Margaret. He was "shocked" by her suggestion that Curveball might be unreliable, the division chief typed. The "CIA is up to their old tricks" and doesn't "have a clue" how hard the BND had worked on the Curveball case.

That same day, the U.N. inspectors' office in New York prepared a nine-page evaluation that eviscerated Powell's presentation. The in-house paper identified eighteen places where his allegations appeared unsubstantiated. Most of Powell's material was out of date, anecdotal, and ambiguous at best, the memo concluded.

Most important, most of the sites that Powell pointed to with such confidence "have been inspected, samples taken, records examined and interviews conducted. No evidence of proscribed material has been discovered."

Still, nothing actually disproved Curveball's account.

BAGHDAD
2003-2004

CHAPTER 26

A few minutes after 9 a.m. on Saturday, February 8, 2003, three days after Powell's speech, a line of boxy white Nissan Patrol four-wheel-drive vehicles with large black U.N. markings on the hoods and doors rolled through the gate from Baghdad's Canal Hotel.

The four cars threaded their way through the heavy morning traffic in the city's southern suburbs. A cold overnight rain still chilled the air and pedestrians bundled up in woolen sweaters and jackets at bustling street stalls and food markets. The drivers picked up speed when they reached a highway leading out of town.

The U.N. issued military-style radio call signs to its weapons hunting teams in Iraq. The chemical warfare specialists belonged to Charlie team, nuclear scientists reported to November team, and missile experts to Delta. This convoy carried a dozen members of Bravo team, the bioweapons contingent.

U.N. inspectors had returned to Iraq in force the previous November after a four-year absence. The official name changed from UNSCOM to UNMOVIC but the work was much the same. Since arriving, the weapons hunters had usually launched a dozen or more missions each day, including Fridays and other holidays. Teams had raided more than 350 factories, military bases, government offices, private homes, and other sites. Most were previously known targets, searched many times in the past. Only a few dozen were new.

Kay Mereish headed biological planning and operations, including Bravo team. Thin and feisty, just shy of fifty, she brought terrier-like energy to her job. She had a Ph.D. in biology and an aggressive curiosity, a perfect mix for an inspector. She had worked nine years inside the Pentagon's high-security bio-defense laboratories at Fort Detrick, Maryland, and knew germ weapons. After joining the U.N., she had rushed to Iraq in the first wave of inspectors, eager to get started. Born in Jordan, she spoke fluent Arabic. But she rarely did so in Iraq. She learned far more if people in the room assumed she only spoke English.

Normally, before a site visit, Bravo leaders prepared a detailed briefing packet to show team members where they were going and why. Not this time. Mereish told the team early that morning only that they were embarking on a high-priority mission to search a new site of extreme interest. It was all very hush-hush.

The CIA and MI6 had imposed those strict limits. If information leaked, they feared, the Iraqis would clean out the site. Mereish and Martin Fosbrook, her British deputy, usually were allowed to share intelligence with fellow American and British colleagues on a need-to-know basis. In this case, the intelligence was so sensitive that they briefed no one, not even the Dutch team leader.

No one wanted to further sour relations between the CIA and UNMOVIC. McLaughlin and other CIA officials deeply distrusted the director, Hans Blix. It seemed a bit unfair. The Swedish diplomat refused to let U.S. intelligence use the teams as spies, as they did in the 1990s. CIA officials grumbled that Blix saw intelligence cooperation as a "one-way street." He wanted their help but refused to return the favor by acting as their eyes and ears in Iraq. Plus, the U.N. leaked like a sieve. Every major intelligence service, including the Iraqis, spied there.

"People didn't want to help the inspectors," said a senior CIA official. "They were afraid information would be compromised. There was a common belief that the U.N. inspectors were penetrated by everybody and their dog. There was a real sense that if you give it to them, it's going to be blown."

But under pressure from several members of Congress, the CIA finally began sharing tips with UNMOVIC in the final week of December 2002. More than a dozen spy services, including the BND and MI6, already funneled material to the U.N. inspectors. The British were especially helpful. They gave Blix's staff about thirty pieces of intelligence, covering nineteen suspect sites in Iraq, under a program code-named Operation Rockingham.

The spy services dealt with James Corcoran, the UNMOVIC intelligence liaison officer in New York. He headed a section named "Outside Information Sources," a euphemism for intelligence collection.

Corcoran had spent thirty-five years in the Canadian Security Intelligence Service and ran Canada's clandestine operations before joining the U.N. His solid credentials and easygoing manner soothed tensions with the CIA. Plus he shared their convictions. "I was convinced we were going to find something in Iraq," he recalled. "I said to the guys here if only 5 percent of the intelligence is correct, we'll find something."

On a bitter cold afternoon in January 2003, Corcoran walked across the street from the U.N. to a bug-proof conference room in the U.S. mission. For the next hour or so, CIA officials briefed him extensively on the Curveball case. They showed him computer designs and diagrams of the germ trucks, some much more technical than those Powell would show.

On January 14, Mereish and Fosbrook hand-carried a thick dossier from Corcoran's office in New York to their operations base at the Canal Hotel in Baghdad. Labeled "Biology," the file focused almost entirely on the germ trucks. It didn't mention Curveball as a source, but included details of the six docking stations that he had identified. "These are the smoking gun sites," Corcoran had told them.

Now, three weeks after getting the file, the convoy of white U.N. vehicles turned off the highway near the giant berms of Tuwaitha, the old nuclear facility. The team members spoke little as they bounced along. They presumed that Iraqi intelligence bugged their cars, as well as their hotel rooms and offices. They assumed U.S. and Iraqi eavesdroppers monitored their Thuraya satellite phone calls as well.

Riding in the lead car, Mereish was excited. The U.S., British, and German governments all had pushed hard intelligence on this mission, according to Corcoran. Three separate countries, including two permanent Security Council members, meant it was top priority, Corcoran had said. This could be the jackpot, the gold mine. Mereish desperately hoped he was right. She wanted to prove that U.N. inspections worked. She wanted to prevent a war.

They rumbled over a narrow bridge over the Diyala River and drove down a two-lane side road lined with grimy factories and foundries. This part of Iraq's desert mostly featured scrub brush and tufted grass between low hillocks of gray stone and grit. It evoked all the charm of a gravel pit. The mid-morning sun already had burned off the early chill. Mud was drying to choking dust.

The convoy passed a gas station before pulling off the road to the right. They parked outside a wrought iron gate on the corner of a large compound. The gate was padlocked, but the security looked surprisingly low-tech. The Iraqis had ringed Al Hakam with guard towers, anti-aircraft batteries, and military outposts. This compound featured only a cement block wall topped with a few rusting strands of barbed wire. Many Iraqi homes are better protected.

The team's QuickBird satellite pictures showed the site had six uneven sides, like a trapezoid twisted at one end. They checked the GPS coordinates to be sure: N 33 16 4.2 and E 44 32 38.6. They were sure.

It was Djerf al Nadaf, the complex where Curveball worked. Powell hadn't mentioned it. It was fresh on their list. No U.N. inspector had ever visited here before.

Fosbrook climbed on the hood of his Nissan and peered over the wall. He wanted to make sure the Iraqis weren't running around hiding stuff, or worse, carting crucial evidence out a back entrance. The Iraqis had done both in the past. But he couldn't see any activity. The place looked dead.

After a few minutes, a befuddled guard appeared. Seeing the U.N. group, he unbolted the lock and pulled the gates open. The cars rumbled past a small whitewashed guardhouse and several small sheds on the right. They passed a truck scale and a junk heap of discarded office equipment on the left. Just beyond, the outer wall doglegged to the right and edged close to an inner wall that bisected the compound from east to west. The angle created an hourglass barely wide enough for their Nissans to squeeze through.

They were getting close. They drove down a narrow path beside a pair of one-story warehouses made of corrugated metal. A larger warehouse stood at the far end, nearly perpendicular to the first pair. They could see that a two-story bay rose at one end. Air and light filtered in from open spaces just under the metal roof.

That was their target. "That's the one where the mobile labs were supposed to be," said Corcoran. "That's the one we were interested in."

Riding in the back of the convoy, Rocco Casagrande, a Bravo microbiologist, stopped beside one of the first warehouses. The car parked inches from the building. Casagrande got out the passenger side and clambered onto the roof of his vehicle. He reached over to bend back a loose flap of metal from the wall. He twisted it several times and finally pulled it loose. He stuck his head inside. The chamber was dark. He squeezed his shoulders through the opening, pulled his slender frame through, and dropped inside.

At twenty-eight, Casagrande had a Ph.D. from the Massachusetts

Institute of Technology with a specialty in agricultural biowarfare. He had a rakish air, with a bushy brown mustache over a small goatee. Before coming to Baghdad, he was convinced that Saddam was building illicit weapons. Now, after weeks of fruitless searches, he wondered. The intelligence looked pretty screwy.

Analysts studying satellite imagery kept reporting Scud missiles hidden on farms. Each time, a U.N. convoy would race to the site, chased by cars filled with Iraqi intelligence officers, followed by reporters and TV crews. Sometimes, to confuse the Iraqis, the inspectors sent two or three teams in different directions. But they would all converge on the same spot. And the poor farmer would watch helplessly as two or three dozen cars and vans filled with jabbering foreigners and surly Iraqis suddenly roared into his yard from all directions and demanded he hand over his ballistic missile.

But the missile always turned out to be a rotating steel drum for drying corn. Or a poultry shed.

"Chickens in Iraq are kept in a long, low half-cylinder coop," Casagrande said later. "We inspected a lot of chicken coops. We found out how chickens were fed. How they live. We found out everything there is to know about Iraqi chickens."

Fed up with wild-chicken chases, Casagrande had a shop print thirty souvenir T-shirts. They showed the U.N. symbol over the words *Ballistic Chicken Farm Inspection Team.* Colleagues bought every one.

Bravo team mostly focused on finding evidence of the germ trucks, however. The two dozen team members raided a brewery, a military hospital, and a public health laboratory. They searched an ammunition dump, an agricultural research center, and the Baghdad Alcoholic Drinks Company. They pored over purchase orders, quality control sheets, and anything mentioning the Mesopotamia State Company for Seeds, which ran the seed program. Wherever they went, they looked for truck repair shops or heavy equipment that didn't jibe with normal biological work. They never found any.

In mid-January, Iraqi officials notified Bravo that they had located several mobile labs. Team members hurried to a government medical lab on the outskirts of a slum in northeast Baghdad. In the back, they found three box trucks, each with a corroded sink and small refrigerator in the back. They were food testing labs. Casagrande took samples of the waste lines to be sure. All the tests proved negative for bio-agents.

On January 19, responding to a tip, four Bravo inspectors sprinted to the Amiriyah Serum and Vaccine Institute—where Curveball claimed they tested product from his trucks—and arrived just in time to stop a refrigerator truck, parked by the front gate, preparing to leave. They yanked open the rear and found neatly packed vials of measles vaccine. It was their third visit to Amiriyah; they found no sign of the quality testing effort that Curveball had described.

Another tip said Taha ran her own secret biological laboratory for ghoulish experiments. The briefing packet included overhead imagery of four office buildings, a garden, and a carport filled with luxury cars. According to a site diagram, Dr. Germ's lab was hidden behind a locked door on the right at the end of an upstairs corridor inside Building #2.

Bravo members raced up the stairs and down the hall, and threw open the door. Inside, several surprised bureaucrats were watching an Arabic version of *Wheel of Fortune* on a small TV. Taha's secret lair turned out to be a government pension office.

The intelligence was leading them nowhere. On February 7, Bravo tried what leaders called a "double bluff" inspection at a pesticide factory in Baghdad. "After looking around, suddenly we jumped in our cars and drove down the street and ran into a vocational college," Casagrande recalled. "We were going to catch them in the act of producing biological agents. Obviously it didn't happen. The school had normal college stuff. And it was Friday, so it was empty."

The next day, when Casagrande dropped into the dim, dusty warehouse at Djerf al Nadaf, he took a moment to get his bearings. Brilliant sunlight streamed in through cracks, shafting through the gloom and illuminating thick particles in the air, A musty smell filled the air. He quickly spotted the cause: moldering sacks of corn and barley scattered on the floor. He opened the door and walked into the yard.

Over at the main warehouse, a couple of team members had propped a ladder up to a grain door on the upper wall. They peered inside while the Iraqi guard fumbled to find the key to the regular entrance. In the rear, bulging white sacks of grain were stacked in enormous piles, nearly reaching the ceiling. The building widened into an L there. A tall array of machinery stood near the wall. No trucks or other vehicles were parked inside.

The guard finally opened the door and Casagrande followed him in. He headed for a pile of loose yellow corn kernels. He could see sections of the floor behind it. Rather than wade through the corn, he climbed on a low concrete wall that ringed the room. He held his arms out for balance, like an aerial artist, as he navigated the narrow top toward the rear.

Climbing down, he opened his backpack and donned his Tyvek, a thin white polyethylene zip-up jumpsuit, and a pair of gloves. Then he got on his hands and knees. Using two cotton swabs moistened in sterile water, he scraped samples of dirt and dust from the tarlike epoxy that filled joints in the cement floor. If the Iraqis produced anthrax or other biological agents here, traces probably seeped or settled deep in the crevices and cracks. The DNA might survive even if the Iraqis had sanitized the site.

Casagrande snapped the tips off the two swabs, put them into a pair of sterile tubes with screw tops, and labeled them. Standing up, he saw Fosbrook, the deputy team leader, point to a nearby wall. He looked over and spotted two large holes for air conditioners. He nodded okay and carefully swabbed cracks around each hole in case an exhaust fan had pulled contaminated dust into the air exchange system. He tubed and labeled those samples as well.

Casagrande then wandered outside and found a discarded shower basin next to the building. Mereish, the chief biologist on Bravo team, instructed him to test that too. He swabbed some goo from the drain.

The warehouse manager finally showed up, a little frightened but eager to help. He led two team members to his office. They grilled him about his work and examined his files. They jotted down the names of company officials, the address of the head office, and other details. Then they shot sixty color photographs of the warehouse compound from every conceivable angle, even old tire tracks they found outside in the mud.

They studied the machinery array in the main warehouse. It clearly didn't cook germs. A funnel at the top fed loose seeds into a rough-edged thresher that removed the husks. The seeds were fed into a mixer that treated them with pesticide, and then into a spin drier. The seeds finally were bagged and sealed. Thick dust covered everything. Birds that apparently ate the treated grain lay in feathered heaps on the floor nearby.

The intelligence packet had described two small rooms tucked in a corner. Mereish found marks on the floor indicating that walls once stood there. At least some information checks out, she decided. Same for the low interior wall, the one that Casagrande had traversed. That was in the packet. She also found an underground room, just as Curveball had said. She found two, in fact.

They were maintenance bays under the seed handling equipment. They allowed technicians to repair the gear from below, the way a mechanic stands in a garage pit to drain the crankcase of a car.

Two Bravo members pulled out a portable ground-penetrating radar unit and switched it on. They tromped up and down the concrete floor. They dragged it over the sacks and the loose corn. They took further readings in the two smaller warehouses and on the dirt lot outside. A retired U.S. Air Force colonel on the team climbed atop the sacks and scraped samples from the overhead fluorescent light fixtures. He also cracked the cement floor at the joints to see if special wires or plumbing were somehow hidden. No one found anything unusual.

Given her excitement on the drive down that morning, Mereish was deeply disappointed. Corcoran's intelligence packet had seemed so strong. But they had found nothing solid.

According to the intelligence, the germ trucks entered the docking station through a huge garage door at the southeast end of the building. But there was no garage door. The wall was a continuous sheet of silver gray corrugated metal on concrete footings. She studied it intently, inside and out, searching for signs of welds that might hide a truck-sized door. She saw none.

The exit door was more mystifying. The entire northwest corner of the L supposedly worked on a huge pivot of some kind and swung to one side. This was Curveball's beloved door. Except it wasn't there. The base of the wall was solid, unbroken concrete. It had no hinge, no swivel, no clamshell door or device. A seed bagging chute, two stories high, hung on the outside. A small garage door, barely wide enough for a farmer's pickup truck, not a tractor-trailer rig, opened beside that.

She and Fosbrook ran their hands up and down the surface of the walls inside and out, searching for hidden seams or alterations. They pressed their weight against it, pushing with all their strength to see if it moved. They looked for hidden levers, handles, or switches, anything they could pull or press to open a secret door like in a haunted house movie. The Iraqis in the room watched them quizzically at first. Then they began to laugh.

Mereish went back outside to look for the generator shed and pump house. They were supposed to feed power and water to the docking station. She spotted a small shed nearby. She walked over and pulled open the door. Dirty plates and old magazines lay inside. Otherwise it was empty.

She peered around the yard. The hourglass entrance path meant vehicles had to make a hard-angled turn to reach the warehouse. The Nissans had squeezed through. A farmer's pickup could make it. But no eighteen-wheeler or other large truck could make that tight turn. No way. There was no room.

She kept looking. A solid, six-foot-high wall flanked three sides of the warehouse. It stood only a few feet from the building. The wall blocked both the end with the missing garage door and the supposed corner exit. Mereish didn't know it, but it was the same wall that British and Israeli photo analysts had spotted in satellite pictures from 1997 and that the CIA weapons center analysts had dismissed as temporary. But the wall was permanent.

"This is all wrong," Mereish told Fosbrook.

She left him and got in her car. She had an idea.

CHAPTER 27

Mereish headed back to the front of the compound, near the entrance gate. Maybe she had missed a clue. She would retrace her steps and start again.

She drove back through the hourglass turn and passed the truck scale and a junk heap in the front courtyard. Then she looked to the left. She craned her neck to be sure, then pulled out her U.N. radio and called Fosbrook, her British deputy.

Romeo 1 to Romeo 2, she said, using their call signs. She told him to come quickly to the front courtyard. She got out of her car. When he got there, she pointed.

Three steel shipping containers baked in the winter sun near the guardhouse. They hadn't noticed them when they first drove in because they were rushing to the docking station out back. The trailer closest to them looked about twenty feet long, but the other pair seemed twice as big. They were gunmetal gray and appeared to be standard, metal-ribbed trailers, each about eight feet wide and slightly higher. They stood side by side in the red dirt, one slightly behind the next and at slight angles, as if they were dropped in a hurry.

Corcoran's intelligence packet had clearly referred to three trailers linked together into a small but efficient bioweapons factory.

Mereish and Fosbrook strode across the yard.

When they reached the first trailer, they could see it was unlocked. Fosbrook unfettered the latch and yanked at the double-hinged door. It creaked as it slowly swung open. A blast of heat hit them in the face, as if they had opened an oven.

Mereish stepped forward and peered inside. Fosbrook pulled open the other door. The mid-morning sun only illuminated the front of the trailer, leaving the back in shadow. But they could see enough.

"Oh my God, Martin," she exclaimed. "We found it."

She grinned happily, beaming with excitement.

"We found it," she repeated.

They entered the trailer.

They could see a half dozen or so large pieces of steel machinery, all painted fire engine red. Labels indicated most of the pieces were imported from Germany.

The equipment was mounted in two rows along the walls. What appeared to be a large fermentor, about six feet high and about the diameter of a 55-gallon drum, stood upright in the right rear. It had a funnel-shaped bottom, a flat top, and a hinged door on top. Another door on the side looked like a sampling port. Two of the vats seemed to be mixing devices, while another apparatus with gauges clearly was an oven drying mechanism. A tangle of wires and hoses appeared to connect them all.

A metal control panel carried twenty-three switches, lined in four horizontal rows, to monitor the system. A small round light was attached to each switch: a dozen white lights, the rest red or blue. Each would glow at different stages of the process. It looked like a controller for a biological fermentor.

Under a top coat of dust, the equipment gleamed dully in the light. Nothing was marred or scratched. It looked brand-new. It looked like someone set it up, closed the creaking doors, and forgot about it.

The thrill of discovery lasted only a few seconds.

It was seed processing equipment. The machinery was designed to thresh seeds, mix them with fungicides, and dry them. Everything still sat on raw wooden pallets, waiting for installation at crop warehouses. When Mereish and Fosbrook opened the other two trailers, they found more equipment and spare parts.

Mereish had a Bravo team photographer shoot color pictures of the control board and equipment, with a U.N. inspector with a blue cap climbing around inside the container to provide scale. Someone drew up a detailed line diagram to show where the three trailers stood relative to the warehouses and other buildings.

She was disappointed. Nothing was going right.

After three and a half hours at Djerf al Nadaf, Bravo team packed up their gear, loaded their vehicles, and headed back to the Canal Hotel.

Casagrande ran a four-person laboratory, called the on-site biological analysis unit, at the hotel. He put on thick gloves and extracted his cotton swabs inside a biological safety cabinet, which uses an airflow to keep contaminants inside. He knew what to test for. Each pathogen has different DNA, and reacts to different chemicals called reagents. He had reagents for the most likely diseases and toxins: botulinum, anthrax, tularemia, and bubonic plague. The process was sufficiently sensitive that he could detect remnants of long-dead bacteria or deactivated viruses. If the Iraqis produced pathogens in bulk at Djerf al Nadaf, polymerase chain reaction, known as PCR, almost certainly would find genetic proof.

He first subjected the samples to a process called lysis, in which cells are beaten in a vortex of tiny glass beads. It makes cells release their biological molecules prior to DNA extraction. He then inserted each sample into the PCR thermal cycler, which heats and cools the solution. The process is relatively simple and surprisingly quick. Each time the DNA comes close to boiling, its intertwined strands unravel. As it cools, the DNA makes a copy. By heating and cooling the sample over and over, a single molecule can replicate itself billions of times in a few hours.

If the target DNA was present, it would multiply rapidly to a detectable level. He'd have proof of a biological weapons agent.

He tested the two samples he'd swabbed from the floor. Then he checked the swab from the walls. Then the old shower drain. It took him about twenty minutes to prep the samples, and another forty minutes or so to run the tests. Afterward, he filled out his lab notes for samples B0081–B0085. He described where he took each swab and then noted the results.

"All samples were subjected to RAPID-PCR and no presence of C. botulinum, B. anthracis, F. tularensis, or Y. pestis was detected," he wrote dutifully, ticking off the most likely pathogens.

That night, he recorded the unrewarding search in his computer journal. "Another inspection of an undeclared site," he wrote. "This one treated seeds with pesticide. Got to climb on a jeep and crawl into buildings and played second story man, but otherwise spent the day in the lab. . . . No threat agents detected."

Several Bravo members drove back to Djerf al Nadaf on February 28.

This time, they carefully measured all the buildings, walls, and doors. They photographed and measured the sheds, the guardhouses, and three warehouses in the adjoining compound. These stood locked and empty. They moved slowly, carefully, cataloguing everything in sight.

The U.N. experts in Bravo team also searched the other sites in the intelligence packet.

Eleven inspectors raided the Al Nasr Al Azim State Company, about ten miles south of Baghdad. Curveball had said the factory welded fermentors and other components for germ trucks. The Bravo team grilled the factory manager, inspected storerooms and records, and tested metals and other materials. Nothing seemed amiss.

Team members searched for a docking station at the Al Ahrar Seed Purification Facility, about ninety miles southeast of the capital. They found seed processing units in a high-bay building and a garage door too low for large trucks, just like at Djerf al Nadaf.

Eighteen experts raided the State Crop Protection Board depot at Suwayrah, twenty-five miles southeast of Baghdad, another Curveball site. Someone had daubed the name in English and Arabic in black paint on the rusting gate out front: Iraqi Company for Seed Production. The germ trucks supposedly docked in the main warehouse, near a large mound of corn against a back wall. They found the corn and the wall but no sign of bio-production around or under the cement floors. They checked records and grilled employees. It was a bust.

On their way out that afternoon, Mereish spotted a large building down the road. She slowed down and stared. It had huge doors, heavy power lines draping in, and giant water pipes. She could see refrigerated trailers in the rear. Maybe someone had confused this with Djerf al Nadaf. Maybe Corcoran's package was wrong.

"Bingo! We found it," she exclaimed to Dimitri Perricos, Blix's chief deputy, who joined the inspection that day. He grinned, just as excited, as she wheeled the car around and sped into the courtyard. Leaping out, they charged into the building.

It was an ice factory.

A Bravo team rode a helicopter north to the Huwayjah Agricultural Facility, north of Tikrit. They checked warehouse logs and interviewed the manager about farmers' trucks and "where the corn originated from and where it was received. They then inspected the company site, both inside and outside, and checked the production lines." Nothing.

Mereish and her colleagues knew time was running out. If they didn't find the weapons of mass destruction, if Saddam refused to come clean, war seemed certain now. The only question was when, not if. They raced to investigate every possible clue.

On March 1, Mereish headed north again to inspect the Tikrit Industrial Facility, a former plastics factory now used by a construction company. Curveball had said two mobile bio-units docked in the main warehouse. At first glance, it looked like he was right.

The team found two container-like trailers. Each was marked on the outside in large letters: "Mobile Workshop." They stood on concrete blocks, however, long abandoned. Prying the doors open, the U.N. team found rusting hammers, wrenches, screwdrivers, and other tools. They were mobile carpentry shops.

Five days later, Bravo headed to Aziziyah, southeast of Baghdad, to see two more corn drying and handling facilities. Another bust. They caught a helicopter north to search the locomotive repair yard at Mosul. If Red River, the British intelligence source, was correct, a fermentation unit was hidden on a railcar there. Negative. Teams launched four separate raids at the Chemical Engineering and Design Center, Curveball's old office in Baghdad, to search for records of germ trucks among project documents. That was futile too.

Mereish wasn't about to give up.

CHAPTER 28

In the first week of March 2003, a month after Powell's speech at the U.N., Mereish sat down with Brig. Gen. Mahmud Farraj Bilal. Educated in Scotland, the plump Iraqi had helped run Iraq's bioweapons program with Taha before the 1991 war. He had supervised testing on animals and the filling of munitions and warheads with anthrax and botulinum. Now he was deputy defense senior minister. Bilal knew as much about Saddam's germ weapons as anyone.

She got right in his face.

"Where are the mobile labs?" Mereish demanded. "Show us! This is the end. Don't you understand? Don't you know what's happening? Show them to us!"

Bilal understood full well what was coming.

"I am in charge of these things in the military," he told her. "I would know of these things. There were no weapons like this. None. We don't have them. Nowhere. Nowhere in heaven do we have them."

He insisted that Iraq could not build such complex systems.

"It's impossible," he told Mereish. "We can't do this. It's not within our capability."

"The U.N. is your last chance to stop the war," she pleaded. "You are a good soldier. Save your country."

He looked crestfallen. He just shrugged.

Perricos, the deputy head of the U.N. inspectors, had slightly more luck when he telephoned Lt. Gen. Amir Hammudi Hasan Saadi and asked him to lunch on March 5.

Saadi had told the Gang of Four in 1995 that he once had urged Taha to build mobile systems. Now Saadi was Saddam's chief scientific advisor and a powerful figure in his own right. He was the chief point of contact for the U.N. weapons teams.

Perricos was no neophyte on Iraq. He had helped unravel and destroy its nuclear program in the early 1990s. He now felt certain Iraq possessed no stockpiles of WMD. He had watched Powell's U.N. speech from Baghdad and was skeptical. Only one allegation impressed him—the detailed description and illustrations of germ trucks and the eyewitness account of a deadly bioweapons accident. That surprised and unnerved him. That was new. The Americans must know, he surmised. They've got the goods.

Perricos and Saadi had sparred for years but they shared grudging respect for each other.

They met for lunch at a stylish French restaurant with starched white tablecloths. It was Friday so government offices were closed. Saadi suggested making it a social affair. He brought his German wife and Perricos invited an attractive young Frenchwoman on his staff. She had a terse, no-nonsense style, and recently had supervised the destruction of an Iraqi cache of Al Samoud rocket engines that the U.N. team deemed illegal. Perricos hoped that the icy presence of "Madame Destruction," as the Iraqis called her, would remind Saadi that the time was closing fast for long lunches over French wine.

Perricos was worried. The Americans and British were all over him to find the damn germ trucks. Perricos's aides had drawn up a plan to impose U.N. roadblocks at strategic choke points to stop and search suspect vehicles. They could move the checkpoints quickly if needed. They would search freight trains as well, not only at loading platforms, but at railway crossings or between stations.

But the task seemed impossible. Iraq had countless trucks and a spidery network of roads and railways. Which roads should they choose? Which trucks or trains? How often? What about at night? They would require air assets to monitor traffic around the checkpoints, and to chase errant trucks if necessary. They could use U.N. helicopters with night vision cameras, or drone surveillance aircraft that the Germans would provide. The CIA had offered to send pilotless Predators to help. But Perricos was certain the Americans would use them to spy, so he refused.

He hoped to find an easier solution.

"Tell me about the mobile labs," he urged Saadi. "Please."

Saadi shrugged, his shaggy eyebrows arched in frustration.

"We don't have any," he said firmly.

Saadi repeated his denial several times, growing more and more exasperated. The Gang of Four had misunderstood his comments back in 1995, he said. They had totally exaggerated his concept. He had sketched a wild idea in the air, nothing more. Chemical engineers do it all the time, he explained. They're creative and imaginative. That's why they're engineers.

"It was blue-sky thinking," he told Perricos. "That's all I was doing. There never was such a plan."

Perricos looked skeptical.

"We have nothing," Saadi repeated. "How can we prove a negative? These trucks don't exist."

Saadi admitted that he was alarmed when he watched Powell speak at the U.N. Most of it struck him as nonsense. But then he saw Powell's vivid description and diagrams of germ trucks. He panicked, afraid that the CIA knew something he did not. So he had ordered an urgent inventory of any Iraqi government or military vehicles that the Americans might have confused as germ trucks.

"Okay," Perricos replied calmly. "Show us what you do have."

Saadi promised to get him the list. That afternoon, Maj. Gen. Eng. Hossam Mohamed Amin, who ran the directorate created to work with the weapons inspectors, sent a one-page letter to the U.N. office at the Canal Hotel.

"You are fully aware that a lot of partial and unfounded allegations have been raised," he wrote. "The most flagrant allegation was that of the U.S. minister of foreign affairs Mr. Powell . . . on the existence of mobile laboratories for biological agents production. We strongly deny the existence of such laboratories."

He described the trucks they had located so far. The Ministry of Health used 139 large refrigerated trucks, all imported from France and Spain, to transport drugs and vaccines. Iraq's mobile fleet also included field hospitals, labs for disease analysis, field kitchens, ovens used to "produce pastries and bread" for the army, and more.

Two days later, on March 7, Blix returned to the Security Council to deliver a progress report. He briefly described the frustrating hunt for "mobile production units for biological weapons," but noted the discovery of wheeled food testing labs and mobile workshops. "No evidence of proscribed activities has so far been found," he admitted.

In response, Powell accused Baghdad of not cooperating and referred to the proposed U.N. roadblocks. "If Iraq genuinely wanted to disarm, we would not have to be worrying about setting up means of looking for mobile biological units—they would be presented to us," Powell grimly told the council.

A week later, Amin sent an envelope stuffed with four videotapes and thirty-seven photographs, each with small labels attached to the back, to the Canal Hotel.

The pictures included "Mobile Ice Factories" in a shed with a corrugated tin roof, like the warehouse at Djerf al Nadaf. Other photos showed boxy Renault and Avico refrigerator trucks used to transport food for the Ministry of Commerce and medicines for the Ministry of Health. In an accompanying letter, Amin wrote that they also had found thirteen mobile military field hospitals, plus X-ray trucks, refrigerated morgue vans "to transport cadavers," and more.

From the outside, several vehicles resembled the trucks in Powell's illustrations. One photo of a truck interior even showed a big dome-topped, stainless steel vessel that looked suspicious, like a fermentor. It was a dough mixer in a bakery truck.

Perricos studied all the pictures closely. "The only thing we didn't find is what Curveball described," he said later.

Corcoran, the U.N. liaison for intelligence, gave the CIA only a cursory rundown of the searches at Djerf al Nadaf and the other sites because of Blix's ban on sharing intelligence. It didn't matter. The U.N. experts had checked every factory, vaccine plant, seed warehouse, military camp, and other site on the CIA's "high" and "medium" priority list. They found no stockpiles, no sign of bio-trucks, and no clear evidence of programs to produce chemical, biological, or nuclear arms.

The U.N. teams did, however, finally solve the mystery of the growth media. Investigators long had warned that they could not account for seventeen tons of nutrient mix that Iraq had imported before the 1991 war. The missing tonnage led President Bush to warn in his 2003 State of the Union speech that Saddam could mass-produce 25,000 more liters of anthrax, "enough doses to kill several million people."

But since returning to Baghdad, Mereish and the Bravo team had accounted for all but 140 kilograms—negligible enough to be a simple weighing or bookkeeping error, small enough to be forgotten in a closet. It was still potentially dangerous if it existed. But it wasn't seventeen tons. The threat of Saddam's germ weapons was evaporating by the day.

But time had run out. Diplomacy had failed to convince Saddam to surrender his germ trucks and other illicit weapons. The U.N. teams were given the order to evacuate on March 17. Mereish, distraught at the unfinished job, was one of the last to leave.

The first salvos of American satellite-guided Tomahawk cruise missiles and bombs rained into Baghdad and other targets before dawn on Thursday, March 20, sparking fiery explosions and sending plumes of smoke into a black sky. The Pentagon called it "shock and awe."

It was still Wednesday night in Washington, and Bush announced the invasion on prime-time television. America and its allies, he said, were fighting "an outlaw regime that threatens the peace with weapons of mass murder." Up to 150,000 American and British troops had deployed around Iraq and the first combat forces soon were battling their way to Baghdad, carrying gas masks and sweaty protective suits to protect against poison gas or germ attack.

CHAPTER 29

The annual White House Correspondents' Dinner is the closest the nation's uptight capital comes to hosting the Oscars. Reporters and their bosses don tuxes and evening gowns to hobnob for a boozy night at the Hilton Washington with cabinet secretaries, members of Congress, and imported Hollywood celebrities. Groupies line up along a red carpet at the entrance to snap pictures.

The president usually attends, tells a few jokes, and then submits to a good-natured roast. But on April 26, 2003, five weeks after he invaded Iraq, President Bush appeared in no mood for levity. He delivered a moving eulogy to two American reporters who died in the rush to Baghdad. Later, Ray Charles wailed and pounded at his piano. But the crowd was too restless to listen. Their chatter and table hopping in the huge ballroom almost drowned out the music.

McLaughlin and Powell both sat at a round table near the front, guests of the *Los Angeles Times*. During a break, McLaughlin agreed to perform a few magic tricks at his seat. He clearly came prepared to dazzle. Distracting his audience with glib patter, he conjured coins out of thin air and transformed a single dollar into a $100 bill. He commanded a card to rise from a deck and hover in the air. Those around the table broke into delighted applause.

But Powell, resplendent in his tuxedo, barely clapped. He seemed tense and out of sorts. Perhaps he just saw Blix, the chief U.N. weapons inspector, chatting amiably several tables over. The U.S. military and the CIA now owned Iraq. They could go anywhere, do anything. And they still couldn't find the weapons of mass destruction. Powell stared at McLaughlin. Then he requested another trick.

"Let's see you find the WMD in Iraq," Powell demanded. He wasn't smiling.

McLaughlin looked up in surprise. His broad grin faded.

"We will," he replied, nodding his head. "They're there and we'll find them."

But the weapons search in Iraq was a shambles. Before the war, White House officials and the CIA had treated Blix with near contempt, mocking him and the other U.N. sleuths as blundering Inspector Clouseaus who would never find Saddam's concealed arsenal. Yet the Pentagon proceeded on the assumption that combat troops would stumble into trenches and warehouses "full of shiny things with pointy ends," as one officer called it, that U.N. experts had blithely missed. A senior DIA official acknowledged the arrogance early on. "Some people thought we'd just drive in and find fields of WMD, with neon signs saying, 'Look here.' We had to get expectations under control," he conceded.

At first, tips flooded in. The military had issued soldiers copies of a pocket-sized laminated flip chart, more than a hundred pages long, with descriptions and pictures of Iraqi bombs, chemical suits, fermentors, and dozens of other items. The invading soldiers and Marines responded with enthusiasm, passing endless rumors and reporting scores of false alarms. So did reporters.

One platoon was overcome by the "effects of a nerve agent" near Karbala. But the soldiers were just dehydrated. An Army unit reported fourteen barrels brimming with nerve agents at a dusty military camp along the Euphrates River. "This could be the smoking gun," Major Michael Hamlet of the 101st Airborne Division excitedly told a reporter. It wasn't.

Every powder, from sugar to bathroom cleanser, suddenly looked sinister. A Marine officer in the desert called for a helicopter after he found a jar of suspected anthrax. The powder was innocuous, however, apparently from a high school science project. Another officer reported "suspicious glass globes." They contained cleaning fluid. A foul-smelling liquid in a drum turned out to be used motor oil. Army Rangers hit the alarm when they broke into a sealed concrete bunker and detected poison gas. It was hazardous waste that U.N. teams had entombed for safety a decade before. Fox News "confirmed" that Marines "may have found weapons-grade plutonium" at Tuwaitha. They hadn't.

"We're getting lots of Elvis sightings," a CIA spokesman said with a sigh, "but nothing compelling yet."

The confusion began at the top. The U.S. military never had

organized a search for stockpiles of weapons of mass destruction, no less scoured a nation the size of California. The Pentagon's Central Command, which was in charge of the hunt, had focused on planning the war, not the aftermath. Once U.S. forces controlled the country, the thinking went, they would quickly discover Saddam's illicit armories. Getting rid of it all safely would present the biggest worry.

Planning, such as it was, began quietly in the summer of 2002 when a group of experienced U.N. inspectors, all Americans, attended a closed-door session with military and government officials at the National Defense University in southwest Washington, D.C. The U.N. veterans volunteered to help plan a careful search. But Pentagon officials wanted credit for finding the weapons and barred the outside experts. They didn't need help. Stephen Cambone, undersecretary of defense for intelligence, was in charge. He soon approved a plan to deploy sequential waves of specialized military units that could identify, test, and disable Iraq's chemical, biological, and nuclear weapons.

In January 2003, the Pentagon reconfigured a field artillery brigade from Fort Sill, Oklahoma, as the Exploitation Task Force–75, or the 75th XTF. It would provide coordination and logistics, meaning everything from medics to trucks, for the postwar hunt. But planning quickly went awry. When the war began two months later, only four of the twenty planned "site assessment teams" had been trained or equipped. They served as WMD scouts during the invasion, following the front line and checking suspect sites with chemical detectors, radiation meters, and other handheld gear.

If the first tests came back positive, they were supposed to call in the next wave, which was led by the DIA, the Pentagon intelligence agency. These so-called mobile exploitation teams would conduct more sophisticated field tests and run "wipes and swipes" of biological material. Once they got a hit, they were to signal the third wave. Explosive experts and other contractors from Raytheon Company or Kellogg, Brown and Root would follow behind to disable or eliminate the actual dangers.

But the effort foundered from the start. The site teams lacked satellite phones and communications gear. The DIA mobile teams lacked helicopters. Everyone needed Arabic interpreters. Shipping containers filled with DNA fingerprinting equipment and other lab gear were left on a runway in Kuwait. The teams operated in virtual isolation. Daily missions seemed ad hoc and haphazard, cobbled together at the last minute.

Back in Washington, officials at the White House, CIA, DIA,

Energy Department, and other agencies squabbled over the disorganization and delays. They traded angry memos and organized contentious video teleconferences to launch complaints about the screw-ups. "It was like a food fight," one participant recalled. "Everyone wanted to be in charge. But no one was. And then, when it all went bad, no one wanted to be in charge."

The Pentagon went back and forth on using the U.N. veterans. Two weeks after the invasion, Dick Spertzel, who was one of the original Gang of Four U.N. bio-inspectors, was told to report to a DIA staging ground at 5 a.m. on a Sunday for training at Fort Benning, Georgia, and then deployment to Iraq. He kissed his wife goodbye, left his hilltop home in northern Maryland at 3:30 a.m., and drove down to the DIA base at Bolling Air Force Base. No one was there to meet him and no one called to explain the screw-up. After an hour or so, he drove home thoroughly angry.

Two weeks later, Spertzel got another call. The DIA was rescheduling him. He went to Langley for a CIA briefing and then attended another at a White House situation room filled with video screens flashing the latest reports from Iraq. "The concept was I would go to Iraq as a senior bio-guru," he said. But a few days later, his DIA contact called again: Forget it, we changed our mind. Later, Spertzel got yet another call.

"They asked me if I was still interested and I said, 'Yes, but on one major condition. That I don't get screwed around like I did in April.' And I never heard from them again."

David Kay, who had led several high-profile U.N. inspections after the 1991 war, railed in frustration when a reporter called. "Unity of command is not present," he charged. "There's not even unity of effort. My impression is this has been a very low priority so far and they've put very little effort into it."

The chaotic looting then sweeping Baghdad and other cities frightened him. For all anyone knew, important blueprints, weapons parts, and crucial chemicals or biological agents were being spirited out of Iraq for sale to terrorist groups. The Pentagon had totally botched the hunt.

Donald Rumsfeld, the secretary of defense, conceded in Washington that his "personal view" was the teams would recover Saddam's weapons "only when they find people who will say precisely where things are." But that search seemed a joke as well.

Saadi, the Iraqi general who had met Perricos for lunch in early March, didn't flee the country or hide in a bunker after the invasion. Listed as the Seven of Diamonds on the Pentagon's most wanted deck, Saadi sat for a week in his large Baghdad villa, waiting for a knock on the door. A German TV crew finally arrived to interview him. His German wife then arranged his surrender to U.S. forces.

No one had prepared for high-level prisoners. Harried U.S. military police were forced to pair captives two by two, like creatures on the ark, and stuff them in stifling rooms in a wooden barracks out by the airport to await interrogation. It became a circus, or as a CIA official ruefully called it, "the petting zoo."

Military and intelligence officers came and went but no one kept track of who they were, or taped the early interviews. After they left, the detainees shared their stories through ventilation pipes. Later, some of Saddam's most senior aides complained that unidentified Americans wandered in at all hours. Some pulled cameras out and ordered high-ranking prisoners to pose for trophy pictures.

The deputy prime minister, Tariq Aziz, turned himself in days after Baghdad fell. After years as Saddam's loyal factotum, he immediately offered his services to the Americans. "Just tell me what to say," he beseeched his interrogator. The erudite Eight of Spades—white-haired, dignified, fluent in English, one of the most recognizable figures from the deposed regime—began to weep as he described the indignities of his detention. One of his captors, he complained, stole his gold watch as a souvenir.

CHAPTER 30

In early May, six weeks after the invasion, the weapons hunting teams under the 75th XTF moved up to Camp Slayer, at the eastern edge of the Baghdad airport.

It previously had served as Saddam's favorite residence and holiday compound. Five palaces, plus banquet halls, guesthouses, and amusement facilities lay along three man-made lakes. Air strikes sheared open most of the palaces during the invasion, and looters then stole what they could, but most of the nine-square-mile complex lay more or less intact when the Americans arrived. Given the chaos outside, Slayer seemed placid and serene. At dawn, white swans glided across the blue-green lakes while fish jumped and broke the water's calm. At dusk, wrought iron Victorian-style gas lamps twinkled along the palm-lined causeways, drawing swarms of mosquitoes.

The military flew in six thousand golf balls, and off-duty soldiers took turns aiming drives toward a beached fleet of plastic paddleboats that Saddam had provided his guests. Others shanked their shots toward the dictator's former houseboat, a wonderfully ornate affair. It made an easy target until someone, a Marine supposedly, took a midnight joyride and ran it aground in the mud, leaving it to rust in peace, safe from the duffers.

The search teams and other military units, nearly one thousand troops in all, put their cots in or around looted villas and cabanas. For furnishings, they scavenged the bombed-out palaces. One team hit the jackpot. They had no power or running water, but they sat on gold-brocade wingback chairs atop a magnificent Persian carpet. They ate their foil-packed MRE rations on a polished black marble slab the size of a Ping-Pong table. For ambience, someone pulled out a boom box and cranked up a Puccini opera.

Another team bunked in a former bordello. A harem from Eastern Europe supposedly had served Saddam's most favored guests there. For reasons unclear, that required extensive piscine decor. Or perhaps the architect just liked fish. Inside the front door, a school of giant marble carp swam down one side of a curving staircase and frolicked back up the other. Nearby, the gaping jaws of a huge marble fish created a fireplace. Tinted skylights overhead bathed everything blue-green, like the inside of an aquarium. Not unreasonably, the Americans called it the "Fishbowl."

Other troops set up cots inside Saddam's "Victory over Iran" palace, which commemorated Iraq's disastrous eight-year war with its neighbor. Helmets of Iranian solders, apparently gathered off the battlefield, were embedded like metal pimples in the facade. A thick steel door, with a second steel door behind that, was hidden off the entrance hallway. Behind the doors, a staircase led down to a two-bedroom bomb shelter with gold-flecked wallpaper and a pink marble bathroom.

An even grander citadel hid behind metal scaffolding next door. The structure was only half built but Saddam already had engraved the name above the front door. It was to be his "Victory over America" palace.

For translators, the Pentagon teams relied on several dozen young linguists from the 142nd Military Intelligence Battalion of the Utah National Guard. Most had learned languages while serving abroad as Mormon missionaries. The guard unit routinely assisted the eavesdroppers at the National Security Agency, or worked as interrogators or interpreters in other intelligence operations. They were eager and dedicated. But their abilities in Swahili, Urdu, and other exotic languages offered limited utility in Iraq.

"I'm a translator and interpreter," Sergeant Micah Thompson, a fresh-faced restaurant manager from Salt Lake City, said proudly one afternoon at Slayer. "That would be okay if I spoke Arabic. But I speak Portuguese."

He pointed to a fellow linguist who sat on a thronelike chair in their lakeside cabana. "He speaks Norwegian."

In mid-May, the weapons hunt changed shape. The "site assessment teams" were reconfigured and renamed "sensitive site teams."

They were ordered to use a master list of suspect facilities that the CIA and DIA had prepared before the war. Over the next few weeks, they searched more than three hundred sites in far-flung corners of Iraq.

In nearly every case, they revisited sites that U.N. inspectors had raided repeatedly in the past. During the war, however, air strikes targeted nearly all the sites. The teams would drive eight hours across the desert to find a crater in the ground, or an office looted down to the wall studs. Even odder, the master list included little or no information from the earlier U.N. searches. Many U.N. inspectors spent years in Iraq, and were experts in their field. The Pentagon teams mostly relied on inexperienced soldiers who grew disillusioned as they chased one futile mission after another.

The impact was clear one brutally hot morning in late May when two dozen Americans and Australians gathered under the shade of a brown and green camouflage net in a corner courtyard at Slayer.

"Okay, listen up everybody," the military briefer shouted.

Satellite photos and other intelligence indicated that Iraqi engineers had built drone aircraft at the Ibn Firnas Aeronautics Research Center, he said. The pilotless planes were rigged to spray chemical or biological poisons. The factory also armed medium-range FROG-7 battlefield rockets with the same stuff.

The team's mission was to drive to Ibn Firnas, recover the drones, and use portable X-ray gear to peer into the warheads.

Donning heavy flak jackets and helmets, the team climbed into six rumbling Humvees and SUVs. They roared out the camp gate and sped northward, finally passing stinking mountains of trash at the Baghdad city dump. Nearby, Ibn Firnas looked no better. U.S. air strikes had pulverized most of the seventeen buildings. Steel skeletons rose from broken concrete and shattered glass.

The team drove through the front gate and dismounted. The roadway shimmered in the heat, and the air hung thick and heavy. Papers, blueprints, and files lay scattered on the ground. About fifty yards in, they found the remains of the supposed drones: five fiberglass wings, each nine feet long. They were blackened by fire but still recognizable.

U.S. Air Force Captain Libbie Boehm, the team expert on unmanned aircraft, squatted down and carefully examined the wings, turning each one over in her hands. She shrugged as she stood up.

"It could have been a student project, or maybe a model airplane," she said, wiping her hands on her pants. "It's nothing."

An Army sergeant on the team picked up several papers from the dirt. They appeared to show aircraft diagrams. "Do we need these documents?" he asked the others. "Do we care?" No one answered. He tossed them back on the ground.

The group headed for a scrap heap out back. The FROG missiles were supposed to be here amid twisted helicopter blades, broken instrument panels, and other debris. They split up to poke among the wreckage. "I got it," someone shouted after a few minutes.

The others came over. The supposed missiles were discarded casings of old artillery rockets. An Australian missile expert named David Warren screwed up his face in disgust. Every intelligence report he'd seen since arriving in Iraq was garbled or wrong. "All we're doing is looking through a rubbish dump here," he said glumly.

Not everyone was discouraged. A dozen or so bedraggled Iraqis patiently pillaged the skeletal buildings, wrenching and cutting away window frames and pipes. They tossed their booty—radio parts, pipes, light switches, and other scrap—aboard two donkey carts and a rusting flatbed truck before they finally rattled off down the main road.

"The looters had a better day than we did," concluded Lt. Col. Michael Kingsford, the mission commander. He ordered everyone to mount up and head back to base. "One thing I can say for sure is there's no smoking gun here."

The team didn't know it but U.N. missile experts had searched Ibn Firnas three times in the month before it was bombed. They didn't find anything worthwhile either.

Several days later, Army Major Ronald Hann Jr., an arms control expert, got what looked like a plum assignment.

Hann led his team to a villa on the shores of Lake Habbaniyah, north of Baghdad. Intelligence indicated that Saddam's oldest son, Uday, stored chemical and biological agents at the compound. A diagram in the target folder highlighted a warehouse and tanks filled with poison gas.

Hann's team approached carefully, assault rifles and bolt cutters in hand, ready for anything.

"The target folder was real clean," Hann said later that week. "This was supposed to be solid intelligence. 'Here's the warehouse, here are the tanks, go here, turn left there.' Well, the warehouse was a carport. It still had two cars parked inside. And the tanks held propane for the kitchen."

Hann checked fourteen sites in as many days, from bombed palaces to concrete bunkers. At Fallujah, his team broke open a locked storehouse and discovered stacks of green and blue barrels. Suddenly their portable chemical detectors all started beeping and flashing and a dozen guys all started slapping each other on the backs and shouting, "This is it! A hit!"

Hann came over to check out the ruckus. "Calm down," he told them. "Let's see what it is."

It was pesticide. They were in a pesticide factory.

The Pentagon search teams hit all the priority sites by the end of May, ten weeks after the invasion. After that, they spent most days back at Slayer washing clothes, taking naps, and fighting boredom. "We're here to answer the big question," said Lieutenant Cody Strong, a tactical intelligence officer, lounging by the lake one sweltering afternoon. "You'd think if this was really a priority, we'd have nonstop missions. Our last mission was eight days ago. Sitting here doing nothing is a waste."

Even the military brass acknowledged the obvious.

"Everybody was sleeping with their boots on and their gas masks close" during the invasion because intelligence predicted a poison gas or germ attack, Lt. Gen. James Conway, commander of the 1st Marine Expeditionary Force, told reporters. He was surprised, he said, that they had failed to spot any WMD. "Believe me, it's not for lack of trying. We've been to virtually every ammunition supply point between the Kuwaiti border and Baghdad but they're simply not there."

But other U.S. troops had just made an exciting discovery.

CHAPTER 31

On the afternoon of April 19, one month after the start of the war, Kurdish militiamen manning a highway checkpoint at Tall Kayf pointed their rifles and ordered a military heavy-equipment transport truck to pull over. It hauled a trailer with a green canvas cover.

Opening the canvas, they saw a large stainless steel vessel with a domed lid, a crude control panel with wires and switches, a metal stand for gas cylinders, and assorted equipment bolted to the metal floor.

The hapless Iraqi driver couldn't identify anything. He had just stolen the rig from a parking lot at a nearby ammunition plant, he confessed. The Kurds let him go but kept the truck. Then they notified a U.S. Special Forces team in the area, near the northern city of Mosul.

After all the humiliating false alarms, all the early disappointments, U.S. officials reacted warily when reports filtered in suggesting Kurds had captured the first mobile germ factory. No one wanted to claim a smoking gun just yet. But the news was flashed to the Pentagon and CIA. The White House was quickly notified. Everyone understood the significance.

The failure to find Saddam's WMD had become a growing embarrassment. Few reporters had challenged the administration's rationale for war before the invasion. Now they were starting to ask awkward questions. So were foreign governments. Discovery of a mobile weapons lab could restore the Bush administration's battered credibility. President Bush could claim vindication of his war to disarm Iraq.

Experts raced north from Baghdad to examine the trailer, parked at an air base at Irbil. The military's CBIST unit, the Chemical and Biological Intelligence Support Team, was first to reach the site. They spent four days measuring and studying the equipment. The team leader found it perplexing. The fermentation unit looked like a rush job done on the cheap, he thought. The trailer was dented and scraped, and carried no shock absorbers to protect sensitive lab equipment from rattling around.

A solid, light brown sludge lay several inches deep at the bottom of the fermentor vessel, if that's what it was, and a liquid pooled in some connecting pipes. A set of crude scrubbers, used to collect emissions from the equipment, suggested the trailer was designed to operate in secret. But everything was freshly painted a dull gray-green, and masking tape still covered one of the dials. It clearly had not been used recently.

The team ran tests, using handheld assays for toxins, and polymerase chain reaction for DNA. They proved negative for anthrax, plague, smallpox, and five other major biological threats. Still, the team reported, the trailer appeared "capable of supporting a limited biological batch production process." To be safe, the reporting officer conceded that vaccine production or other civilian uses "could not be ruled out."

A British and American special operations unit called Joint Task Force 20 also hustled to Irbil. They were more confident, deeming the single trailer "part of a process to produce biological weapons." It clearly was not Curveball's truck. According to a metal data plate, the Al Nasr Al Azim State Company built the fermentor in 2002. Curveball had left Iraq in 1999. The trailer therefore was "probably the latest generation" of a TBWAPT, or "transportable biological warfare agent production trailer," the task force concluded.

The special ops team also shot color photographs of the equipment. Someone in Washington hatched the idea of showing them to Curveball to see if the trailer matched his. Drumheller and his crew at the CIA launched a rearguard action when they heard the plan. They proposed slipping in a few phony pictures to test Curveball's truthfulness.

If the defector picked out an oversized trash can or the beeping R2D2 robot from *Star Wars* instead of the real thing, they'd know for sure he was lying. Just showing him the real pictures was like putting only guilty guys on a police lineup, Drumheller groused to his aides. What did they expect the defector to say?

But the CIA and DIA analysts refused. "We know what we're doing," one official responded huffily. Testing Curveball's veracity was unnecessary, he said, and the Germans would go ballistic if they found out the Americans had tried to trick or trap their source. So Defense

HUMINT gave the BND the clean set of photos. Back in Munich, Schumann and Meiner arranged an emergency meeting with Curveball.

The brooding Iraqi greeted them truculently, still defiant. Swaddled in smoke, he berated them as before. The BND still hadn't gotten his wife out from Baghdad. What was taking so damned long? They still couldn't get him a job. They still refused to pay him more money. They were pathetic, he muttered.

The handlers finally calmed him down. After a suitable silence, they spread the photos on a table and cautiously asked if anything looked familiar. Is this the kind of trailer you told us about? He stared at the pictures, leafing through them slowly. He seemed uncertain. He finally pointed to a few photos and issued a response. The BND notified the DIA, which rushed out another intelligence report in U.S. channels: Curveball has identified components on the trailer.

The good news began to leak in Washington. Stephen Cambone, Rumsfeld's intelligence deputy and chief of the weapons hunt, made it official on May 7.

U.S. and British experts "concluded that the unit does not appear to perform any function beyond . . . the production of biological agents," Cambone told a news conference. It appeared "very similar" to the diagrams Powell showed the U.N. in February, he said. The primary source of Powell's information, he reminded the reporters, "had a hand in the design and operation of this type of facility. He was even knowledgeable of the deaths of a number of people who had been working on such a facility." The source had identified the trailer, he added.

Cable TV channels headlined the news. The Pentagon had finally found evidence, if not quite proof, of WMD. Over at the State Department, Powell and his aides grinned and applauded in relief. "We were all cheering," he said.

Then, two days later, on May 9, a U.S. Army infantry patrol turned a dusty corner in Mosul and found a second trailer. It stood outside the main gate of the Al Kindi State Company, a missile factory. Looters had stripped away the canvas cover and removed most of the piping on the trailer. Even the tires were missing. But it still carried a large reactor vessel, a 5,000-pounds-per-square-inch compressor, a small feed tank, a 3,000-liter water tank, and a water chiller. A data plate indicated it was built in 2003, but unfinished welds suggested the work was incomplete. The layout appeared almost identical to the first trailer.

The discovery fueled further excitement at WINPAC, the CIA weapons center. A highly-strung, middle-aged analyst named Jerry had helped champion Curveball's story the previous fall, backing Beth during her fracas with Margaret. A loyal member of the geek squad, Jerry ardently believed in Curveball. He tended to see the world in black and white and brought an emotional, almost religious, fervor to the case. Jerry was thrilled but not surprised when the trailer reports came in. He had never doubted Curveball.

In mid-May, Jerry and two other analysts flew to Baghdad. By then, U.S. forces had hauled the first trailer down to Camp Slayer. The visiting CIA team compared the design, equipment, and layout with Curveball's original account and their own data. They also checked the second trailer. They reported back to Langley that they "agreed with the conclusions" of Task Force 20.

After returning home, Jerry and his colleagues prepared a detailed analysis of the two trailers. The CIA forwarded a copy to the White House.

Another influential figure also weighed in.

David Kay had headed three wildly successful U.N. raids on Iraq's nuclear facilities after the 1991 war. He famously led a four-day standoff in a Baghdad parking lot after his team refused to surrender crucial files to Iraqi soldiers who surrounded their cars. Unruffled by pressure, Kay gave a giddy running commentary of the crisis to CNN and other media on his satellite phone. The U.N. Security Council was called into emergency session. The Iraqis finally backed down and Kay's triumph over Saddam was front-page news around the world.

Kay became a respected policy wonk in Washington after that, giving speeches and testifying frequently on Capitol Hill. He wrote op-ed pieces and gabbed on Sunday talk shows. He was perfect for TV. With a slight drawl and a load of academic degrees, he presented a potent mix of folksiness and gravitas. He could break complex issues into witty sound bites. He sported a bright smile, a jaunty air, and a full head of hair edging to silver. Plus he loved the limelight.

Now, in May, Kay worked as an on-air consultant for NBC News. They had flown him to Baghdad after the invasion and he was working at the network's bureau when NBC got wind of the second trailer in northern Iraq. The 101st Airborne Division was guarding it in Mosul.

"I know who to call," Kay volunteered. He had friends in high places and soon got Army Lt. Gen. David Petraeus, commander of the 101st, on the phone.

"We understand you found one of the mobile labs up there," Kay told him. "Can we come up and see it?"

"Sure," Petraeus replied. "C'mon up. I'll have my guys meet you at the gate."

So Kay and a crew drove up to Mosul. And Petraeus's chem-bio team led Kay and the TV crew over to see the germ trailer. The axles were propped on concrete blocks. With the canvas cover gone, dust covered everything. Most of the metal frame for the canvas was bent or missing. It looked like a pile of junk. Kay didn't know what to make of it. He was supposed to be the expert but this was new to him. His background was nuclear, not biological.

Kay looked over and spotted a team of the CIA Secret Squirrels, including an operative he knew from his U.N. inspections a decade earlier. She had just evaluated the trailer. Stay here, he told the camera crew. Kay sidled over and, after a few pleasantries, quietly asked for help. What is all this stuff? How is it supposed to work? The CIA officer showed him how the Iraqis had arranged each piece of equipment and why.

That night, May 11, Tom Brokaw, the NBC anchor, broke the news that a second trailer looked "more and more like a major find in the search for weapons of mass destruction." Kay was presented as the network's expert, and he acted as a chatty tour guide in the news story that aired.

Walking beside the trailer, he pointed to the fermentor and other hardware and explained how they fit together. He showed no doubt whatsoever. The compressor "keeps the fermentation process under pressure so it goes faster," he said, pointing to the pump. The gravity flow tank over there—he pointed up at that—feeds bacterial seed into the nutrient mix, creating a warm broth in the fermentor. "Think of it as sort of chicken soup for biological weapons," Kay observed with a slight smile.

Could the equipment be used for something else? the reporter asked him.

"Literally, there is nothing else you would do this way on a mobile facility," Kay said confidently. "That is it."

CIA officials were jubilant.

John McLaughlin, the number two CIA official, was especially excited by Kay's confirmation on network TV. He wished his people had found DNA or other indisputable proof. But now a respected independent figure had touched the equipment, seen it up close, and given an unqualified thumbs-up. Kay's TV appearance helped McLaughlin make up his mind. There was no point in the CIA not taking credit. He decided to go public, a rare step for the spy service. He knew it would boost Tenet's standing at the White House.

On May 28, the CIA posted a nine-page White Paper on its Web site. It was essentially the report from Jerry, the true believer from WINPAC, and his two colleagues. The title stated the conclusion: *Iraqi Mobile Biological Warfare Agent Production Plants.*

The two trailers provided "the strongest evidence to date that Iraq was hiding a biological warfare program," the paper began. They appeared "strikingly similar" to trailers that the chief source, meaning Curveball, had described. The source recognized "a mobile BW production plant similar to the one that he managed, even pointing out specific pieces of equipment that were installed on his unit."

In the paper, the CIA excused the failure to find any DNA or other biological material as proof that Iraqis had flushed the vessel and pipes with ammonia or bleach. Other trailers, yet to be found, probably carried the equipment needed to prepare and sterilize growth media, and to concentrate and dry the slurry, the paper noted.

Most important, the document rejected suggestions that the trailers might serve a more conventional purpose. Iraqi officials had insisted that both trailers were designed to chemically produce hydrogen gas to fill weather balloons for a Republican Guard artillery unit. The Iraqis had handed over a thick sheaf of documents—written contracts, purchase orders, status reports, and even an operator's manual on how to produce hydrogen. But the CIA paper dismissed hydrogen production as a "plausible cover story" designed to deceive the outside world.

Bush administration officials had begun hedging their bets in recent weeks, suggesting that U.S. forces might only find "weapons programs," not actual weapons, in Iraq. But now the White House happily tacked back. The president was leaving the next day for a week-long trip to Poland and five other countries. The theme of his diplomatic tour, aides promised, was "What does President Bush do with his military victory in Iraq?" This news fit perfectly. Aides arranged for television reporters from TVP in Poland and TV3 in France to interview the president in the White House library. He appeared in high spirits.

"We found the weapons of mass destruction," Bush announced, clearly pleased with the news.

"We found biological laboratories. You remember when Colin Powell stood up in front of the world, and he said, 'Iraq has got laboratories, mobile labs to build biological weapons.' They're illegal. They're against the United Nations resolutions. And we've so far discovered two.

"And we'll find more weapons as time goes on," he continued. "But for those who say we haven't found the banned manufacturing devices or banned weapons, they're wrong. We found them."

Two days later, Bush hailed the find again at a press briefing with Russian president Vladimir Putin in a palace in St. Petersburg. "We've discovered a weapons system, biological labs, that Iraq denied she had, and labs that were prohibited under U.N. resolutions," the president said.

He wrapped up his trip with a brief visit to U.S. troops at the Al Udeid air base in the deserts of Qatar. "We recently found two mobile biological weapons facilities which were capable of producing biological agents," he told them.

Powell, en route to Europe, seemed visibly relieved when he ventured to the back of the plane to talk to reporters about the trailers.

"We didn't just make them up one night," he said. "Those were eyewitness accounts of people who had worked in the program, knew it was going on, multiple accounts."

He sarcastically dismissed the Iraqi explanation. "'Oh, it was a hydrogen-making thing for balloons.' No. There's no question in my mind what it was designed for."

He was even more expansive on one of the Sunday talk shows.

"I would put before you Exhibit A, the mobile biological labs that we have found," Powell argued. "People are saying, 'Well, are they truly mobile biological labs?' Yes, they are." Tenet, the head of the CIA, he added, "stands behind that assessment."

In London, Blair announced the good news in Parliament. "I would point out to you we already have, according to our experts, two mobile biological weapons facilities," he declared.

Behind the scenes, a battle was raging.

In New York, U.N. bio-inspectors downloaded the NBC video on their computers. They scrutinized it frame by frame. Based on David Kay's height, they roughly calculated the dimensions of the fermentor and other equipment. They studied the shapes and handles. On the morning of May 28, several hours before McLaughlin released the CIA report, Kay Mereish and an Australian colleague briefed Dimitri Perricos and the panel of commissioners who oversaw the U.N. operation.

The two U.N. experts told the panel that the trailer "almost certainly could not be for BW," Perricos recalled.

The steel vessel had a flat base and rounded top, Mereish pointed out. Bio-fermentors need round bottoms so microbes can't collect in cracks to contaminate the next batch. Either the Iraqis installed the fermentor upside down, in which case it didn't work, or they hid another vessel inside it. That made no sense. The U.N. experts also pointed to a large round door on the front of the vessel. The door should be on the top. If you opened a pressurized fermentor from the front, they said, you'd get sprayed in the face with germs. Or the slurry would pour onto your feet.

Hans Blix, head of the U.N. inspectors, authorized aides to share the assessment with the CIA and DIA. The report was ignored.

Another dissent also arrived in Washington that week.

A special DIA-led technical team had examined the trailers. The nine American and British scientists and engineers all worked for defense contractors or at national defense laboratories. The secret group, known as the Jefferson Project, specialized in analyzing and countering biological threats. After flying into Baghdad, they drove over to inspect the two trailers, now parked in the motor pool beside the "Victory over Iran" palace at Slayer.

They clambered all over the equipment, probing and tabulating. They disassembled the fermentors, the exhaust and filtration systems. They tested inside everything. They turned valves, tapped gauges, and measured pipes. After two days, they wrote a three-page classified field report that landed in Washington on May 27, the day before McLaughlin released the CIA report. The group followed up with a 122-page technical report.

The equipment "could not be used" to produce biowarfare agents, the scientists concluded.

"The first question was where was the containment," said one member of the group. "There was no shielding. These were just canvas-covered trucks. There was no airlock or any other protection to keep the material from spreading into the countryside. If there was an outbreak of anthrax downwind, everyone would know about it. The Iraqis didn't care about killing people. But we would find out. It made no sense."

He added, "The labs that I saw were not for biological weapons. They were for hydrogen. It was obvious."

A CIA scientist in the group e-mailed the summary back to Langley, where Beth and the other WINPAC analysts learned of the direct challenge. They refused to budge. On June 6, Jerry and his colleagues helped write an assessment, called *Update on Iraq BW Trailers*, for Condoleezza Rice, Bush's national security advisor. The CIA's judgment "has not changed," they assured her. No one has found "a credible alternate use" for their trailers other than brewing biowarfare agent.

The analysts gave Rice two pages of talking points to use if reporters asked about the DIA-led team's findings. The configuration of the equipment was "almost identical" to Powell's descriptions at the U.N., according to the first point. Powell's presentation "was based on an account of an eyewitness who had firsthand experience with these BW systems."

The Jefferson Project report was shelved.

The CIA's White Paper on the trailers provoked even sharper criticism.

"It caused an immediate hue and cry in the analytic community," said Carl Ford, head of the Bureau of Intelligence and Research, the State Department intelligence unit. "People were saying, 'What is this thing?' It came out of nowhere."

Normally, before intelligence is released to the public, a classified version is first prepared. As a safeguard, experts from several agencies vet the evidence and review the conclusions before the paper is released. That didn't happen here. Only a handful of analysts had examined the evidence. There was no outside fact checking or editing.

Ford was irate that the analysis appeared so one-sided. In his view, the CIA stacked the evidence to support its conclusions, and included no objections or questions from outside experts. There was no attempt to challenge the hypothesis, to rethink the analysis. "Here was a rush to judgment that was unprecedented in my thirty-five years in the business," he said.

Sitting at his desk, Ford typed a sharply worded memo to Powell: "Boss, we take great exception to this on both procedural and substantive grounds," he wrote, as he recalled it later. "You should be very careful about this."

Powell was concerned enough that he asked Tenet about the warning. Tenet responded by calling Ford out to Langley and chewing him out for causing trouble.

"I was taken to the woodshed for having the audacity to talk to my boss about my questions," Ford said. Tenet "had talked to his people and they had no questions. I said that was his problem, not mine."

The DIA finally gathered experts from across the intelligence community to conduct a painstaking review of the evidence. They agreed to start from scratch to see if they reached the same conclusion as the authors of the White Paper.

"The fact is they didn't come to the same conclusion," Ford said.

After they finished the study, the DIA manager of the study took an informal poll of the fifteen intelligence analysts who participated.

"Twelve analysts concluded that the trailers definitely were not bio-related," Ford recalled. "They looked like they might be related to hydrogen production. Two believed they definitely were not bio-vans, but didn't know what they were."

Only one member of the group insisted that the trailers were mobile weapons labs. It was Jerry, the true believer who had drafted the original CIA analysis. Ford was astonished. The CIA analysts were fanatics on this issue, he decided. They adjusted the evidence to fit their hypothesis. "It had to be true because it proved they were right," Ford said.

In Berlin, Werner Kappel and his aides at the BND studied the report on the CIA Web site and watched President Bush's pronouncements with alarm. Kappel wondered why the CIA pinned confirmation of the trailers on their "chief source." That meant Curveball.

Since the Iraqi provided the original description of the equipment, he was only confirming himself. That was circular logic, not proof, Kappel thought.

A day or so later, the head of Meiner's group, the science and technology division in Directorate Three, telephoned Kappel. He had just read the CIA report. What were the Americans talking about?

Curveball didn't confirm anything substantial when they had showed him the pictures, the division chief said. The defector was his usual sulky, irritable self. Sure, he had recognized a few things. But nothing solid, nothing that clearly matched up to the trailers he designed.

"He did not authenticate anything," the division chief said.

They had showed Curveball a photo of the control panel found on the first trailer. A standard piece of factory equipment, it was lined with electronic switches, starters, relays, and lights on a flat metal panel. Similar control panels are widely used to monitor and operate machinery and processes.

Sure, Curveball grunted. He had seen that before. Lots of places. Half the factories in Iraq used control panels like that, he told them.

He studied the photograph of the compressor on the trailer. He recognized that too.

It looked like an air conditioner, the Iraqi guessed.

He couldn't identify the steel tank with the round door. It looked upside down and it didn't match the fermentors he knew. The picture of the nutrient feed system, perched up on stilts, looked screwy too. He'd never seen that before, he said. Most important, the configuration of the equipment on the truck beds bore absolutely no similarity to his trucks, he insisted.

The two trailers in Iraq "have nothing to do with Curveball's design," the division chief told Kappel. "These are not the same at all."

Kappel was taken aback. According to the CIA, the chief source had identified equipment on the trailers. It wasn't true. The Americans are taking a big risk, he thought.

The CIA surprised him again a few days later. Tenet selected David Kay, who had just endorsed the biological trailer on TV, to find the rest of Saddam's weapons of mass destruction.

CHAPTER 32

Even Kay considered himself an unlikely choice as the CIA's top man in Iraq.

Before the war, he was what the intelligence agencies called a "graybeard," a senior outside brain that analysts sometimes invite in to give an independent look at a particularly vexing problem. Washington was full of graybeards. But Kay's expertise was nuclear weapons, and that, plus a reputation for clear-edged thinking and top-level security clearances, kept him in demand.

He would drive down to CIA headquarters, get escorted into a secure office, and read the latest take from spy plane readings of isotope emissions off North Korea. Then he would render his judgment, tear up his notes, and go home. Or a strategic planning group would lock a few graybeards into a conference room and run a tabletop war game: Okay, it's dawn and India and Pakistan are loading their nukes. What do we do?

Kay was a political scientist, a think tanker, and a technocrat, not a spy. He never served in the military and never attended CIA boot camp. And with his TV appearances, he hardly fit the anonymous mold. But Kay was an outspoken hawk on the war. Finding Iraq's elusive weapons had obsessed him for over a decade. He had read every major report, attended endless conferences, and written academic tracts, at least one of which the CIA used as a training text. He didn't doubt that the WMD existed. His op-eds, media interviews, and, most important, his testimony to Congress had provided crucial support for the White House as it rallied the country for war.

"Unless we take immediate steps" to remove Saddam, Kay warned the House Armed Services Committee in September 2002, "we will soon face a nuclear-armed Iraq." Doing nothing, he added darkly, "is to accept the almost certainty of a successful first attack against the U.S. and its friends."

Kay worried that the administration seemed far too blasé about the invasion. In January 2003, two months before the war, Kay was quietly offered a job running civil administration in the postwar occupation authority. He would be responsible for public order, justice, education, courts, and cops. It was a huge job, way outside Kay's expertise, but he wanted to help so he went to the Pentagon for briefings. He was underwhelmed.

"I was assigned exactly one deputy and no working computer," he recalled. "We had no resources. The whole operation was slung into a largely vacant, almost abandoned part of the Pentagon. I couldn't get anyone's attention as to how large the task was or what was going to be necessary. I kept getting the answer, 'Don't worry. It's not going to be a big deal.'"

The military usually excels at planning for contingencies. This was the opposite, Kay thought. No one was making backup plans in case their rosy scenario didn't materialize and looting broke out or civil war filled the vacuum. What if he had to assume civil administration for all Iraq? This was worse than no planning at all. He quit after two days.

He watched the invasion from home and then flew to Baghdad in May for NBC. On June 5, shortly after he returned to Washington, Kay drove to Langley to graybeard a new estimate on North Korea. As he got ready to leave, he was told that the deputy CIA chief wanted him to stop by. Kay walked down the long seventh-floor corridor and poked his head into McLaughlin's large suite. The two men greeted each other pleasantly. They had met once before. Now McLaughlin laughingly thanked him for confirming the bio-trailer on TV. He had really helped them out.

Then he asked Kay about his trip to Iraq.

"What's going on out there?" he asked.

Kay's words tumbled out in a rush. The weapons hunt was a farce, he said. The officers in charge were utterly unprepared. The teams still relied on the prewar lists. Almost no one spoke Arabic. No one knew what the U.N. had done. "They just sort of go to the sites and say, 'Any WMD here?' and sort of leave," he said. "They're wandering around without a clue."

Kay said that most likely, the Iraqis had not produced stockpiles. They simply prepared factories and scientists so they could churn out chemical or biological bombs on short notice or when the world wasn't watching, he said. The mobile weapons labs were a good example.

After listening, McLaughlin asked his visitor to repeat the impromptu briefing for Tenet, his boss. Their offices shared a private inner door and McLaughlin led Kay in. Kay noticed that the CIA chief lacked a computer in his huge corner office. An aide screened his e-mails. It seemed a throwback to an earlier era. But so did Tenet. Jacket off, sleeves rolled up, he chomped on an unlit cigar. He was characteristically gruff.

"The president is unhappy," Tenet announced, as Kay recalled the conversation. "The Pentagon totally screwed this up. I don't want to take over. It's a real mess. But I may have to."

Kay's spirits rose. At least the White House recognized a problem, he thought. He recapped his assessment of the search.

"What would you do differently if you were king?" Tenet abruptly demanded when his visitor had finished speaking.

Kay was startled. But he threw out a few ideas.

"First," he said, "start all over. Forget the old sites. The Iraqis wouldn't do anything at sites we know about. They're worthless."

Next, he continued, let intelligence drive the process. Make a plan and use it. Put Arabic speakers and case officers on the street. Spread money around. Find the scientists and engineers, the guards and the truck drivers. They will tell you where to go next. Set up a proper triage to exploit documents. Bring in linguists. Do it now before security disintegrates.

"Make it your top priority until you're done," he concluded. "If you do all that, you'll find the answers and can go home in six months or so."

Tenet watched Kay carefully. "Yeah, that's right," he interrupted once or twice. "Yeah, that's what I'll tell the president."

The CIA chief leaned back and chewed his unlit stogie in contemplation. Then he popped a surprise. Would Kay be interested in taking over the WMD hunt? Would he consider being king?

Kay was wary. Tenet had a reputation for telling people what they want to hear. He's a bullshit artist, Kay's CIA friends had warned. He'll charm you but don't trust him. Still, Kay was flattered.

"Possibly," he ventured in reply. "But only if you guarantee that we do it my way." Otherwise, he said, he'd quit.

But upbeat by nature, Kay chuckled as he spoke and they all

laughed and gossiped for a while, and Kay was unsure when he departed if Tenet was serious. Over dinner that night, he worried to his wife, Anita, that he probably appeared too confident.

"I should have kept my mouth shut," he told her.

Kay didn't know it, but Bush already had ordered the CIA to take over the hunt. During his stopover in Qatar several days earlier, Bush had convened a meeting with his Iraq commanders. He was getting hammered around the world. All America had found were the two battered trailers. He demanded an update on the search for the other weapons of mass destruction.

A day or so later, Bush told Tenet what happened. The president had first turned to his Baghdad proconsul, Paul Bremer, and asked, "Are you in charge of finding the WMD?" Bremer said no, that wasn't his job. Bush then put the question to his military commander, General Tommy Franks. Was he in charge? Franks said it wasn't his responsibility either.

Bush looked at them in exasperation. He asked again. Who was running the search?

After a moment, an aide offered the name of Stephen Cambone, Rumsfeld's little-known deputy for intelligence. There was an awkward silence.

"Who?" Bush asked.

Tenet roared with laughter as he described the finger pointing exchange to McLaughlin. Except it came with a kicker.

"At that point the president points to me and says, 'George, you're in charge now,'" Tenet told him. "We got the job because no one was doing it."

The weekend after his meeting with Tenet, Kay and his wife headed out to the Poplar Springs Inn, a spa in the wooded foothills of the Shenandoahs, to celebrate his sixty-third birthday. They liked the quiet isolation: no TVs or Internet. But cell phones worked and when Kay's suddenly chirped during dinner, his contact at the interagency National Intelligence Council was on the line.

"The president has taken the search away from the Department of Defense and is assigning it to the CIA," he said. "George wants to know if you will take the job. You'll be in charge."

Kay couldn't say no. He had given Tenet his job description. Plus now it involved the White House. Even his wife urged him to go. "You've got to do this or you'll never be happy," she told him that night.

To be fair, he couldn't resist. He was fixated on solving the mystery of Iraq's missing weapons. Even if they didn't exist, he wanted to know that too. A friend later likened Kay's pursuit of the truth in Iraq to the search for the Holy Grail. Kay would call it his quest for the unicorn.

Plus Kay's ego wouldn't let him refuse. He enjoyed playing hero. He was a sort of Walter Mitty character except his daydreams came true. He never applied for jobs; they landed in his lap, each more adventurous than the last. He had been lionized when he stared down Iraqi troops back in that parking lot in 1991. Now he could swoop in and save the day again. Now he could be king, as Tenet put it. If it didn't lead to cheering throngs and the thanks of a grateful nation, at least he'd have fun. He liked Iraq.

So, of course, he said yes. And two days later, when he showed up at Langley, they strapped him to a polygraph for a CIA employment screening. During his days as a U.N. nuclear inspector in Iraq, Kay dealt with spy services from around the world. It was part of his job. Now he answered honestly about his experience.

"Have you had access to classified information outside of government employment?"

"Yes." Kay's pulse stayed steady.

"Have you dealt with a foreign intelligence service?"

"Yes." Same result.

"Have you ever shared classified information with a foreign intelligence agent?"

"Yes."

Kay easily passed the test but the operator eyed him suspiciously, as if he had just interrogated Benedict Arnold. Confessions like this usually led to prison.

"You're going to have to shoot the poly guy," Kay joked to Tenet later that day. "He probably thinks I'm a security risk."

By 3 p.m., Kay had passed his psychiatric examination ("My wife said this morning," he joked to the shrink, "that anyone who takes this job ought to be declared mentally incompetent") and his medical exams. Cameras clicked as Kay was sworn in as special advisor to the director of central intelligence for strategy for Iraqi weapons of mass destruction programs, his official title. He got the same high SIS-4 rank as Drumheller, equal to a four-star general.

After the ceremony, Tenet grinned and strutted like a peacock in his office. The CIA had never screened anyone in a day. The chief of human resources had insisted it was impossible. But Tenet gloated that he beat the bureaucrats.

The CIA chief lost the next battle. He ordered his new special advisor to leave the next day for Iraq. Kay refused. "It's absolute insanity," he told Tenet. "I'm an outsider."

He needed to meet the main players at the agency and elsewhere, and study the latest intelligence on Saddam's weapons. He would stay a week. So WINPAC set up briefings on the mobile weapons labs, the poison gas factories, and all the rest. Pavitt and other senior officials made time to talk. Tenet introduced Kay to his senior staff at his "prayer meeting," as the CIA chief called it, a weekly intelligence roundup on Iraq, in a large conference room outside his office. Everyone at the table welcomed Kay, cheerfully commiserated about the challenge ahead, and wished him luck.

One afternoon, an aide stepped into Kay's temporary office to say someone from the Pentagon had phoned to ask his size. The supply division wanted to send over a set of standard Army fatigues and boots for him. They'd carry no name, no rank, and no insignia. Kay bristled in response.

"You make it very clear to them that I am not going to wear a military uniform with no rank in Baghdad," he instructed. He was going as chief, not some anonymous grunt. He didn't plan to hide.

He couldn't refuse the next request, however. The CIA issued Kay a cover name to use on internal communications. Every agency officer who heads overseas, even for a quick trip, is issued an alias. Supposedly a computer at Langley spits out random names from an old London phone directory.

Kay, who had lived in Europe, liked the idea. Stiff upper lip and all that. And Bond. James Bond.

Except Kay's official CIA cover name was Buford S. Vincent.

It certainly didn't sound British. Or glamorous. It conjured up, to him at least, a pudgy salesman gulping iced tea on a rocking chair on a plantation porch. In fact, it wasn't too far from the truth. Kay grew up in East Houston but his family roots were in Winona, a tiny town in the steamy flats and pecan fields of East Texas. Generations of Kays—farmers, preachers, shop clerks, and railway workers—had lived and died in Winona, population never more than a few hundred. Their graves filled a small cemetery behind the sole Baptist Church.

Back when Kay worked as a U.N. inspector in Iraq, CIA reports had referred to him as Ramrod. Colleagues teased him for it. But Kay loved the macho name.

Ramrod. Rambo! Now that was more like it.

But Buford S. Vincent? It bothered him.

As the week drew to a close, Kay and Tenet were driven down to the Pentagon for lunch with Rumsfeld and his chiefs.

Defense Department officials already had pulled the hapless 75th XTF out of Iraq and created a larger DIA-run operation called the Iraq Survey Group. The Pentagon's search teams, now in their third iteration, were abolished. It was a whole new ball game.

Maj. Gen. Keith Dayton was organizing the new group in a hangar at the Al Udeid air base in Qatar. The graying Army officer had trained in artillery but shifted to intelligence and rose swiftly through the ranks. He had just finished six months as chief of the Defense HUMINT Service, the DIA operations division. Under pressure to professionalize the much maligned service, he signed off on a plan that for the first time required DIA operatives to train at the Farm, the CIA boot camp in the bracken and swamps near Williamsburg, Virginia.

Still, like most DIA officers, Dayton was suspicious of the CIA.

Now, just weeks after arriving in Qatar, he discovered that he was about to share his command with an egghead that the CIA had pulled off the TV. Dayton, a two-star general, didn't outrank Kay. So he moved to outflank him.

Kay should fly to Qatar on an inspection trip for a week or so, Dayton advised in a private note to a Navy captain who served as Tenet's military liaison. They would arrange briefings and show him around the hangar, and then Kay could fly his CIA butt back to the safety of Washington. He could work on broad strategy issues, write policy papers and procedures to his heart's content, and monitor the weapons hunt from half a world away. He could mail them the strategy papers if he wanted and maybe, if necessary, if he had no other pressing concerns, he could visit periodically. That, at least, was Kay's take when he saw the note.

Subtle it was not. Tenet and Kay complained to Rumsfeld. And the Pentagon chief told them the CIA now had complete control. He wanted no part of running the Iraq Survey Group. Kay asked if Rumsfeld at least wanted to see his reports from Iraq.

"Absolutely not," Rumsfeld responded firmly. "You're George's man. You report to George. I don't want anything to do with this."

On the drive back to Langley after lunch, riding up the parkway, Kay mused aloud that Rumsfeld sounded surprisingly eager to wash his hands of the WMD search.

"Smart Rummy," Tenet said stiffly. He sounded envious.

Tenet doesn't want this job either, Kay realized with a start. Nobody wants to stick their neck out on this anymore. If this goes sour now, he thought, forget Tenet's offer to be king. I'll be the joker. I'll be the fall guy.

Kay shook off his doubts. He had built his career on aggressive self-confidence. Still, he reminded Tenet of his promise make the weapons hunt an absolute priority. Kay emphasized again that he didn't want to be left high and dry in Iraq. He needed the authority to draw on CIA resources until he finished the job.

"It's got to be my call," Kay insisted. "I'm not of the agency. I have nobody back here to watch my backside. If I get out there and people here start nickel-and-diming me, cutting me apart, I don't have anyone to protect my interests."

Tenet assured him that he'd have whatever he needed. But Kay pushed further, looking for leverage. The CIA chief had guaranteed the White House and the Congress that Iraq possessed WMD. Tenet had backstopped Colin Powell at the U.N. when he put America's credibility on the line. Now the president had ordered the CIA to find the damn weapons.

"I'm taking on your moral hazard," Kay warned. "Your credibility rests with me."

CHAPTER 33

On June 20, exactly three months after the war began, Kay stood in the hangar at the air base in Qatar and introduced himself to an all-hands meeting of several hundred Iraq Survey Group staffers.

Pack up, Kay ordered as his first command. We are moving to Baghdad. Saddam hid his weapons in Iraq, not here in Qatar. Kay explained his ideas for the new search. Any questions?

A DIA analyst raised his hand. "What happens if there are no WMD?" he called out.

Kay was startled to hear such doubts. Others seemed surprised as well. The assembly grew silent. He chose his words carefully.

"We're here to find the truth," he promised the group. "If there are no WMD, we'll say so."

Kay next flew up to Camp Slayer. He got a rude shock. The 75th XTF, the Pentagon's weapons hunting group, had returned to Oklahoma without arranging any transfer of files or information to their replacements. They left no logs or reports of who went where or what they saw. Kay rarely got angry. But he was mad now. The Pentagon had searched Iraq for three months and no one kept an official account? They just blew this off, he fumed.

Another surprise also hit hard. Rumsfeld's deputy, Stephen Cambone, had announced that the Iraq Survey Group would deploy "some 1,300 experts." But most were support personnel: administrators, military police, logistics, even a recreation director and a chaplain. When Kay tallied his roster, he had about 120 intelligence analysts and subject experts. Surprisingly few had focused on Iraq's weapons, however. Worse, he could draw on only about forty case officers trained to recruit sources and collect intelligence. Fewer than a dozen or so spoke Arabic. Unbelievable, Kay thought.

Sure, some Iraqi scientists and government officials spoke English. But Kay wanted to scrounge for the truck drivers who carted the weapons and the janitors who held keys to the storerooms. They knew the real secrets. Finding them required savvy operatives who could work the streets. It wasn't like the CIA could look up someone's address in the phone book. Baghdad had no phone book. At the moment, Baghdad didn't even have a phone service.

Kay's first priority was finding a secure workspace. The 75th XTF commanders had operated from a lakeside cabana just up from the Fishbowl, the former brothel. The survey group needed much more space. During the war, U.S. warplanes had ignored one of the biggest buildings at Slayer. They apparently mistook the large multicolored dome for a mosque. But Saddam actually had used the huge hall to host grand banquets and parties. Stylized Arabic script inscribed above the massive oak doors poetically suggested Saddam's presence was as sweet as perfume. The new headquarters of the Iraq Survey Group was quickly dubbed the Perfume Palace.

It looked like an early Hollywood version of an Arabian Nights palace, the kind of place where Valentino might keep a harem in gauzy veils. Shaped like an arena, it perched on the edge of one of Slayer's broad lakes, with grand views across the water. A watery moat and a line of graceful palms wound around the palace, like the fringe of a tonsure. Brown turtledoves cooed softly in eucalyptus trees and crapped on those walking below.

A pool shaped like spreading palm fronds beckoned just inside the main doors. Enormous chandeliers, dripping with faux crystals and pearls, glittered high overhead. Gleaming marble lined the walls and floors. A grand staircase of more marble, flanked by faux-Babylonian columns, rose at the far end of the chamber and then split at the landing into two wings. The only other staircase had impossibly low ceilings that forced those going up or down into a painful crouch. Saddam apparently had required his servants to kowtow even when he couldn't see them.

The grand hall was upstairs, a cavernous ballroom under a dome that loomed overhead like a vast planetarium. It glowed the soft blue of a new morning sky. But a two-story-high mural of an imperial Saddam, waving a golden sword on a prancing white charger and leading his armies of the night, dominated one long wall. The artist had done something with Saddam's coal-black eyes. No matter where one stood in the room, they seemed to glower back.

Survey group engineers boarded up the pool and covered the awful murals. They drew plans to convert the second-floor ballroom into an enormous intelligence vault so those inside could handle highly classified information. Halliburton got the contract to construct a SCIF, a sensitive compartmented information facility, a vastly larger version of the prefab model the CIA had airlifted to the V.V.I.P. compound.

Workers raised a false floor over the marble and snaked computer and communication cables beneath it. They lined the roof with special copper shielding and built an indoor grid of conductive wire to block spy satellites or enemy agents from eavesdropping on conversations or sucking up electronic emanations from computer monitors, magnetic discs, keyboards, and cables.

Inside the vault, they hung huge plasma screens on a central podium and constructed concentric rings of computer stations and desks. They hooked up independent power, air conditioners, and alarms. Then they sealed the bug-proof ballroom with thick steel doors. But they took so much time and blew so many deadlines that Kay erupted in anger at the construction manager one afternoon. He threatened to complain directly to Vice President Cheney, the former chief executive officer at Halliburton. Kay never made the call but the contractors got their revenge.

They finished everything but the plumbing. The Perfume Palace possessed not a single working urinal or toilet. When nature called, Kay and others working from offices on the third floor—including the entire Curveball team—had to hike down ninety-eight hard marble stairs and tromp outside in the thick dust and baking heat to a bank of portable plastic outhouses beside the moat. When they were finished, they had to climb those ninety-eight steps back up. It was brutal. Everyone watched their fluid intake after the first day.

Kay faced a more fundamental problem: CIA infighting with the DIA was undermining the weapons hunt.

CIA security officers insisted on isolating agency staffers from everyone. No one could see a CIA computer monitor without a special security clearance. Among other things, that entailed passing a "lifestyle" polygraph. It focused on suspect social habits. Do you snort cocaine? Like sex with animals? The rules were rigid, no exceptions allowed. Kay couldn't budge the "security Nazis," as he constantly derided them.

After the early clash over his authority, General Dayton, the former head of Defense HUMINT, had accepted reality. He played a loyal second fiddle to Kay, running security and logistics for the operation. "Dr. Kay provides the guidance, I make it happen," Dayton told his British deputy.

Dayton couldn't make everything happen, however. He had commandeered a marble cabana fronting the lake as his living quarters. Aides imported bags of grass seed from Qatar and ordered a crew to plant and water a lawn out front. It would provide a welcome reminder of home, of suburbia, of America itself. It was folly, of course. Dayton's green lawn soon withered and died in the smothering heat and choking dust.

The CIA's security rules and culture infuriated Dayton. He stormed into Kay's office one afternoon and unleashed a diatribe against what he called the agency's "cowboy attitudes."

"Your CIA guys won't work with us," he protested. "They refuse to share intelligence. They refuse to work in the same facility. They won't even eat with us. It's bad for morale. People resent it."

Kay fully agreed. Even the super-secret eavesdroppers from the National Security Agency ran a bullpen inside the upstairs ballroom. Everyone there was cleared for access to material rated Top Secret or higher. The DIA and CIA were squabbling like children. Kay wanted everybody to play nicely in the same sandbox. So he imposed a compromise.

The DIA and the technical teams—code breakers, digital map makers, overhead imagery analysts, and so on—would work together in the big ballroom as planned. But Halliburton would build a separate secure workspace for the CIA in a nearby conference room.

Work crews ran more cables, installed another thick steel door, brought in more alarms and shielding, another power supply, and all the rest. The twenty-five or so CIA staffers finally fired up their laptops around a coffee urn and everyone relaxed, except that unlike the main ballroom, their private vault had windows. So the security zealots worried about incoming mortars and rocket-propelled grenades as well as enemy eavesdropping. At least they were safe from the DIA.

After the 9/11 attacks, U.S. intelligence officials had vowed to blow up the so-called stovepipes that prevented agencies from sharing critical information. But in Baghdad, the CIA and DIA still barely talked. They used completely different communications systems. It drove Kay crazy. He'd be talking on a secure video link back to Langley and the Pentagon, or half a dozen other places, and he'd mention a new classified report that he had just issued and either the CIA or the military side would interrupt to say they had not seen it. Often as not, he'd next hear a voice mumbling apologetically off screen, "Ahhh sir, it's on the other system. It came in last week . . ."

A new CIA camera at Langley didn't help. Voice activated, it swiveled to focus on whoever was speaking. But when more than one person spoke at once, or someone offered an aside, or cleared his throat, the camera whirred toward the noise and then panned back, focusing here and there, in and out, desperately searching for the voice. To anyone watching the feed, it was a high-tech headache, another overpriced, useless CIA toy.

Kay stayed in an air-conditioned shipping container at the CIA station out at the airport because Tenet or McLaughlin sometimes called at 2 a.m. Iraq time and needed to talk. The CIA shut its communications vault at the Perfume Palace each night, locking away the hard drives and setting high-tech alarms. Plus agency phones there kept crashing. Jamming, sunspots, dust storms, nobody knew why. If an important call came in, Kay had to rush to the CIA station anyway. So he figured it was easier to just live there.

Someone would pound on Kay's trailer door in the middle of the night and he would pull on his pants, strap on his Glock sidearm, and stagger over to the communications trailer. The White House seemed especially oblivious to the nine-hour time difference.

In July, when U.S. troops shot and killed Saddam's two adult sons, Uday and Qusay, Kay was assigned the job of ensuring a legal chain of custody to ensure no one switched or tampered with the DNA samples. He had never met Saddam's sons but he identified the bloody, bullet-riddled bodies as they came off the plane from Mosul. Then he watched a doctor take blood, clip hair samples, and seal the material in a container aboard a CIA plane. The samples would go to the FBI laboratory in Quantico, Virginia.

That night, way past midnight, someone ran up to Kay's trailer and pounded excitedly on the thin door.

"The vice president's office wants to know if Dr. Kay has identified the DNA samples," shouted a voice.

"Tell them I'm not that kind of doctor," Kay hollered back. His doctorate was in political science.

Soon after, Scooter Libby, Cheney's chief of staff, phoned in the middle of the Baghdad night and left an urgent message for Kay. Libby wanted the survey group to immediately search a series of caves where Saddam's aides supposedly had stashed chemical and biological weapons. Libby even left the precise geographic coordinates to guide the search. Startled by the request, Kay instructed his deputy to investigate. When the aide's report came back, Kay burst into laughter. That afternoon, he sent a carefully barbed message back to Langley:

"Please advise the Vice President's office that the coordinates are in the Bekaa Valley in Lebanon and we are not authorized to operate there," Kay wrote.

Lebanon doesn't even share a border with Iraq. So much for crack White House intelligence, Kay thought.

Before the invasion, the CIA had tapped a former Iraqi general living in Virginia to lead the Scorpions, a clandestine army with a comic book name.

Scorpion officers sported nicknames like Alligator and Cobra. The CIA spent millions of dollars on the Scorpions, training them in sabotage at secret bases in Jordan and even giving them old Soviet Hind helicopters. But most of their major missions—spray-painting graffiti on walls, cutting electricity, and "sowing confusion," as one put it— went awry or got canceled during the invasion due to poor planning.

All was not for naught. The Scorpions scouted out and captured a mansion near the enormous crossed swords of the Hands of Victory monument in Baghdad. They brought in private chefs and served lavish meals. After enjoying a sumptuous dinner one night, Kay asked the Scorpion leaders to check railroad switching yards for boxcars or containers that might hide bio-production equipment. He also requested their help tracking down several former Iraqi weapons scientists who had moved or were in hiding. The Scorpions seemed reluctant until Kay offered a reward.

"If someone comes in with a warm weapon, I would pay big," he assured them. Kay controlled a $10 million revolving fund that he could use to pay rewards. About $1 million in cash sat in a safe at the CIA station. The Scorpions happily agreed to help him spend the money. They produced very little of value, however.

Out at Slayer, the weapons hunters focused on finding evidence and sources. Following Kay's directives, teams hauled in troves of documents from government ministries and offices so translators could help analysts search for clues. Soldiers in the field sometimes lent a hand. One morning, a well-dressed Iraqi couple drove a dented pickup truck to a U.S. military checkpoint in Baghdad. Several large boxes lay behind them in the truck bed.

The driver disclosed that the boxes contained Saddam's personal papers and documents concerning WMD. He wished to give them to America. His wife, who had worked for Saddam, had ordered her to destroy the papers, the driver added. But now the despot had run away and they were happy to turn them in.

The young Army lieutenant running the checkpoint thanked them and accepted Saddam's private stash. But he didn't write down the couple's names or address, or ask any details of where the woman had worked or exactly what Saddam had told her. And it took days to push the hoard up the military chain of command until somebody finally thought to call the Iraq Survey Group.

When the dictator's personal papers finally arrived at Slayer, Kay cursed and ordered translators in his document exploitation unit to drop everything. "Consider these twenty thousand pages your top priority," he instructed. "Let me know as soon as you find something."

It took days and all they found was a mix of Iraqi government files with no proof of provenance. Maybe they were real, maybe not. Nothing on them suggested they came from Saddam. It didn't matter since none of the information concerned weapons of mass destruction or much else of value. After that, Kay asked every U.S. military commander he met to instruct the troops: if an Iraqi brings in a weapons document, hold him until we know what it is and where it's from.

To help the overworked linguists, the CIA flew out sophisticated new translation software that a contractor in Arizona had developed. Scan the paper in, the computer does the rest, simple as pie. But the computers constantly crashed trying to decipher handwritten Arabic. Half the time, clerks in the document exploitation unit scanned the Arabic script in upside down or backward. So the translators had to eyeball everything. And it was painfully slow. Each time an urgent report of a dramatic new find landed on Kay's desk, he'd order them to double-check and, as often as not, someone had screwed up the translation.

But more truckloads of documents kept pouring in. Thick bales and boxes and heavy plastic bags of confiscated files, some tied with string or frayed ribbons, overflowed into the corners of a lakeside warehouse at Slayer. It was a mountain of paper. The backlog was such that no one yet realized that the haul contained crucial files about Curveball.

CHAPTER 34

The "bio-babes" worked the Curveball case.

At least that's what the two top CIA biological weapons analysts at Slayer called themselves. Neither petite nor shy, Rita and Martha regularly introduced themselves to newcomers at the HVT Bar with raucous, defiant laughter. "We're the big, buxom bio-babes," the two CIA women boasted, and their knot of male admirers usually bellowed approval.

Rita, chief of the bioweapons team in the Iraq Survey Group, was short, dark-haired, and spirited. In her mid-twenties, she bubbled with energy and ideas, talked nonstop, and seemed to work just as hard. She was fearless or foolish enough to take awful risks when she left the camp. The security teams who guarded her grumbled that they'd be blamed if she got killed. But she was headstrong and ambitious and she produced solid results that got noticed back in Washington, and that's what counted.

Rita grew up in New Jersey in an Italian-American family but went south to attend Texas A&M University, where her East Coast accent must have seemed exotic. Run by a former CIA director, Robert Gates, the school maintained exceedingly close ties to Langley. An agency talent spotter on campus liked Rita's adrenaline-charged style and her undergraduate degree in biology. After passing the CIA entry interviews and polygraphs, she studied biowarfare at the Dugway Proving Ground in Utah, where the Army develops and tests chemical and biological defense systems on a base the size of Rhode Island. Since Rita spoke Italian, the CIA weapons center assigned her to focus on weapons programs in Libya, a former Italian colony. They added Iraq as an also-ran to her portfolio but after the invasion, she was among the first to volunteer for the weapons hunt. She was single and couldn't wait to get into the field.

No one at the Perfume Palace questioned Rita's competence. But her inexperience sometimes showed. One morning, she excitedly told a staff meeting that an Iraqi tribal sheikh gave her a fabulous lead. He swore that Saddam's aides had buried a secret cache of biological weapons in farmland that he owned outside Baghdad. Rita wanted to dig it up.

Others in the room rolled their eyes. Hundreds of screwball tips poured into the Iraq Survey Group. Saddam seemingly buried his weapons under every other basketball court, hospital, and graveyard in Iraq. The survey group even posted a "Scam Chart" to record the latest, most ludicrous hoaxes. People kept showing up trying to sell beakers of plutonium and vials of anthrax that turned out to be soap powder.

But Rita kept pushing the sheikh's story. Finally one day she got her way.

"The guy promised me that if they're not there, we can bury him," she announced dramatically. So Kay approved her request.

They had to truck in front-end loaders and bring in armed troops to ensure perimeter security. They needed mobile chemical and biological testing gear and emergency demolition and disposal teams for whatever they dug up. But Rita finally got everything organized and, a few days later, the big machines roared to life and dug where the proud sheikh pointed. And after shoveling awhile in the blistering sun, they had scooped out an enormous hole in the sand.

"Aaargh, maybe I'm wrong about the location," the sheikh confessed. He slapped his forehead in embarrassment. "No, now I remember, it's over there." He pointed to another area.

So the big machines shoveled and scraped a huge hole there too. Then he pointed over yonder, and they dug a third dry hole before giving up in disgust. Rita drove back to see the sheikh two weeks later and discovered he had pumped water into the holes and filled his three new ponds with carp for a commercial fish farm. Kay, the scion of East Texas, teased Rita unmercifully about how the CIA put a damned Texas Aggie in charge of biology and all she could do was advance aquaculture in the desert.

Martha, Rita's best friend and bio-team mate at Slayer, sported a wolfish grin and a temper to match. Now in her fifties, she had survived two bad marriages and a tumultuous CIA career. She had little respect for the boneheads and bean counters back at

WINPAC and didn't care who knew it. She spoke from the gut and told people what she believed, not what they wanted to hear. Her voice blared like a klaxon, grating enough to rattle fragile egos, especially since she usually was cursing. She cursed so loudly, so exuberantly, and so frequently that supervisors both in Langley and Slayer repeatedly tried to rein her in. She usually demurred with a few choice expletives.

The CIA required anyone posted to Baghdad to be "weapons qualified." Before coming, Martha took the test at a CIA firing range and instructors dove for cover after her first few shots. As she cheerfully told the story later at the HVT Bar, she had shot the floor, the ceiling, everywhere but the damned target. But she begged to join the weapons hunt and the CIA desperately needed bodies. Her supervisors let her go as long as she promised not to touch a gun or leave the safety of Slayer. Once she had arrived, Martha found endless excuses for field trips off base that absolutely required her presence. Kay, a good sport, gave his approval as long as qualified shooters went along. And the knuckle-draggers from security adored her so, they tried to teach her to shoot, but she still couldn't pass the test.

Martha thrived in the chaos of post-invasion Iraq. She had focused on the Iraqi bioweapons program for years so she recognized the major players and the key facilities. She understood how fermentors work and other technical details. She worked hard by day and played hard at night, usually holding down one end of the HVT Bar.

Unlike the Army, the CIA couldn't order anyone to go to Iraq. It was a civilian agency. Most CIA officers volunteered for sixty or ninety days, some only for a few weeks. Rita packed up and flew home from Slayer after her initial three-month assignment, vowing never to return. But Kay, who constantly struggled to retain experienced staff, begged her to reconsider. She gave in after two weeks and flew back to Baghdad. Martha was the opposite. She kept extending her tours. Kay was taken aback when he discovered that Martha's supervisors did not want her back at Langley anytime soon. The more sedate analysts did not miss her constant swearing and loutish jibes.

Kay repeatedly tried to convince Beth, the WINPAC analyst who fought so fiercely with Drumheller's aide over Curveball, to join the team at Slayer. He filed requests, and then complaints, with her superiors but the geek squad chief who had pushed hardest on Curveball would not or could not come. Nor would the chief DIA analyst on the case show up.

Kay believed Powell's description and illustrations of the bio-trucks had formed the most potent part of his U.N. Security Council speech.

He was worried that U.S. and British intelligence experts still couldn't agree on the purpose of the two trailers they had found. The CIA jumped the gun with the White Paper, he feared. Worse, the president told the world that America had found weapons of mass destruction. It was hugely embarrassing. Kay knew he was partly to blame. He deeply regretted naming the equipment that cooked "chicken soup for biological weapons" so confidently for NBC. He really hadn't recognized the system. He kicked himself for appearing so certain in his judgment. He shouldn't have trusted the Secret Squirrel.

Unraveling the mobile program, he resolved, should be an early goal for the Iraq Survey Group.

In the first week of July, Kay asked for a meeting with the bioweapons team—Rita and Martha from WINPAC, two CIA clandestine case officers, and a technical expert from the National Ground Intelligence Center, a military intelligence support agency. Since the team was mostly CIA, they didn't work in the main ballroom vault at the Perfume Palace. Their desks clustered right outside Kay's third-floor office and he saw them all the time. But he had not yet gotten a full briefing. At the prearranged time, they filed into his office. General Dayton had neglected to order any furniture for Kay's office, so they pushed together around a small table that one of Kay's aides had scavenged.

"Where are we?" Kay asked. "Tell me what's going on."

Rita updated them on CIA fears that Saddam's scientists secretly produced the variola virus that causes smallpox. They especially worried that someone deliberately or inadvertently stole the deadly virus during the postwar looting. But the prewar intelligence on smallpox now looked very shaky. She and Martha also were checking other biowarfare issues, including reports of human testing and small laboratories run by Iraqi intelligence.

The conversation quickly turned to the germ trucks. Kay showed them a printout of a multicolored spreadsheet that he had compiled on his computer. It broke down Powell's U.N. speech into specific charges and sections. He had highlighted Powell's claims about the mobile weapons labs and copied the illustrations.

"I want to see the supporting intelligence for all this," Kay began. He was doing this with the nuclear, chemical, and missile teams as well. "Where did he get all this?"

Kay confessed that despite his interview on TV, he no longer felt certain about the two trailers. In any case, they formed only part of Saddam's germ weapons program. Where were the other trucks? Why couldn't they find them?

He pointed again to his spreadsheet of Powell's speech and turned to Rita, the bio-team leader. He asked about the eyewitness, the chemical engineer who managed the program. Powell said the defector had witnessed an accident that killed twelve people.

"Tell me about him," he said.

Rita blanched slightly. She seemed discomfited. She paused to prepare her thoughts.

"He's under German control," she replied evenly. "But he's given us the complete story of the mobile program."

She outlined the defector's account—he was hired out of Baghdad University, was sent to the Chemical Engineering and Design Center, and personally designed and built the mobile biological production units at Djerf al Nadaf. His information was very solid. His code name was Curveball.

Kay laughed. He had never heard the code name before. Who came up with these wack-job names?

He asked what the germ trucks actually produced. Anthrax? Botulinum? What? Powell had sort of danced around the question.

It's a little unclear, Rita admitted. Curveball really wasn't sure. He insisted everything was kept secret.

"We think it was anthrax because it's the easiest," she explained.

Kay chewed on this for a moment. Intelligence was usually piecemeal, he knew, more an art than a science. But still. It seemed odd that the guy who managed the program wasn't sure. He pushed on.

"What is the source like when you talk to him?" he asked.

"Well, we've never actually talked to him," Rita told him. "The Germans keep him under wraps."

Kay's jaw dropped. They hadn't talked to him?

"You're kidding me, right?"

"I don't doubt Curveball's account," Rita added defensively. "No one does. His reporting is very detailed. It's all credible stuff."

"But you've confirmed it, right? This guy is reliable?"

"His information is very credible," Rita repeated. "Everybody says so."

Kay felt a sinking feeling in his stomach. "Credible" is one of those squishy words in intelligence. To analysts, it means the information makes sense. To operatives, it means the source is reliable. Rita was an analyst. Was Curveball trustworthy or wasn't he?

Kay checked his spreadsheet again. Powell had cited three corroborating sources for the eyewitness who managed the germ trucks.

"What about the three other sources?"

Rita took her time in replying.

"There really are no other sources," she said.

She sounded sheepish, almost apologetic. The other sources were on the edges, she said. They all claimed different things. Their information did not really match up with what Curveball said. There was essentially one source for all the mobile information.

Kay fell back in his chair. For one of the first times in his life, he was speechless. This can't be real, he thought. One source. And we haven't even talked to him. Was the CIA really so reckless they would hang everything on a single source? Why didn't he know this before?

He recalled his briefings in Washington. No one—not McLaughlin, not the analysts at WINPAC, not a single person at the CIA or DIA— had hinted at doubts about the mobile program. He had held lengthy discussions with James Pavitt and Jamie Miscik, who headed the analyst side of the shop, and with Alan Foley, head of WINPAC.

He remembered his warning to Tenet. *I'm taking on your moral hazard. Your credibility rests with me.*

Tenet hadn't mentioned Curveball. No one had admitted that so much prewar intelligence rested on such thin ice.

Kay wondered if Powell knew. Powell had borne the full credibility of the United States. He had paraded the germ trucks before the world as if Saddam himself were dishing out anthrax from the back like ice cream. It was the centerpiece of his speech. If Powell had confessed to the Security Council, "Hey, it's really only one source, we never actually interviewed him, and we don't know his name," people would have laughed him out of New York, Kay thought.

Kay got a grip on himself. He didn't want to let the others see his dismay.

Okay, he told the team. Let's start with Dr. Taha, General Saadi, and any other Iraqi who worked in the pre-1991 BW program. Check the old U.N. reports. Check the CIA files. Go back to the Germans. Check anything you can.

"Let's do this the intelligent way," Kay said. "Let's go to our human sources and see who was involved in the program and follow the leads."

He shook his head. He still couldn't believe it.

"Let's figure this out," Kay commanded the bio-team. "This is the highest-priority investigation."

That Friday, he wrote the first of a series of private weekly e-mail assessments back to Tenet. They had agreed to set up a back channel, and Kay didn't share his private cables with General Dayton or anyone else. Some were short, others ten pages. He signaled his concerns about Curveball in his first e-mail.

"The emerging picture here is by no means complete," Kay later recalled writing. "But the emerging picture is very different from what I expected."

He reluctantly signed it Buford S. Vincent.

CHAPTER 35

Even inside the Perfume Palace, few knew about Curveball.

Rita's biological unit was smaller than the five other survey group teams, and she deliberately kept the case on close hold. But Hamish Killip, one of the original Gang of Four biological experts, arrived from London on July 12 and quickly was briefed on the investigation.

Bald and rumpled, Killip sported a growing paunch and a crooked grin that suggested little fazed him. In his mid-fifties, he had recently retired from a long career as a combat engineer and a biowarfare analyst for the Defence Intelligence Staff, the British equivalent of the DIA. Killip had visited Iraq more than fifty times as a U.N. inspector in the 1990s. That made him "the walking encyclopedia," as he put it, for the survey group in general and Rita's biological team in particular. Killip was an agnostic on the trucks. He didn't trust Saddam for a second. But he also recalled Scott Ritter running in circles trying to find the mobile weapons labs.

For now, military checkpoints were under orders to watch for germ trucks. Patrols regularly pulled over eighteen-wheelers and other vehicles for spot inspections. One afternoon, an urgent message came into the Perfume Palace: U.S. troops had stopped a large box truck with a generator, electronic control boards, and other hardware mounted in arrays in the back. It had exited the back gate of a mosque and the driver said two other vehicles just like it were still parked inside the compound.

Killip and a few others jumped in a convoy and raced to the mosque. The message had said three trucks loaded with equipment. That's what the intelligence always predicted. After all this time, maybe we finally got them, he thought. Against his better judgment, he let his hopes rise.

A bearded Muslim cleric greeted them graciously. He looked quizzical when they asked permission to check his parking lot, but he led them to the rear of the mosque. Killip laughed as the supposed germ trucks came into view. They were satellite transmission trucks for Iraqi state television. Regime officials hid them at the mosque during the war so Saddam could broadcast taunts after air strikes destroyed the city's TV tower.

Everything looks like a mobile weapons lab now, Killip thought.

After Kay's meeting with the bio-team, they instructed linguists to search more carefully through the jumbled bales of captured files and documents for anything they could use to check Curveball's story.

Since MI6 had provided the defector's identity to U.S. intelligence, the translators had a name to work with. Rummaging through the morass of documents, they finally discovered personnel records seized from the Military Industrialization Commission and other material taken from a storeroom at the Chemical Engineering and Design Center, where Curveball had worked. Digging deeper, they found his file.

It included his home address.

In late July, three deep-cover operatives—two from the CIA and one from Defense HUMINT—climbed into an unmarked car and drove out of Slayer to search for Curveball's parents.

The team leader, Mohammed, was in his twenties and a newly minted member of the CIA clandestine service, a proud graduate of the first post-9/11 class. An Egyptian-American, Mohammed had managed to get past CIA counterintelligence officials who normally distrusted anyone with foreign roots. The 9/11 attacks finally had opened their eyes to the advantages of diversity. He spoke fluent Arabic. Better yet, he could fake an Iraqi accent, which made him invaluable on the streets.

The three case officers had studied the case file, and Rita and Martha briefed them extensively before they set out, going over a list of basic questions that the CIA weapons center in Langley had e-mailed over.

When you meet the parents, find out anything you can, Mohammed's team was told. Where did he work? What did he do? Why did he leave Iraq? Where did he go? What are his attitudes toward the United States? Anything.

Crossing to the east bank of the Tigris and weaving northward, the three spies quickly lost their way. Baghdad has few street signs, and many streets are unnamed or change names after a few blocks anyway. Many buildings lack numbers. The Americans felt increasingly conspicuous in the narrow streets. The previous weeks saw the first major bombings and shootings of the post-invasion period, ostensibly by Saddam's Sunni supporters, and several survey group teams had come under attack.

Mohammed stopped several times to ask shopkeepers for directions. His team fiddled with handheld GPS units and checked satellite pictures of the area to figure out their location. A German company had prepared digitized maps of Baghdad for Saddam's regime and the CIA had obtained a set. Mohammed tried to plot their route using a laptop. But it was getting late and they finally gave up and drove back to Slayer, totally discouraged.

They restudied their maps and geo-spatial data that night and realized they had been close, only several blocks off. They agreed to try again early the next morning. This time, they found the right dusty street and the right dingy building, an ocher apartment block near a small Sunni mosque. They climbed up the cool, dark steps inside and knocked. A middle-aged woman answered the door.

Once her initial surprise wore off, Curveball's mother welcomed the three Americans courteously and invited them into her home for tea. The father greeted them sullenly and mostly sat watching, suspicion etched over his face, saying nothing.

The CIA team had agreed to shade the truth. They didn't want to barge in and say, "We want to ask questions about your son, the defector." They concocted a cover story and now they spread it out, like fishermen casting their net. The goal was to get the parents to drop their guard and talk.

"Your son is in good health," Mohammed assured the mother. "He asked us to look in on you."

"Have you seen him?" she asked excitedly.

"Ahhh, no," Mohammed admitted. "But my friends have. He seems very happy."

Then the three CIA operatives perched together on a couch and they chatted in a roundabout way about the weather, the war, and Saddam, but they always worked in a question. So where did her son work before? What did he do there? When did he leave Baghdad? And so on, gently guiding the conversation rather than grilling the mother.

And she could not have been sweeter or more hospitable, pouring more tea and all but showing his baby pictures. She told them what little she knew of his travels, which, she was sad to admit, wasn't very much. She shared a mother's lament. Her boy lived so far away now and he hadn't called in such a long while. She missed him so. His wife still lived in Baghdad but they didn't see her much either, she said.

But her older son had just returned home from Europe, she went on. He worked for Ahmed Chalabi's group, the Iraqi National Congress, she added, although she wasn't sure of his position. The news shocked the CIA team. It was the first hint that Curveball might be tied to Chalabi, who was detested at the CIA.

The mother carried gamely on, not noticing their alarm.

Her older son got in trouble many years ago and had to leave the country, she said sadly. Her younger boy bravely took responsibility and worked hard to pay off the debt. Such a good boy. Then he left Iraq too.

And the three Americans commiserated at her travails. The team leader finally decided it was safe to broach another, more sensitive topic.

"We understand your son really doesn't like Americans," Mohammed wondered aloud.

She seemed startled, almost insulted, Mohammed later reported.

"No, no, he loves Americans," she replied indignantly. "He always has dreamed of going to America. He always talked of going to America. He learned English at school. He loves America!"

And she proved it too, leading them down the dim hallway to see Curveball's old bedroom, which still waited for him, neat and clean.

"Look," she said, pointing proudly.

And they saw American posters all over his walls—music stars, rock bands, basketball teams, pop pinups. It looked like a typical American teenager's bedroom except, Mohammed would say later, there were no dirty clothes on the floor.

"See, he loves you," the mother trilled happily, smiling at the Americans.

Mohammed and the others took it all in and fired a cable off to Washington when they got back to the Perfume Palace. The news hit the CIA like a stabbing chest pain.

Now that they knew Curveball's older brother worked for Chalabi, CIA officers grew fearful that the defector had been coached to poison the intelligence. The thought that Chalabi had planted Curveball to trick them, as he had done with other defectors, seemed too awful to contemplate. It was a nightmare scenario.

Even worse, perhaps, the BND, their partner and ally, had fed them a crock of lies.

"Curveball doesn't hate Americans," Mohammed angrily told his colleagues in the Perfume Palace. "It's all bullshit. His mother says he loves us. He speaks English. He wants to move to America. I think she means it."

Mohammed went to see Kay. "We need to push the Germans hard for access," he urged. "This is total bullshit."

The CIA quickly found a way to get even. In early August or so, the chief of the BND clandestine service, part of Directorate One, sent word that he wanted to visit Iraq to formally reopen their Baghdad operation and reestablish their own Iraqi spy networks. Germany had political and economic interests in postwar Iraq. Since the United States served as official occupying power in Iraq, the BND formally asked for permission to resume spying.

And CIA management, from the chief of station in Baghdad to the spy chiefs at Langley, refused the request. Not once, but over and over.

"The agency made damned sure they were not going to let him in," Kay recalled. "It caused great pains for the DIA because they had this long-standing relationship with the BND. But the agency said absolutely not, no way in hell. So while we're trying to get access to Curveball, the agency is slamming the door in their face."

It would cost them later.

CHAPTER 36

Mohammed's interview with Curveball's mother kicked the bio-babes' investigation into high gear.

None of the WINPAC analysts in Langley or in the Perfume Palace was openly calling Curveball himself into question. The Germans had caused the problem, they believed. CIA supervisors pushed Rita and the rest of the unit even harder to find the bio-trucks, not to disprove the defector's account.

"At this point, the analysts were not saying, 'He's a fabricator. We have to retrench.' They were just saying, 'We really need to run this to the ground because he's the story,'" a former CIA officer said later. "And the reaction they got from WINPAC was, 'Hey, we invaded, we're there. It's a fact on the ground. There's nothing to be gained by going back now and trashing the source who was one of the primary reasons for the war.'"

But Kay complained that the team needed help, and Langley finally sent reinforcements in late August or early September. Two analysts showed up in Baghdad with orders to work full-time on Curveball.

One was Jerry, the zealous geek squad member who had championed Curveball early on and had flown to Iraq to examine the two trailers. The CIA had briefed Jerry's report at the White House and used it for the public White Paper. It was a major achievement for a midlevel analyst.

Jerry had trained for the clandestine service when he first joined the CIA. But the intense stress of overseas operations didn't suit him. So he had shifted to the bioweapons backwater at WINPAC. Until Iraq, and Curveball, his career seemed stalled in slow motion. It seemed unfair. In his mid-forties, with dark hair and a gray mustache, he brought a keen mind and extreme focus to his work. He considered intelligence a calling, and he poured his heart into it.

His colleague, Tim, was thin and shy, only in his twenties, with boyish good looks. He looked so young, in fact, and used an alias anyway, that others in the unit nicknamed him "the Kid."

Kay made it a point to meet and brief every new arrival to the Perfume Palace. Jerry's fervor and the Kid's timidity left a lasting impression after they talked in his third-floor office.

Jerry confided that back at headquarters some CIA officials had begun blaming Kay for failing to find the germ weapons and bio-trucks. The Iraq Survey Group had been screwing around for two months, people were saying. What were they waiting for? The evidence was glaringly obvious in Iraq. The WINPAC chiefs figured Jerry and the Kid could bring fresh thinking, fresh energy. So they volunteered.

Kay listened with mild amusement. He wasn't offended. He had his own doubts about Curveball and the germ trucks, but as a manager, he certainly didn't want to dampen anyone's hopes or expectations. So he welcomed the eager new recruits.

"Let's hear your ideas," he said with a smile. "We'll make the resources available. What's your plan?"

"We want to collect the ground truth on Curveball," Jerry announced. It came out sounding a bit silly, as if no one else had tried.

But he knew the case cold, he explained. Not every piece of evidence fit, he realized, but pieces in an intelligence puzzle never line up exactly. He felt absolutely convinced, he said, that Saddam built a fleet of bioweapons factories, just as Curveball had claimed. Jerry admitted no reservations. He brought faith and zeal, not just expertise, to the case.

"I'm a true believer," he confessed to Kay.

He would run the case to ground, he promised. He would investigate all of Curveball's claims. He would figure out what happened at Djerf al Nadaf and Suwayrah and all the other docking stations. He would unearth proof of the testing at Amiriyah, the bio-accident that killed people, everything.

Curveball was the key to unraveling the whole mobile program, to finally finding the weapons of mass destruction, Jerry said. He brimmed with optimism.

"Let's really nail this program," he told Kay excitedly.

The early insurgency was complicating the hunt.

The six-mile highway from Slayer and the airport to downtown

Baghdad had become known as "Ambush Alley." Gunmen hid in the scrubby brush or in cement-block buildings along the four-lane road and fired assault rifles and rocket-propelled grenades at passing convoys, like in a shooting gallery. Powerful explosives, buried in the median or along the verges, began shredding cars and bodies, spreading gore on the road.

Two Defense HUMINT officers based at the Perfume Palace won notoriety for fighting back. The two women were driving out from Slayer one morning in September when an Iraqi vehicle sped up beside them. Three men inside pointed guns at the women and tried to force them off the road. The women yanked out their own weapons, however, and started firing. In the excitement, they quickly shot out her own windshield, windshield and two side windows before they popped a U-turn and fled, leaving the attackers behind. That night, everyone at the HVT Bar raised toasts to the crack DIA team who shot up their own car in self-defense.

A few days later, a drive-by squad of assassins shot a crucial informant, an Iraqi weapons scientist called Source Alpha, shortly after members of the bio-team had visited his home. He miraculously survived, and Kay used CIA funds to buy the man a car and resettle his family in a safer area. But another survey group informant, shot in the back of the head, died instantly. Mortars began to target the Perfume Palace and the CIA station at the airport from outside the walls.

The first CIA chief of station at the V.V.I.P. terminal had served in Baghdad before the 1991 war. Fluent in Arabic, he ran covert operations into Iraq as U.S. troops deployed for the 2003 war. He was a veteran, a pro. But he rotated out three months after the invasion.

His successor, another Arabic speaker, was younger and less experienced despite tours in the Middle East and South Asia. In October, seven months after the invasion, he moved the CIA station from the airport to the garrisoned Green Zone downtown. The CIA had outgrown the old V.V.I.P. compound and needed to be closer to American occupation officials.

As the insurgency caught fire, the CIA began pouring staff into Baghdad. The station would soon become the largest since Saigon at the height of the Vietnam War. New recruits were shipped over by the dozen for on-the-job training. They doubled and tripled up in trailers and converted shipping containers, but the CIA was fast running out of room again. So the new station chief had an idea.

He proposed stacking the container apartments atop one another and running metal stairs up the outside. It seemed an ideal solution until headquarters sent an engineer out to run some calculations. The trailer towers, he discovered, would rise above the perimeter blast wall, creating an easy target for insurgent fire. They might as well paint a bull's-eye on the side. The plan fizzled, trailers stayed on the ground, and the station chief was transferred that December, after only six months in Iraq.

When insurgents started to shadow U.S. intelligence officers, the CIA barred staff from leaving the Green Zone on their own. Case officers were ordered to take three armored cars, with three people in each, just to drive out to meet a source. It was impossible to stay covert under the circumstances. So people hunkered down in the CIA trailer camp, staring at computer screens all day and each other all night. The result was "a kind of relentless overage frat party in Baghdad," one CIA officer recalled. People were "sort of forced to stay on the compound and party," said another. A senior CIA official called it a "free-fire sex zone". The evening activity, he said, entailed "figuring out how to get laid, not recruit sources."

Business exploded at the new HVT Bar. The seedy saloon had followed the CIA station to the Green Zone. Now it occupied a plush double-wide trailer, large enough to add a pool table and wide-screen TV. People sat at tables and chairs. Well lit and clean, the new bar had little of the squalor—or charm—of the old dive. Worse, State Department and other riffraff crowded in from the Coalition Provisional Authority. The HVT patrons mocked the CPA as Children Playing Adults, and complained of the invasion. What was the point of running an exclusive club if anyone could get in? So the CIA station chief imposed a new rule. Henceforth, the HVT would admit invited guests on Saturday nights only. The CIA owned the other six nights of the week.

One CIA colleague e-mailed a desperate plea to Lindsay Moran, the case officer on the Iraq operations desk back at Langley. "She said she was bored out of her skull and could I please send her the entire final season of *Sex and the City,*" Moran said.

The search for Carrie and Mr. Big, it seemed, had trumped the hunt for Saddam and his weapons of mass destruction.

CHAPTER 37

Jerry had vowed to find "ground truth" on Curveball. It didn't take long.

The bio-team made six separate visits to the dusty grain warehouses at Djerf al Nadaf, where Curveball said he built his germ trucks. The once peaceful mix of Sunni and Shiite villages south of Baghdad increasingly echoed with automatic weapons fire. Jerry's convoy came under fierce attack one day, bullets whizzing by and peppering the sides of their cars, but they escaped unharmed.

The bio-babes, plus Jerry and the Kid, largely repeated the plodding investigation of the U.N. Bravo team from nine months earlier.

They traipsed up and down the red-dirt courtyard at Djerf al Nadaf and stared in disbelief at the six-foot-high wall that blocked trucks from approaching the main warehouse. They walked up and down on both sides, checking to see if it concealed a secret gate. It didn't.

They searched laboriously for welds or other signs that the sheet metal walls at the southeast end of the building concealed a giant garage door. The walls were solid. They pushed and prodded the north-west corner for a hidden lever that could open a secret side-swinging door. There was none.

They used ground-penetrating radar and exhumed samples from every crack and cranny to find DNA or other forensic evidence of the deadly bio-accident. They found nothing.

They visited Suwayrah and other docking stations and depots that Curveball had identified. As at Djerf al Nadaf, the buildings generally matched Curveball's description. But once they went inside and checked the machinery or records, or tested for biologic evidence, it all fell apart. Managers and workers all denied any knowledge of mobile germ factories.

The team also searched the sites that the three corroborating sources had mentioned. Nothing supported their stories either.

Jerry threw his files down in frustration when he returned to Slayer from one trip. Another leg of the case had collapsed. His faith was being tested. He turned to Killip, who worked at the next desk in the Perfume Palace.

"If this is wrong, what the hell is right?" Jerry asked bitterly.

Killip, the "walking encyclopedia" of the Iraq Survey Group, didn't have an answer.

Killip was facing his own problems.

He had become obsessed with the two trailers. He had dropped his bags the day he first arrived and rushed over to examine them. He crawled over every inch of the equipment, even climbing inside the steel fermentor vessels. By nightfall, he was sure. The fermentors were "singularly inappropriate" for producing biological material.

"One mistake and the whole truck would be covered in anthrax," he said later. "We were in hysterics over this. You'd have had better luck putting a couple of dust bins on the back of the truck, lighting a fire, and brewing it in there."

The former British Army officer studied the CIA's White Paper on the trailers. He reddened in anger each time he read it. The CIA paper reeked of "dishonest science and shoddy intelligence," he railed to his teammates. Jerry didn't argue. He never told Killip that he had helped author the report.

Under Killip's direction, the survey group renewed its investigation of the two trailers.

Guards escorted five of the High Value Targets out of their detention cells to give their opinions. Each had worked closely with Saddam's bioweapons program before the 1991 war. None of them recognized the equipment.

Taha, the head of the former program, said she was "quite sure" the trailer could not produce anthrax spores or other biological agents because it lacked a steam generator, instrumentation, and fermentor sampling ports. General Saadi, who first had told Killip and the other Gang of Four members about his idea for bio-trucks, was especially dismissive.

"Anyone who told you this is bio should be fired," he declared.

Killip wrote up his assessment in late September. The equipment could not brew biological agents, he wrote. Nothing in the so-called fermentor drained properly. It was impossible to sterilize the vessel and the pipes. The hardware was designed to chemically produce hydrogen, just as the Iraqis said, he argued. The traces of ammonia were easy to explain: someone had pissed in the equipment.

Killip found that Al Kindi, the manufacturer, had prepared paperwork to declare the trailers to U.N. inspectors in 2002. But officials in Baghdad didn't submit the forms because U.N. resolutions did not prohibit hydrogen-generating trucks. During one of their prewar raids at the Chemical Engineering and Design Center, a U.N. Team even had noticed "Renovation of mobile hydrogen generation plants" on a project status board, records showed. When the inspectors asked for clarification, the Iraqis had described their plan to produce hydrogen gas on military trailers, and the U.N. experts agreed the vehicles were of no concern.

But Rita, head of the bio-team, refused to back Killip's demand for a CIA retraction of the White Paper.

"I'm not an engineer," she said. "I really don't know."

Back in Langley, WINPAC refused to consider withdrawing the paper. This issue is settled, Killip was told. It's been put to bed. Leave it be.

Killip only grew more determined. He kept measuring and testing the trailer equipment, collecting more documents, interviewing more Iraqis. He kept pushing.

By late September, the bio-team at Slayer quietly shifted gears and began to investigate Curveball himself.

No one told Langley at first because they all knew what it meant. For the first time, they were questioning the official CIA position as well as their own assumptions. They were admitting doubt. The CIA did not welcome doubt.

Jerry decided to start by double-checking Curveball's résumé. Someone retrieved the records from the Engineering Department at the University of Baghdad. Jerry groaned aloud when he read the translation. According to the original CIA file, Curveball had boasted to the Germans that he had graduated first in his class. His Iraqi academic file showed him number forty or so, near the bottom.

On other days, the bio-team pored over the defector's official government employment records. They showed Curveball was irascible and hard to work with, which came as no surprise. But Jerry and his colleagues were staggered to read that supervisors at the Chemical Engineering and Design Center had fired the young engineer in late 1995 for unspecified sexual offenses.

It was the most serious blow yet. It meant Curveball did not work at the Baghdad center for four years as he had claimed. Nor could he possibly have constructed germ trucks at Djerf al Nadaf in 1997 or witnessed an accident there the following year.

Curveball's mother had told them he went to Jordan in late 1998, a trip he had not disclosed to the Germans. Iraqi immigration records confirmed that he left Iraq from July to December 1998. They also showed he had traveled abroad several times between 1995 and 1998, the period when he supposedly was working full-time on the germ trucks.

He also had spent time in prison.

As best the team could determine, his older brother had skipped the country after borrowing money or running up a debt. When collectors came after his parents, Curveball apparently stole or embezzled money to pay the debt. He was caught and briefly jailed. The details were not clear but it explained why he hung up the phone on his brother in 2001.

With help from his mother, they found the brother at the Baghdad Hunting Club, a lush estate that Chalabi's group had seized after the invasion. The brother told the CIA team that he had phoned Curveball two years earlier and he recounted their chilly conversation. Later, Chalabi and his top aides all denied any knowledge of Curveball, and the CIA didn't identify either brother to them. But the CIA obtained phone records or an eavesdropping report that proved the telephone call had occurred.

"Whether he couldn't stand his brother, whether he didn't like the Iraqi National Congress or their politics, or whether he just felt he didn't need Chalabi's help, was not clear," an investigator said later. "All we know is Curveball pretty definitively turned him away."

The Chalabi connection didn't fit the usual pattern in any case. Chalabi's group didn't deliver Curveball to the Germans. The BND found him on their own at Zirndorf after they reviewed his asylum paperwork. Chalabi normally brokered his defectors directly to spy services, especially the DIA. And he never hid his hand: he used Iraqi informants to court American and British media, doling out interviews to scoop-hungry reporters.

They would "shop their good sources around town, but they weren't known for sneaking people . . . into some asylum system," said a CIA analyst. It wasn't how they operated.

"If you were going to try to influence the United States government, would you send someone to Germany and then say he refused to meet the Americans? That's enormously sophisticated. You'd make more certain it would get into U.S. hands," agreed a DIA official.

CIA operations officers still worried whether Saddam's intelligence agency had sent Curveball out as a double agent to confuse them. The Mukhabarat had run a special unit, Department 44, which deployed agents to deliberately create false trails leading to dead ends. In some cases, the CIA believed, the Iraqi spy service had even manipulated legitimate defectors. "They were shown bits of information and led to believe there was an active weapons program, only to be turned loose to make their way to Western intelligence," said a U.S. official. "Then, because they believe it, they pass polygraph tests . . . and planted information becomes true even if it was all made up to deceive us."

But Jerry and the bio-babes found no trace of Curveball in the Mukhabarat files in Baghdad. He was no double agent or secret plant.

Kay had promised to give an interim progress report to Congress.

He flew back to Washington and, on October 2, the CIA released his thirteen-page report. Kay admitted that the Iraq Survey Group had found no anthrax, no smallpox, no biological weapons of any kind. The survey group was "not yet able to corroborate the existence" of mobile weapons labs, he conceded. Nor had they found any sign of chemical or nuclear arms programs. Still, Kay argued, Saddam never gave up his "aspirations and intentions" to acquire weapons of mass destruction someday.

As proof, Kay cited the discovery of "dozens of WMD-related program activities." He especially highlighted the recovery of a vial of biological material, C. botulinum Okra B, from an Iraqi scientist's home. The scientist had stored the single vial, about two inches high by half an inch wide, in his kitchen refrigerator for ten years. It was the only suspect biological material the Iraq Survey Group had found.

Kay's closed-door testimony to three congressional committees went badly. Even Pat Roberts, the dour Kansas Republican who chaired the Senate Intelligence Committee, announced he was "not pleased by what I heard today." Roberts admitted he was frustrated by the failure to find the WMD. "There has not been a breakthrough."

Stung by the criticism, the White House swung into action: it blamed the media. Condoleezza Rice called in reporters the next day to complain about morning headlines that stressed Kay's failure to find any WMD. Desperate to respin the report and regain the initiative, the White House unholstered its biggest guns to argue that Saddam's illegal weapons program had flourished until the invasion. Speaking on the South Lawn of the White House, the Washington Monument rising majestically behind him, Bush hailed Kay's alarming discovery of "a live strain of deadly agent botulinum."

He didn't mention that the vial of C. *botulinum Okra B* could cause food poisoning, but posed little danger if inhaled. No one, not Iraq or any other country, had ever managed to turn *Okra B* into a weapon. It was the wrong strain of botulinum.

CHAPTER 38

As October wore on, members of the bio-team fanned out from the Perfume Palace each morning to chase new leads. They tracked down and interviewed more than sixty people who knew Curveball or might have worked on the mobile bio-factories.

None of the senior designers or managers at the Chemical Engineering and Design Center seemed to know who Curveball was. The records indicated that, rather than being a project manager, he had served as an assistant in a filing office. The evidence suggested he never worked with fermentors at all.

The former chief of the Military Industrialization Commission, sitting in a detention cell, cooperated extensively on other topics. But he denied that Curveball or anyone else built germ trucks. He knew because he had to authorize and pay for each project.

Rita, the chief bio-babe, interrogated Huda Salih Mahdi Ammash in another holding cell. Dubbed "Mrs. Anthrax" for her role in the pre-1991 program, she served in Saddam's inner circle and was the only woman on the Pentagon's most wanted list. Mrs. Anthrax swore that she knew nothing about mobile production systems.

Rita got even less help from Taha, the former chief of Iraq's bioweapons program. Dr. Germ angrily denied building bio-trucks as a backup production system. The CIA invented these trucks, not Iraq, she snapped. Taha also haughtily dismissed Curveball's claims that he met her several times and worked for her.

"These are lies," she insisted. "I never met this man. I don't know who he is."

But Taha refused to provide further details. Despite the CIA's best efforts to break her will, she sat in defiant silence and barked only stony yes and no answers, most of which only confirmed what they already knew.

Rita came up with the idea of playing Taha's child against her. While Taha stewed in a foul detention cell, her daughter was staying with a grandmother. Rita tried to tap Taha's maternal instincts. If Taha gave them the information they needed, Rita promised to let her visit her daughter.

The subtle approach went nowhere. Taha glared back and refused to say a word. Her daughter and her mother would have to survive on their own.

So Rita tried a cruder tactic. Taha's husband, the Missile Man, kept two wives in separate homes and Taha was #2. Apparently the two women hated each other. The interrogators told Taha that wife #1 was out living the high life in Baghdad while she rotted in a cell. This time, the pitch worked. Taha exploded in anger. She began talking her head off, desperate to win quick release. Her husband sweated in panic when he got the news. As they were about to free him, he pleaded with the Americans not to let Taha loose as well. "You can keep her," he said.

Taha didn't get out for months.

In Washington, intelligence authorities had begun what they called a "hard scrub" of the prewar intelligence, from human sources to written analyses, from assumptions to tradecraft.

The DIA began reinterviewing the corroborating sources for the germ trucks and other claims "to see if false information was put out there and got into legitimate channels and we were totally duped on it," a senior intelligence official said.

In October, Defense HUMINT officers reinterviewed the Iraq civil engineer who had claimed in 2001 that Saddam hid biological production vehicles in underground bunkers at Karbala and other sites. Now the defector recanted his earlier statements. He knew of "no equipment for the production of biological weapons at this facility," he admitted, and "had no knowledge" of bio-production or stockpiles at other facilities.

They couldn't find Mohammed Harith, the intelligence major from Chalabi's group. But an internal CIA review finally had uncovered the paperwork showing that the DIA had disavowed him as a fabricator nearly a year before the war. It turned out that Defense HUMINT had filed the burn notice in a computer message system separate from the actual intelligence reports. They didn't recall or correct the original reports. They didn't stamp "fabricator" in red letters on the original reports, or reissue them with a warning banner on top as the CIA does. An analyst called up the original Harith reports would see no sign that U.S. intelligence had declared him a fraud.

Then MI6 sent word from London that they no longer believed Red River's hearsay claim about bio-fermentation units on railway cars. They told the CIA he showed deception on a polygraph. It was the final confirmation that all three of Curveball's supposed corroborating sources had lied.

Back in the Perfume Palace, Killip borrowed a copy of the Curveball file and read it cover to cover.

The BND still refused to supply any transcripts of the Curveball debriefings. But the file contained at least ninety-five reports from Defense HUMINT, six from the CIA, plus satellite photos, diagrams, and other material. Killip studied them all. The more he read, the more confused he became.

"I could never put my finger on precisely what he did," he said. "It was difficult to sort out. He knew a lot, an awful lot. But what was he really talking about? I couldn't figure out what he actually did."

He wondered if Curveball stayed in touch with colleagues after he was fired in 1995, people whom the Iraqi could quiz about Djerf al Nadaf. He noticed something else. Curveball had passed countless details to the Germans and yet he always covered his tracks with caveats and disclaimers.

"He did not claim special technical expertise," Killip said. "He was a friend of Fred, the great fermentor guy, or he knew Bert, the pipes and valves guy. He was quite careful not to pin himself down."

Studying the files further, comparing early interviews to those that came later, Killip saw that Curveball adjusted his answers over time to reinforce whatever his questioners asked. His ability to mix verifiable facts in with "water cooler gossip" gave the impression that he knew a great deal, Killip believed. It enhanced his credibility.

Killip began seeing similarities in Curveball's files to material he knew well—reports that he and other U.N. bio-inspectors had filed back in the 1990s during their search for Saddam's biological weapons. The defector, Killip realized, had used his time in Internet cafés to research the old reports. "A lot of this information was on the U.N. Web site," he said.

Mostly, the British expert was startled to read Curveball's specific denials that his trucks produced biowarfare agents. It meant that the intelligence officers who wrote up and analyzed Curveball's account pushed their own conclusions. The analysts, not the defector, decided that Djerf al Nadaf and the other sites were docking stations. The analysts, not Curveball, concluded the trucks brewed anthrax. Like a children's game of telephone, or what the British call Chinese whispers, Curveball's words had changed and grown in the retelling.

Whether the distortions in the intelligence file flowed from poor translations, analytic sloppiness, or willful deception, the outcome was the same. The whole case was a fraud, Killip now was convinced. They were chasing phantom trucks, ghost weapons, tricks of the mind.

Jerry wasn't there yet. He still held out hope. He pulled Kay aside one afternoon in early November and pleaded for help. The only way to get to the bottom of this is to meet the source, he said emotionally.

"We can't take this further unless we talk to Curveball."

So Kay, who had to make a quick trip back to Washington, briefed George Tenet, the CIA chief, and his deputy, John McLaughlin. He harangued them about the CIA's inability to gain access to the single most important human source of the prewar intelligence.

"This thing is unhinged," Kay said. "It's inexcusable. You've got to call the Germans."

Tenet agreed to telephone August Hanning, the BND chief, and demand CIA access to Curveball. "Yes, yes, I'll do it as soon as you leave," Tenet promised.

It is rare for the heads of spy services to talk on the phone. In this case, it was unprecedented. Tenet had never called his German counterpart before.

Tenet's office first sent an "eyes only" note to Berlin to propose the call, and one of Hanning's aides passed it to his boss with a laugh. It didn't take a genius to know what the American wanted. The aide sat by Hanning's side when the call came in on a secure line from Langley. The conversation was polite but brief. Tenet made no threats.

"We need to see Curveball," Tenet said stiffly. "We need your help."

"I understand," Hanning replied. "I'll see what I can do."

Afterward, the BND director turned to his aide. They both knew that Tenet had swallowed his considerable pride to make the call. Spy services rarely, if ever, allow other services to meet their sources. It just isn't done.

"Tenet must be under a tremendous amount of pressure," Hanning said. "If he is personally making the call, it must be vital."

He thought about it for a moment. Directorate One, the operations branch, wasn't going to like this. The case officers would go ballistic. It wouldn't be easy.

"I don't think we can resist this time," he said finally. "I think we have to do it."

Word quickly filtered back to Langley and Baghdad.

The WINPAC geek squad assembled another list of questions. Jerry added his own ideas in the Perfume Palace and then jumped on the CIA plane to Amman and boarded a flight for Munich. And he and a case officer from the CIA's local base drove over to Pullach in high spirits early in the morning because they finally would interview the English-speaking, American-loving Iraqi defector who was driving them all crazy.

Instead, the Directorate One chief settled the score for the CIA's refusal to let him open a German spying station in Baghdad back in September. The Germans led Jerry and his companion to a cramped side office and pointed to two chairs. They were facing a closed circuit TV monitor, not Curveball. They watched the flickering screen for two agonizing hours as BND handlers in another room with a hidden camera chatted with their informant in German using an Arabic translator.

Jerry didn't speak Arabic so his colleague translated the German blaring through the speaker. The BND handlers didn't ask all the questions on Jerry's list and the Iraqi ignored or deflected most of them anyway. Even when he said something odd or intriguing, the Germans blundered on without picking up any cues for follow-up questions. They appeared to be just going through the motions.

Jerry stared at the TV in a mix of disbelief and rage. Everything hung on this interview. It was Curveball's last chance to explain his story. It was probably Jerry's last chance to salvage his faith, to find some solid ground in this swamp, to attain some vantage point for clarity. And it was turning to shit.

When it ended, the BND handlers refused Jerry's pleas to arrange another session for follow-up questions. They wouldn't agree to sit Curveball down again later that day, or the next day, or any time in the foreseeable future. They would let him know if anything changed. Jerry flew back to Baghdad in abysmal spirits.

He seemed inconsolable at the next bio-team staff meeting at the Perfume Palace.

"It was a charade, a complete charade," he complained. "It was a total waste of time. We got shafted by the Germans."

The trip to Germany really knocked Jerry for a loop, Killip thought. The American looked awful. He stared out from bloodshot eyes, sunk in their sockets, and his broad shoulders sagged beneath an invisible weight. His voice sounded strained, and deep stress lined his face. Killip worried about his health.

"Poor old Jerry was having a rough time," Killip said later. "He had lost his last hope. He seemed more and more depressed. He came out a true believer and now he's peeked behind the curtain and nothing is there. He knows the whole house of cards is built on this. And it's falling down right on his head."

Killip wondered if Jerry was going to make it.

The final interviews with Curveball's friends and colleagues proved devastating.

Curveball's best friend in college called him a "congenital liar." His childhood friends described him as a "great liar" and a likable "con artist" who was always looking for the next scam. The sentiments "appeared to be universal," the bio-team noted in a report. "People kept saying what a 'rat' Curveball was."

Some of the defector's former colleagues found it hilarious that the Americans thought he might be responsible for one of Saddam's secret weapons programs.

"The Iraqis were all laughing when we asked about him," said Kay. "They were saying, 'This guy? We wouldn't hire him.'"

Curveball, the team was told, drove a taxi.

CHAPTER 39

Kay posted a large chart on one wall of his office to show staffing levels at the survey group. Aides updated it each day to keep track of who was coming or going from which team. The first post-invasion wave brought in the Iraq experts, Middle East aficionados, and weapons specialists. As they rotated out, the next wave drew recruits with more eclectic interests. Kay, as always, tried to meet them all.

"What's your specialty?" he asked one new arrival.

"Chinese air defense systems," came the reply.

"Ahh, great. Welcome to Baghdad."

And a month or six weeks later, just when the newbie had gotten used to the heat and the danger and the ninety-eight stairs to the toilets, he'd be gone. Kay needed more experts, not fewer. He begged and battled constantly with CIA headquarters to fill the gaps. He couldn't complete his job if he kept losing linguists, analysts, and case officers.

One afternoon a week or so after Jerry's trip to Germany, Kay looked up at the wall and saw that Jerry and the Kid's names were scrawled on the big chart. They were ticketed to leave Baghdad the next morning on the CIA flight to Amman and then change to a commercial flight to Washington. They did not book a return ticket to Baghdad.

"What the hell is this?" Kay shouted at his office assistant. Jerry and the Kid were scheduled to work at least another month at Slayer. The bio-trucks case was still open, still officially unsolved.

Kay was livid. Two of the six people on his bio-team were going home. They were pulling out without his permission and without arranging replacements. He had nobody in the pipeline to replace them. It was a revolt of his team, and he was furious.

He complained to WINPAC officials back at Langley. "A couple members of the bio-team are taking themselves out of theater," he griped over the videoconference call. "We have no replacements on the board for them. You have to send me somebody soon."

After the call, he ordered Jerry and the Kid into his office. He was still steaming, totally pissed, ready to rip a piece of skin off their backsides.

They shuffled in and took seats around Kay's little table. And he lit into them. Maybe they felt frustrated or miserable or missed their families, he declared. Everyone felt that way. But no one just decides to pack up and leave a war zone on his own. They could not just quit. What the hell was going on?

Jerry grabbed the table but his voice choked. He had trouble speaking. Alarmed, Kay observed him closely. Red-rimmed eyes stared back over dark circles. Jerry's face was flushed. He looked feverish, or perhaps he was fighting back tears.

He's losing it, Kay suddenly realized. He's crashing in front of me. He's having a nervous breakdown. Kay softened his harsh tone.

"Tell me what's happening," he said. "What's wrong?"

"I totally believed in the mobile labs," Jerry stammered. "I totally believed in Curveball. We went to war because of that."

He clenched his fists, his knuckles white and bloodless.

"I was wrong," he blurted out. "All wrong. I wrote all those reports. I'm responsible."

The Kid slouched in his seat. He nodded in agreement but said little. He looked as haggard as Jerry.

Kay's anger dissipated. He couldn't help himself. Jerry had been so hard-core, so driven, when he had come to Baghdad. Back then, he knew all the answers. Now his black and white world had collapsed. Mr. True Believer sees what the rest of us see, Kay thought. And it's tearing him apart.

"Calm down," Kay said sympathetically. "Let's talk about it."

Jerry simmered down enough to review the disaster for the next two hours. He recalled how he had first embraced Curveball's claims and knew every detail in his file. And even though Curveball's story changed over time, Jerry never lost his devotion, his unshakable faith. He knew the germ trucks were real. So he wrote incisive analyses that carried Curveball's claims all the way into Congress, the White House, and the U.N. Security Council. And America went to war.

But Curveball had fooled them. His open source stuff could be confirmed. But none of the material that was unique to him held up. The whole case was built on lies. And he, Jerry, fell for them all. Not a single piece of evidence pointed to a mobile weapons program. Even the two trailers were worthless. Jerry admitted that now. He had only seen what he wanted to see. He had lied to himself. His expectations had blinded him, twisted his logic, distorted the evidence in front of him.

Jerry kept talking. He couldn't just let this go. He was consumed by guilt. He was responsible for all this, he repeated. He couldn't live with himself. He had to do something. He had no choice. If Curveball was a fraud, people needed to know.

"I've got to get out of here," he said hotly. "I'm going to come apart. I've got to make this right."

He's right on the edge, Kay reckoned. His plane is scheduled to leave tomorrow. And he may not make it. The sooner this guy gets back home, the better off we are. He could lose it any minute.

"I just can't push this ahead any further from here," Jerry repeated, more determined than ever. "The problem isn't in Baghdad. It's back in Langley. I've got to go back home. And tell them the truth."

Kay slowly nodded assent.

"Good luck," he said. You're going to need it, he thought. The CIA doesn't like people who bring bad news.

"Be sure he gets on the airplane," Kay warned his aide the next morning. "This guy is at the end of his rope."

The CIA welcomed Jerry back as a pariah.

Returning to WINPAC, he confronted his bosses with his thick file of pictures, interviews, and other evidence proving they were dead wrong about Curveball and dead wrong about the two bio-trailers. There were no agnostics in Jerry's world, and like any convert, he argued with a fervor bordering on obsession.

Curveball fabricated his story, Jerry emphasized. There was no doubt anymore. Curveball lied about his access to Taha and he lied about being fired in 1995. He lied about the 1998 accident. And he lied about the wall and the doors at Djerf al Nadaf. Jerry laid out his anguish and concerns just as he had outlined them for Kay.

Jerry proposed a solution. The CIA should own up to its mistake and withdraw support from Curveball. They shouldn't let something so totally wrong just sit there. Since he was partly responsible, Jerry offered to help them confess. He would write a formal reassessment to explain how they had erred so badly on a matter of such critical importance.

But Alan Foley and the other WINPAC managers refused Jerry's offer to play penitent. They feared how a wholesale retreat would look to Tenet and his aides on the seventh floor, as well as to the White House. They had invested their credibility in Curveball too. He had rocketed to such stellar heights—he had starred in the 2002 National Intelligence Estimate, in Powell's U.N. speech, in the president's 2003 State of the Union speech—they would not back down just because Jerry had doubts. Kay's survey group might still find something. Or Curveball might clear it up. And amazingly, Beth and the other geek squad bioanalysts who wouldn't go to Iraq still believed in the defector. Maybe he was a jerk or even a liar. But he was credible. The germ trucks had to be real. No way had they fallen for a hoax.

So the CIA banished Jerry. He found someone else sitting at his desk when he came to work, his belongings stuffed in a box. He was reassigned to an office cubicle reserved for visitors, an isolated booth without a classified computer or secure telephone. He was given no work. People barely acknowledged his presence.

He was a turncoat, a traitor. His supervisors couldn't order him not to write his reassessment but they made clear he was wasting his time: they would not publish or disseminate it. He was "read the riot act" by his office director, who accused him of "making waves" and being "biased," Jerry said later. The Soviets used to exile dissidents to asylums. The CIA was more subtle. They ostracized him and urged him to seek therapy.

Distraught at his internal exile, Jerry sought out an aide on the House Select Committee on Intelligence, who put him in touch with Michael Scheuer, a veteran analyst who had suffered similar CIA banishment for challenging counterterror tactics.

"They wouldn't let him do anything," recalled Scheuer, who later quit the agency. "They just put him in a corner and wouldn't let him work. So he sat there day after day. There was a tremendous amount of pressure on him not to say anything. Just to sit there and shut up. He was like a nonperson."

Later in November, Jerry also complained to the CIA ombudsman for politicization, an in-house arbiter who is supposed to protect analysts from outside interference. It was a waste of time. His inquiry focused only on whether Jerry had been pressured to change his analysis. It did not consider whether Jerry was punished because he wanted to expose CIA mistakes. The ombudsman ruled that no impropriety had occurred.

Following procedures, he referred Jerry's complaint to Jamie Miscik, who headed the Directorate of Intelligence, which ran WINPAC. She met Jerry and told him that a reassessment of the Curveball case was not needed.

"They basically said to him, 'Okay, I hear you but I reject your position,'" said an official who later investigated the case. "At that point he was expected to shut up and stop protesting. And he didn't. Jerry wouldn't shut up. I think that speaks very highly of him. But it made management pretty angry."

So WINPAC managers pushed Jerry out of the CIA. He wasn't fired, but they made clear the weapons center was "no longer an appropriate place for me to work," he told the investigator.

"I think it was petty," the investigator said. "I think it was pretty small-minded, especially in an organization that relies so completely on the honesty and integrity of its officers. It was the tried-and-true, passively aggressive cowardly way of dealing with someone you want to get rid of in government. You make them want to leave and you encourage them to look elsewhere. If you look at the paper trail, you won't find anything written saying he was fired from WINPAC. He just got bad reviews for not being a team player. Those are code words. That way you can say you weren't fired and they can say you left on your own."

Kay was outraged when he heard the news. Jerry dared to challenge authority so Tenet's CIA all but put him in front of a firing squad. "Jerry went back to bring truth to power. Instead he got taken out and shot."

Kay would soon discover firsthand just how unforgiving the CIA could be.

CHAPTER 40

Kay's battle with headquarters over staffing at the Perfume Palace intensified as November 2003 drew to a close.

His teams were being whittled away. His executive assistant, a fluent Arabic speaker, was transferred to work on counterinsurgency. The head of the nuclear team decamped for home. A brilliant Arabic-speaking case officer got yanked to Morocco. Kay spent part of every day pleading with people to stay. He had only two CIA clandestine operatives left who spoke Arabic and they were being reassigned.

New recruits were not lining up to replace them. It was clear inside the CIA that no one would be crowned with glory for finding Saddam's weapons of mass destruction if none actually existed. Few people saw career advantages in volunteering to investigate what increasingly appeared to be an intelligence calamity. Plus it was hard to argue that "a history project in the middle of a war," as a DIA officer derisively called the fruitless search for WMD, should take precedence over stopping the growing carnage in Iraq.

Kay appealed to McLaughlin for help but got nowhere. The CIA was under tremendous pressure to assist the military. Americans were getting killed. In late November, the CIA agreed to a request from General John Abizaid, commander of U.S. forces in the Middle East, to redirect Iraq Survey Group resources to include counterinsurgency. The search for the truth about Saddam's WMD was no longer the CIA's priority mission. Tenet urged Kay not to give up. "If you leave now, it will look like the wheels are coming off completely," the CIA chief told him.

Kay was demoralized. He hadn't signed up to fight a war or to cover up CIA incompetence.

Several days later, Kay summoned Killip and a few other top

deputies to his office at the Perfume Palace and confessed his unhappiness with Washington. He also admitted for the first time that the evidence on Saddam's WMD now appeared overwhelming. They had tested every hypothesis in the book. It was time to reach some conclusions, he said.

He was persuaded, Kay said slowly, that Saddam's regime really did abandon its chemical, biological, and nuclear programs after the 1991 war—and never built any germ trucks at all. Curveball wasn't the only problem. The whole thing stank. It seemed inconceivable. He always assumed that some of the intelligence was wrong. It never occurred to him that all of it was wrong.

Kay looked at them expectantly. He was challenging core beliefs. He waited for an argument, or at least a debate. But no one opposed him.

"No one disagreed," Killip recalled. "We were all reaching the same conclusions. It was not a failure. We didn't find the WMD because there were none."

British army Brigadier John Deverell, who was General Dayton's assistant, thought Kay looked weary and immensely troubled. Saddam's weapons had been an article of faith for Kay. He had believed in them passionately. He wasn't as emotionally agitated as Jerry. That wasn't his style. But still, to Deverell's eyes, Kay now looked "like a man who had suddenly found there was no God."

Back in Washington, the CIA leadership still denied any mistakes. At the end of November, Stuart A. Cohen, vice chairman of the National Intelligence Council, staunchly defended the prewar National Intelligence Estimate, the authoritative assessment that formed the foundation for Powell's U.N. speech. So far, the evidence collected in Iraq appeared to disprove almost every key judgment in the October 2002 estimate. But in an op-ed printed in the *Washington Post* and a longer piece posted on the CIA Web site, Cohen argued that it was unfair to criticize the judgments just because they were wrong.

"I remain convinced that no reasonable person could have . . . reached any conclusions or alternative views that were profoundly different from those that we reached," wrote Cohen, who had thirty years' experience at the CIA.

Cohen called it a "myth" that major judgments were "based on single sources" even though the estimate relied almost entirely on Curveball for its verdict on biological weapons. Another myth, he argued, was that U.S. intelligence "relied too much" on U.N. inspectors. Actually, the U.N. findings had proved far more reliable than the CIA estimates. In any case, Cohen called for patience before assuming the prewar intelligence was wrong. "David Kay and the Iraq Survey Group must be allowed to complete their work," he urged.

Kay was stunned to see the CIA still refused to acknowledge its blunders. Tenet and his aides were in denial, he thought. The system was broken. They were still holding on to the lies.

So Kay, like Jerry, decided he needed to shake their cages. This wasn't about being noble. His own integrity was at stake. He had stood in that hangar in Qatar at his first all-hands meeting of the Iraq Survey Group and promised he would speak the truth, and he meant it.

Kay still hoped to come back to Baghdad to answer the remaining questions about the WMD when he boarded the CIA plane to Amman on December 6. He told only a few aides at the Perfume Palace that he was departing. He left most of his clothes in his trailer. If he got more resources, if he got Tenet and McLaughlin to live up to their promises, he'd be back.

But his constant carping preceded him at CIA headquarters. He was treated upon arrival as if he carried a loathsome disease.

On previous visits, Tenet's special advisor for strategy for Iraqi weapons of mass destruction programs was assigned a parking place in the VIP lot in front of the old headquarters building, or a prime spot in the executive garage. Now the guard directed him to the general CIA parking lot, a brutal hike away from the far side of nowhere on a frigid winter morning. It felt like Valley Forge out there.

America's top weapons hunter no longer merited a seventh-floor office down the hall from Tenet and his covey of close aides. Kay now was consigned two floors down to a tiny, windowless office without a secure phone or classified computer. It lay at the end of a distant, deserted corridor undergoing construction. All the nearby offices stood empty, the halls dusty and silent.

So this is what Siberia looks like, Kay laughed. He was more amused than hurt by the bureaucratic humiliation. The CIA was like a religious cult, and management considered him a heretic, an outcast in the wilderness. At least he didn't have to hike ninety-eight stairs to take a leak.

To beat the traffic, he drove in early each morning and stopped by McLaughlin's suite first thing. "I'm in if John wants to talk to me," he told aides in the outer office.

And other than a few brief discussions, nothing happened.

For four weeks, no one asked him to prepare an update or write a final report. No one invited him to sit in on Tenet's "prayer meetings" about Iraq join the videoconferences with the Perfume Palace or other high-level confabs. No one routed papers for him to see or sign. He couldn't read classified cable traffic. No one else worked near his office so it felt a bit eerie. He read the newspapers. He heard of meetings after the fact or, more usually, heard nothing at all.

Over the years, Tenet had sent a clear message to the troops: you're with us or you're against us. Now Kay felt people give him wide berth. When he went to lunch or wandered the halls, people literally avoided him or grew wary as he approached. "I was contaminated, like Typhoid Mary," he said. "It was, 'Don't get too close. He might tell you something.'"

Kay started coming in late and leaving early. Some days he didn't come in at all. And no one said a word. So he gave formal notice that he planned to quit. Tenet quickly offered Kay's job to Charlie Duelfer, a State Department officer who served as the chief deputy of U.N. inspectors for most of the 1990s. Kay bumped into Duelfer walking out of the CIA cafeteria just after he had accepted the job. They were old friends.

"What do you think?" Duelfer asked, standing in the hall.

"I think you're crazy," Kay said simply.

And that was it for the formal handover of the Iraq Survey Group. No briefings, no papers, nothing.

Stanley Moskowitz, one of Tenet's top deputies, asked Kay to hold off on announcing his resignation until after President Bush's 2004 State of the Union address on January 20. The White House didn't want news of Kay's departure to distract from the president's speech. "No problem," Kay replied. "I understand."

He watched the speech on TV and midway through, he was startled to hear Bush hail the "Kay Report" for discovering "dozens of weapons of mass destruction-related program activities." Bush added, "Had we failed to act, the dictator's weapons of mass destruction programs would continue to this day."

Laura Bush, the president's wife, led the standing ovation from the upper gallery. Ahmed Chalabi, dressed in a bulky charcoal gray suit, loomed just behind her in the First Lady's Box, grinning and clapping loudly.

Kay called Moskowitz back the next day. Didn't Bush's people know he was resigning? Didn't they know he had concluded that Saddam abandoned all WMD programs years ago? Didn't they understand that "weapons of mass destruction-related program activities," which Kay had first coined in his October report, meant that he found no weapons or weapons programs? The phrase was close to meaningless.

"Ahhh, yeah," came the response, "they knew."

So Kay quit. He stopped in to say goodbye to Tenet and McLaughlin before he left the building. Neither one tried to persuade him to stay. Nor did they accept his conclusions. "I don't care what you or anyone else says," Tenet insisted. "I know they had WMD."

Kay was astonished. My God, he thought, he's still so invested in this he won't admit a mistake.

The CIA leaders made only one parting request: don't talk to the press. They would handle it now. He could stay on the agency payroll as a consultant and senior advisor. Kay was noncommittal. He suspected they were trying to buy his silence.

He wasn't surprised. They don't want to be laughed at, he thought. That's their main concern now. They want to keep this quiet.

The phone was ringing when Kay got home that night.

A Reuters reporter was on the line. Kay couldn't help himself. He didn't say much but it was enough. "I don't think they existed," Kay said, when asked about the WMD. "What everyone was talking about is stockpiles produced after the Gulf War, and I don't think there was large-scale production in the nineties."

The news rocketed onto the wires. Other reporters reached him for longer interviews. Kay's devastating inside view of the intelligence fiasco was splashed on front pages and led network news shows. Kay was surprised at the reaction. He assumed Americans already knew the scope of the disaster.

Kay's disclosures rattled the Bush administration and its supporters. The presidential election campaign was in full swing. John Warner, the Republican chairman of the Senate Armed Services Committee, arguably the most powerful panel in Congress, telephoned Kay and all but demanded he appear before the committee in two days' time. Warner, a white-haired Virginian in his seventies, had served more than a quarter century in the Senate. Now he looked like one of its marble busts: a jutting jaw, craggy nose, and eyes cranked on perpetual high-beam. He was determined to protect the president.

Kay agreed to testify but told Warner he wouldn't submit a written statement in advance, the usual practice. He didn't have the time. He jotted some notes on a few white index cards as he usually did before a speech. But he knew what he wanted to say. He barely glanced at his cards when he appeared before the full committee in the Dirksen Senate Office Building on the morning of January 28, 2004.

"Let me begin by saying we were almost all wrong," Kay began. He needed to get that off his chest first. If he felt relieved, it didn't show on his face. But it was a stunning admission, a guaranteed headline across the country. No one from the Bush administration, no one from the U.S. intelligence community, had previously conceded any errors in Iraq. Kay took a breath and pushed on, now indicting himself as part of the problem.

"And I certainly include myself here . . . Prior to the war, my view was that the best evidence that I had seen was that Iraq indeed had weapons of mass destruction."

He sat alone at the polished witness table under harsh, bright TV lights. Uncowed by authority, comfortable in the spotlight, he showed no sign of discomfort. Reporters, staff aides, and members of the public filled every seat and lined the back wall in the huge hearing room. Except for the clicking cameras, it was conspicuously silent. Kay continued with his mea culpa.

"It turns out we were all wrong, probably, in my judgment," he emphasized. "And that is most disturbing."

Kay cut to his conclusions. The survey group found no stockpiles of poison gases or deadly germs. They found no trucks or factories that could produce them. Iraq had no nuclear infrastructure. Nor did any evidence indicate that Saddam had assisted Al Qaeda, as the White House had warned.

Questions remained but it was "important to acknowledge failure," Kay urged. The practice was almost unknown in Washington.

Kay cited the two trailers he once had endorsed as an example. The "consensus opinion" among experts was the two looted trailers were "not for production of biological agents," he said. It was a direct shot at the White House.

A week earlier, Vice President Cheney had told NPR's *Morning Edition* that he was "quite confident" that Saddam built mobile weapons labs and the two trailers "were in fact part of that program." Cheney called the trailers "conclusive evidence" of WMD.

Kay ticked off the underlying problems for the oversight committee. The CIA had no real Iraqi spies and had grown "almost addicted" to using U.N. inspectors in the 1990s. Analysts had become prisoners of their inherited assumptions, victims of a "group think" mentality that produced consensus but not truth.

The disaster should surprise no one, Kay told the panel. He cited a long, tortured history of intelligence mistakes. He started with the 1962 Cuban Missile Crisis, when CIA officials assured President John F. Kennedy he could attack Cuba because no Soviet nuclear warheads were stored there. Luckily, Kennedy ignored their advice.

"We got it wrong in World War II," Kay added. American military intelligence had indicated that heavy bombing was "destroying the German will to fight and that German war production was falling. As it turned out, afterwards, the German will to fight increased under the bombing, and production went up until the last two months of the war."

Then there was, "well, skip Vietnam," but Kay noted a few errors there too. He threw in the CIA's failure to foresee the collapse of the Soviet Union and its communist empire despite forty-plus years of effort focused precisely on that goal. "There's a long record here of being wrong," he explained helpfully.

Senator Pat Roberts nodded his shiny bald head in agreement. Kay had testified for two hours to the intelligence committee, which Roberts chaired, behind closed doors earlier that morning. The garrulous Kansas Republican now blamed the CIA for misleading the country.

"We are constantly having these 'Oh my God' hearings on the intelligence committee," Roberts announced in his flat Topeka twang. "As in, 'Oh my God, how did this happen?'"

And he too cited a string of intelligence failures, starting with the failure to foresee India's underground nuclear tests in May 1998 even though a new government in New Delhi had publicly vowed to do just that. Election rallies during the campaign featured mock-ups of an atom bomb garlanded with flowers. The CIA "didn't have a clue," Tenet admitted later.

Roberts recalled the CIA's blunder in sending warplanes to bomb the Chinese embassy in Belgrade during the Yugoslav war in 1999. CIA analysts hadn't updated their database of addresses, or even checked the Belgrade phone book. They didn't realize that Beijing had moved its embassy three years earlier.

Roberts next cited the two zealots who packed explosives into a rubber dinghy in the Yemen port of Aden in October 2000. They crossed the harbor in broad daylight and rammed the USS *Cole,* killing seventeen sailors and nearly sinking a $1 billion guided-missile destroyer. The same pair previously had targeted another American warship, USS *The Sullivans,* in the same port. That attack failed only because waves swamped their little boat.

"And it goes on and on and on—same kind of thing," Roberts mused aloud.

Kay leaned forward, eager to assist, eager to educate. When Senator Edward Kennedy, the Democrat from Massachusetts, asked pointedly if the evidence found in Iraq "justified us going into war," Kay broke into a wide smile.

"Senator, that's probably," he began, but then he chuckled into the microphone before he finally finished, "far more in your realm." Kay admitted he was but a "naïf in the world of politics," and then he let loose another chortle that echoed across the quiet room.

Warner wasn't amused. He hunched his shoulders and glowered down from the raised dais like a bird of prey. He didn't like Kay's glib manner or his definitive verdict about Saddam's lack of WMD. "It is far too early to reach any final judgments or conclusions," he snorted in disapproval.

Kay's face colored but he did not retreat. He leaned forward into the microphone.

"I believe that the effort that has been directed to this point has been sufficiently intense that it is highly unlikely that there were large stockpiles of deployed militarized chemical and biological weapons there," he replied firmly.

"Right," Warner retorted. "But the operative word in your assumption is 'large.' Several small caches could constitute an imminent threat. Am I not correct in that?"

Kay held his ground. They found no stockpiles large or small, he said, nothing that indicated any likely threat. He could not dismiss the "theoretical possibility" that new evidence might turn up someday, somewhere, but made clear he didn't expect it. He couldn't resist throwing in a last jab at the CIA, noting "there are more people in this room" than agency case officers who speak Arabic.

Warner adjourned the hearing and stormed off.

That afternoon, Scott McClellan, the White House spokesman,

deflected all questions about Kay's testimony. "The situation in Iraq was a gathering threat," he insisted. "And the decision that the president made was the right decision then. And what we have learned since only reconfirms that it was the right decision."

Tenet's aides, hiding as usual behind anonymity, savaged Kay in seething calls to reporters. They smeared him as a traitor to the agency, if not the nation. "He's hated here," one senior CIA official growled. "He is shooting off his mouth about things he doesn't understand." Another seventh-floor official sneeringly compared Kay to Saddam, saying neither could be trusted. "He promised he'd keep his mouth shut."

Kay had gone from gun-toting Ramrod to cheerful Buford S. Vincent to despicable dictator. His crime: he had humiliated the CIA. And he hadn't even mentioned Curveball in public.

CHAPTER 41

Tenet dropped the first public hint of the debacle.

Early on February 5, 2004, exactly a year after Powell's disastrous U.N. speech, a CIA convoy of black SUVs pulled up to the graceful hilltop campus of Georgetown University. The ivy-lined chapels and grand study halls have funneled diplomats, bureaucrats, and spies into government since the early days of the republic. Tenet graduated from Georgetown in 1976 and he remained a fervent fan of the Hoyas, the school basketball team. They chose a bulldog, fangs bared, as mascot, and the snarling, stubborn image fit America's top spy perfectly that icy winter morning.

Tenet was livid about Kay's "we were all wrong" testimony and his brutal interviews in the press. Problems in intelligence were best handled behind closed doors. Kay was out of control.

Except for hearings in Congress, CIA chiefs rarely appear in public. But after stewing for several days, Tenet decided to fight back. He'd give a speech. It was a rush job. His staff only lined up the Georgetown hall the day before he was to speak and only finished writing the draft at 10 p.m. that night. They didn't vet the speech with White House staff; Tenet would speak for himself. It would come from the gut.

By 9 a.m., hundreds of students and faculty began filling the long wooden rows. Tenet made sure the setting was friendly. He packed the front pews with family members and a sizable entourage of top aides and old friends. After a brief introduction, Tenet swept across the stage in a dark suit. He donned his reading glasses and arranged his speech on the lectern. He began with a promise to speak "honestly and directly."

Then he launched into an impassioned defense of the CIA's record on Iraq. He cited Kay by name four separate times, but he didn't openly attack his former special advisor. Kay was far too popular after his star performance on Capitol Hill.

Tenet quickly came to the point.

"The question being asked about Iraq in the starkest of terms is: were we right or were we wrong?" He let the query hang in the air for a moment. Kay already had answered the question. Now it was Tenet's turn. Reporters, forced to sit in the rear, strained to hear.

But the CIA chief waffled in his reply, outlining a slippery grade curve that probably shocked the Georgetown deans.

"In the intelligence business, you are almost never completely wrong or completely right," he advised. "That applies in full to the question of Saddam's weapons of mass destruction. . . . When the facts of Iraq are all in, we will never be completely right or completely wrong."

Tenet was wrong. Or more to the point, the CIA had completely misjudged Saddam's chemical, biological, and nuclear programs. Curveball was the worst case but it was hardly alone. The CIA had painted a damning picture of Iraq that came in only two colors, black and blacker. But Tenet used more muted hues on this morning. Rather than admit any errors, he soft-pedaled his answers, spinning them in the best possible light.

U.S. intelligence "may have overestimated" Iraq's progress in developing nuclear weapons, he admitted, a coy way of saying that the Iraq Survey Group and other experts had debunked the aluminum tubes, the supposed hunt for uranium in Africa, meetings of Saddam's scientists, and all the other CIA claims. There was no nuclear program. Saddam had abandoned it in 1991.

Tenet held out hope that Charlie Duelfer, Kay's replacement, still might discover some of the hundreds of tons of chemical weapons agents that Iraq supposedly had produced the year before the invasion. "However we have not yet found the weapons we expected," he conceded. In fact, they had found no sign of poison gas production or planning after 1991.

Tenet acknowledged the failure to find any of the biological weapons that the CIA had so confidently predicted. Nothing supported the prewar warnings that "all key aspects" of Saddam's biowarfare program were active, larger, and more advanced than before the Gulf War. Kay's team had found no evidence of production after 1991, nor any plans to resume the program.

Tenet spun it his way. "My provisional bottom line today: Iraq intended to develop biological weapons," he said. "But we do not know if production took place. And just as clearly, we have not yet found biological weapons."

He admitted doubt for the first time in public about the two looted trailers. "We initially concluded that they resembled trailers described by a human source," meaning Curveball, for "mobile biologic warfare agent production," he said. "There is no consensus within our community today over whether the trailers were for that use or if they were used for the production of hydrogen."

Kay more accurately had told the Senate committee that the "consensus opinion" was the trailers did not produce biological agents.

Tenet next turned his attention to Curveball, although not by name.

"I must tell you that we are finding discrepancies in some claims made by human sources about mobile biological weapons production before the war," he said. "Because we lacked direct access to the most important sources on this question, we have not as yet been able to resolve the differences."

But that finally was about to happen.

It had taken the Germans four months to arrange the interview after Tenet's plea to Hanning in November.

The BND case officers had put up a pitched battle. The DIA reported that several threatened to quit if they were forced to give up their source. Schumann, the chief handler, trotted out all the old arguments. He handled Curveball, not the CIA. The BND had exhausted the defector's information long ago. The Iraqi was a legal resident now and had rights under German law. They couldn't order him to meet Americans. He lived on his own and no one should disturb him. Let the CIA sort out its own problems.

While that fight dragged on, the BND allowed several CIA officers operating from the agency sub-station in Munich to view previous BND videotapes of Curveball. As a temporary compromise, it was a disaster. The team emerged from a February viewing as dissatisfied and frustrated as Jerry had been.

Finally, Schumann was given an ultimatum. Hanning has made his decision: now do it. And Curveball didn't resist. His wife joined him from Baghdad around that time, so perhaps that was a factor. Maybe a cash bonus for his time, his usual demand, convinced him to change his mind. What's clear is he agreed to a face-to-face meeting in the middle of March. The BND still didn't tell him the other face would come from the CIA.

Killip, still at the Perfume Palace, got word in early March that the CIA needed detailed pictures of Djerf al Nadaf for the interview. He grabbed his digital video camera and jumped in a small CIA convoy of armored vehicles. They drove south toward Tuwaitha and over the creaky Diyala River bridge. The area had become a stronghold for Shiite militants. Someone shot out a headlight as they drove along, but no one was injured. They heard isolated shooting when they finally drove in the gate and pulled it closed.

A frightened caretaker greeted them but they saw no other sign of life. Looters had ransacked the compound since the previous summer, stealing office equipment, bags of corn, roofing panels, anything that wasn't bolted down. Several vehicles lay wrecked and abandoned in the courtyard. The place looked desolate.

Killip flipped on his camera and a microphone so he could record a commentary as he filmed. First he panned the courtyard and various side buildings and sheds. He turned and slowly approached the main warehouse with the two-story bay. He zoomed in on the uninterrupted sheet metal siding there and the solid wall where the corner door supposedly hinged.

Inside, he shot the shallow maintenance bays and the meter-high barrier that ran along the walls. Finally, he focused on the six-foot-high wall that hugged three sides of the warehouse and blocked trucks from coming or going as Curveball had claimed.

Killip reviewed the case in his mind as he shot the twenty-minute film. He had concluded long ago that the Iraqi's lies were minor compared to those of the intelligence officers who exaggerated his information. He even felt a grudging respect for the defector's daring and nerve.

"I quite liked Curveball," he said later. "Because he showed real talent and imagination in the way he stretched the truth. He was very charming, very resourceful. There was a spot of James Bond about him. But when I shot the video, I thought, 'You bastard. We got you now.' Because he overreached himself at Djerf al Nadaf."

Killip handed the digital film memory card and a compact disc with his commentary to the lead CIA officer that afternoon. It was Killip's last hurrah. He had fought for eight months to convince the CIA to abandon its bogus claims that the two looted trailers could produce biological agents. But Tenet refused to back down. So Killip gave up. The most experienced biowarfare expert in Iraq quit the survey group and flew home several days after shooting the video.

Back at Langley, Drumheller's European Division was allowed to take charge of the long-awaited Curveball interrogation. The geek squad bioanalysts had done enough damage. Everyone understood that the agency needed to send an experienced debriefer who knew how to exploit the psychology of defectors, not another WINPAC analyst who fretted about fermentation temperatures.

Drumheller chose Chris, a deputy division chief in operations and one of the agency's most talented operatives, for the job. Chris had served in Germany, spoke fluent German, and knew all the BND handlers and senior analysts in the case. His youthful looks belied twenty years at the CIA, most of it overseas in the clandestine service. He wasn't trained as a biologist but had studied enough science to hold his own. More important, he excelled at cajoling reluctant sources to spill their guts.

Chris caught a flight to Munich in mid-March 2004, a year after the invasion. At the appointed hour, he waited in a nondescript office building on a German military base near the walled BND headquarters in Pullach. The BND drove Curveball in through a back entrance, hidden in a dense copse of woods.

A hidden video camera and recorder silently captured the scene. Curveball looked relaxed, far from the emotional wreck or wildly irrational figure Chris had feared. He had put on weight in recent years and looked almost pudgy. They met across a table in a bug-proofed conference room for about six hours that first day, stopping when Curveball visibly tired.

As usual, the BND demanded that the CIA case officer conduct the interview in German and pretend to be German. The defector was extremely hostile to Americans, they warned, and they would not betray his trust. Chris knew it wasn't true but he wasn't going to argue.

So he and the Iraqi started off speaking in German. It was a struggle. Despite five years in Germany, despite countless lessons, Curveball still stumbled and groped for the right words, laboring to communicate.

Finally, after several hours of mental exertion, the Iraqi asked Chris politely if perhaps he spoke English. It came out sounding quite formal, like he was offering Chris a cup of tea.

"Yes, I speak English," the American admitted.

"Why don't we speak English," Curveball suggested. "I speak English a lot better than German."

So they tried that for a few minutes. And the Iraqi heard something that made him suspicious.

"You're not German," he suddenly said. "Are you American?"

Chris conceded that he was. Curveball simply laughed, Chris told Drumheller that night over a secure phone line. The Iraqi wasn't at all upset.

Nor, he added, did Curveball appear to harbor anti-American sentiment. His mother was right. He seemed to love Americans. He showed no animosity at all. He acted as if he had been waiting for the CIA to finally show up.

Chris quickly established Curveball's purpose in telling his story back at Zirndorf more than four years earlier. The Iraqi had no political motives or opposition agenda and wasn't trying to spark a war or topple Saddam. From the beginning, Curveball said, he only tried to get himself and his family out of Iraq. All he ever wanted was political asylum in Germany. And money. And a Mercedes.

A BND officer, a straight-backed older man with a thick mustache, nodded in agreement. It was Schumann.

He had insisted on joining the CIA debriefing and tried directing the questions at first. When Chris insisted on running his own show, Schumann kept interrupting and interpreting and disrupting the flow with his own prompts and answers. Chris asked him to stop several times and then blew his top. He demanded Schumann leave them alone.

Schumann refused to abandon his source. "Why is your debriefing better than ours?" he demanded. "We've already asked all these questions."

So Chris complained to Langley and someone there called the BND brass again and threatened dire consequences if the Germans didn't allow the CIA guy to do his damned job and bring this to completion. Whatever they said, it worked. Schumann grudgingly withdrew to watch the closed-circuit TV from another room, just as they had forced Jerry and other American teams to watch from afar, until the temperamental case officer stormed out in a fit of pique.

Chris met Curveball four or five times in all, stretching into a second week. The Iraqi never showed up drunk or visibly hungover.

Chris used the downtime between sessions to study the thick file and to plan his arguments. He phoned Drumheller back in Virginia each day to brief him on the highlights, and then tapped out a nightly classified report on his computer.

An MI6 officer initially joined the debriefing. But he soon withdrew. A British official later described his role as "firing for effect," suggesting he played bad cop to Chris's good cop in a carefully staged squeeze play to get the Iraqi to cooperate.

That left only the good cop, the friendly CIA officer, with the defector who held the key to understanding how America went to war in Iraq.

Chris decided to go slowly. They faced each other across the conference table and just talked. It was not unlike Schumann's first meeting with the Iraqi back in early 2000 when Curveball was just an eager refugee. Chris kept it light, easy, smooth. He wanted to get to know the Iraqi. He wanted Curveball to trust him. They could disagree later.

When the time felt right, Chris asked Curveball to walk him through his story. "Let's start at the beginning," he said pleasantly.

So they went through his university days, his work at the Chemical Engineering and Design Center, his assignment at Djerf al Nadaf, his instructions from Taha, his escape to Germany, and all the rest. Chris listened carefully, writing notes along the way.

But as he narrowed his questions, he read earlier answers back to the defector, holding them up for closer inspection like a prosecuting attorney building a case for a jury. He asked Curveball several times if he could explain why the records in Baghdad showed he was fired in 1995.

Curveball was unfazed.

"The records are wrong," he explained patiently. Errors and lies filled all government files in Iraq. Everyone knew that.

He deflected questions about his travels to Germany and his disappearances after he arrived. But he talked more openly than Chris expected, appearing calm and composed and utterly unperturbed, except his story still didn't add up.

"This doesn't sound good," Chris warned Drumheller after the second meeting.

Curveball refused to discuss anything about his family. Each time the subject arose, he clammed up tightly or started to get edgy. Chris backed off gently to avoid provoking him. He was afraid the Iraqi would get up and stomp out of the room for good. As a result, he didn't ask Curveball if Chalabi's group sent or coached him, or ask anything about his older brother.

CIA officials already were convinced the Chalabi connection was coincidence. No evidence showed Curveball operated under direction of the Iraqi National Congress or any other outside group. Perhaps it was better not to ask. The CIA would feel doubly burned if Chalabi, whom they loathed, had tricked them again so neatly. So Chris didn't push the issue.

Finally, Chris confronted Curveball with recent photos of Djerf al Nadaf and the other docking stations in Iraq. He kept returning to the wall around the warehouse where Curveball said he had worked. Chris asked how the trucks got through the wall. He didn't accuse Curveball of lying. He wasn't judgmental. He just pointed out the problem.

"This doesn't make sense," he said in apparent confusion. "Show me what I'm missing here."

Curveball obliged. The wall might be new, he suggested. The Iraqis probably built it after he left. Or the pictures showed another wall at another warehouse. They all looked the same.

"I don't know," he said with a shrug. "Your photo must be wrong."

So Chris reached down into his briefcase and pulled out satellite imagery of Djerf al Nadaf from early 1997, and other pictures taken later at the site. They showed when the perimeter wall first appeared and how it barred large trucks from approaching the warehouse.

Curveball paused to ponder that. He stared at the photos and then looked up smugly.

"The pictures are a trick," he countered triumphantly. The CIA must have doctored them. Anyone could do that on a computer.

As Chris bore in, the defector showed no sign of shame, no indication of remorse. He recanted nothing, retracted not a word. It wasn't his fault if others exaggerated or twisted his account, he said. He would not admit deceit. Nor, however, did he appear bothered by all the fuss and questions over his case.

"Your information is different from mine," he said indifferently. "I have said everything I'm going to say."

He folded his arms and stopped talking.

Chris had heard enough anyway.

"This guy is lying," he confirmed to Drumheller that night. "I've got him on twenty different things. He's lying about a bunch of stuff."

Drumheller congratulated him on a job well done. "You might as well wrap it up and come home," he instructed. Before returning home on April 1, Chris compiled a thirty-page report that focused on Curveball's falsehoods. It read like a guilty verdict. The facts were in. The CIA had been completely wrong.

It took nearly two months to identify and double-check every U.S. intelligence report, cable, and technical file that had used Curveball's misinformation. It involved hundreds of documents, thousands of pages.

The CIA issued the recall notice to its stations and bases around the world on May 26, 2004, fourteen months after the war began. The blandly worded assessment was tagged "Key Mobile BW Source Deemed Unreliable."

Investigations "since the war in Iraq and debriefings of the key source indicate he lied about his access to a mobile BW production project," it read. He "was unable/unwilling to resolve these discrepancies; our assessment, therefore, is that [Curveball] appears to be fabricating in this stream of reporting."

Two weeks later, the CIA and DIA formally notified the intelligence oversight committees in Congress that Curveball was a fraud. Tenet personally telephoned Powell over at the State Department to pass the news.

"He was in utter disbelief," recalled Lawrence Wilkerson, Powell's chief aide. "Here we were being told that the last vestige of credibility was sitting on air, on swampland. It was absolutely false."

Powell was steaming when he hung up the phone. The case, he said later, had "totally blown up in our faces."

CHAPTER 42

Kay had just staggered in his front door after a jog along a nearby golf course when the phone rang. It was the morning after his "we were all wrong" appearance before the Senate committee in January 2004.

The White House operator asked him to please hold.

Condoleezza Rice came on the line. He assumed she was calling to complain about his testimony, which was all over the news. But she didn't. Nor did she mention the editorials and pundits who hailed his honesty and audacity. "Give David Kay credit for courage," the *Washington Post*'s lead editorial began.

"The president would like to have lunch with you," she said briskly.

"Fine," he said, a little surprised. "When?"

"Today."

"Yessssss. What time today?"

"Can you be down here at 12:30?"

Kay looked at his watch and sucked in his breath. It was just after 10:30. He still wore grungy sweats. He hadn't shaved.

"If I hang up right now, I'll make it," he told her. He ran upstairs to wash and get dressed.

He and Anita lived in a gated community in Leesburg, about thirty-five miles northwest of Washington. They moved in when the area had horse farms and country lanes. But Leesburg had exploded into one of Virginia's fastest growing communities. Now it was an exurban morass of jammed highways, crowded strip malls, and endless housing developments.

Kay knew from hard experience that the drive to Washington could easily take ninety minutes. He raced down the highway, weaving from lane to lane in his silver-gray Cadillac CTS. He gripped the wheel so tightly it hurt. One thought alone filled his mind: I hope I don't get arrested. He made it downtown in fifty minutes flat.

Parking in a garage, he speed-walked four blocks to the White House, and guards whisked him inside. Kay checked his watch: five minutes early. Not bad, he thought, pleased with himself.

A secretary told him the president was running late. Would he mind waiting? She showed him into the Roosevelt Room, lined with landscapes from the Old West, a collection of cowboy bronzes by Frederic Remington, and tattered pennants and flags from nearly every American military campaign. But then aides from the communications office swept in for a 12:30 meeting to discuss the day's "message." They took seats around the treaty table, and fussed with their files and clipboards. Their chatter ebbed to an awkward silence.

Kay felt their eyes on him. He wondered if their agenda included cleaning up the mess he caused in the Senate. Maybe they planned to kneecap him to reporters the way CIA aides already had. He feigned an intense interest in the pictures and flags.

Rice finally rescued him, appearing suddenly at his side.

"The president is ready," she said simply. She led him into the Oval Office.

Bush rose from his desk, held out his hand, and greeted his guest. So did Vice President Cheney, and Bush's chief of staff, Andrew Card. Bush pushed open a side door and led them all into a small anteroom that he used as a private dining room. Stewards had neatly set one end of a rectangular table with service for five.

The president sat at the head of the table. He motioned Kay to sit to his right. Rice quickly took the chair beside Kay. The vice president sat directly across from Kay. Card grabbed the chair next to Cheney. Simple hand-printed menus lay on the plates, and a steward in a white jacket hovered. The president ordered first, choosing chicken salad and iced tea.

"I'll have whatever he's having," Kay said without looking at the menu. He didn't plan to eat much anyway. He wasn't nervous. He just figured he was there to answer questions, not eat.

Bush took the time to ask where Kay came from in Texas.

"I was born in Houston but my family is from Winona, a little flyspeck town north of Tyler in Smith County. You've never heard of it," Kay assured him.

"But I know Winona," Bush said excitedly. "It's got the one church."

And he described the little Baptist church and even the graveyard where Kay's father and grandparents were buried. And Kay realized that when Bush ran for governor, he probably visited every whistlestop and crossroads in Texas, so of course he knew Winona. (Bush didn't mention it, but he probably also remembered the angry families who wrote endless letters, led loud protests, and made national news in their effort to shut a local hazardous waste facility outside Winona when he was governor.) Kay was delighted.

Bush quickly turned to the intelligence on Iraq. He peppered Kay with questions, pushing him for details. Why did the CIA make so many errors? What was Saddam really up to? What happened inside his entourage? Why did Iraqi officials jerk U.N. inspectors around for so long? Why didn't Saddam simply say, "Come in, look all you want, there are no weapons?" Why was there so much ambiguity, so much confusion? And how do we fix it?

Kay repeated what he had told the senators. Bush listened patiently, interrupting occasionally, and asking follow-up questions. He didn't dispute Kay's answers. He did not ask Kay to temper his views or to recant his claims, as Warner had done. Kay was surprised. It seemed spontaneous and not something that Condi had briefed him on, he thought.

The president showed no sign of rancor or ill will as the discussion deepened. Kay was relieved. "There was no tension, no hostility, and no defensiveness on his part," he said later. "Neither was there a tone of, 'God, you caused me a lot of trouble. Why did you have to do it?' Not that at all. Or, you know, 'How can you be so damned certain there are no weapons there when so many people said there were?'"

The conversation ranged to other intelligence. Bush asked Kay what he thought of the President's Daily Brief, called the PDB. It was a touchy subject. Each day at 7:30 a.m. a special briefer from the CIA goes to the White House, or wherever the president is, to deliver the latest intelligence nuggets and warnings. A huge staff at the CIA produces it every night. The PDB synthesizes the gleanings of the entire U.S. intelligence system and boils them down to the most critical secrets for the commander-in-chief and his closest aides.

President Clinton largely dispensed with the oral briefing, finding it faster to simply read the six or so pages himself. But Bush preferred his PDB in person, and Tenet became the first CIA director to meet the president almost every morning. He had even boasted about it during his speech at Georgetown.

"The president of the United States sees me six days a week, every day. . . . I can tell you with certainty that the president of the United

States gets his intelligence from one person and one community: me." Tenet's unseemly bragging about his access had rankled some at the White House.

Kay had even done a PDB. In July 2003, on Kay's first visit home from the Perfume Palace, Tenet had invited Kay to attend the daily briefing. So he drove down to Langley at dawn and joined the briefer at 6 a.m. for the ride to the White House. When they walked inside, Bush was already waiting in the Oval Office with Cheney, Rumsfeld, Rice, and Card.

The CIA chief introduced Kay with enthusiasm and unexpectedly added, "And David is here to brief you today."

Tenet hadn't warned Kay he would be briefing the president. But Kay rose to the occasion. He gave an off-the-cuff recitation of the highlights of his first month in Iraq and the challenges they faced. He droned on so long and got so many questions that they ran out of time, and on the way back to Langley, Kay apologized to the woman who served as the regular CIA briefer.

"You've got all this material you wanted to show the president and I used all the time," he said. "I'm so sorry."

"No no, thank you!" she replied. "We'll just use it tomorrow." Her material wasn't anything special, she added. They were always hunting for stuff that they could keep and use another day. It was like a newspaper. The CIA needed to come up with headlines every day.

Now Kay told the president over lunch that preparation of the PDBs had become so standardized that they focused on short-term daily developments, not long-term strategic goals and plans.

"It's become like a classified CNN," he told the president.

"Give me an example," Bush asked.

So Kay explained that the need to fill the PDB drove what the CIA and other spy services collected, rather than the other way around. The system had gone haywire. And Tenet's looming presence at the briefing each morning, and his personal approval for each White House request, magnified and distorted the importance and urgency of what sometimes were innocuous comments.

"If you express any interest in anything on the PDB, it's going to appear every week," Kay told the president.

Bush looked startled. Something occurred to him. He turned to Cheney and nodded.

"That's why they keep telling me about that SOB in Mozambique," the president said with a smile.

Bush apparently had asked a briefer an offhand question about President Joachim Chissano, who was running for reelection after ruling the dirt-poor southern African nation for eighteen years. The CIA mobilized its Africa desk and probably sent someone down to Maputo. The briefer followed up with regular detailed updates on the otherwise obscure internecine squabbles of Mozambique's political elite.

Bush turned back to Kay and surprised him with his next question.

"Do you think I should meet less with George?" the president asked.

Kay flinched. What could he say? He was fully convinced, as were many in the intelligence community, that what one senior CIA official called the "damned coffee klatch every morning in the Oval Office" had co-opted Tenet, undermining his independence and sucking the CIA into an untenable political vortex. Tenet had become a yes-man. But Kay held back. This was not his fight.

"Mr. President, that's not what I'm saying," he replied, carefully backing away. "And please, the last thing I need is for George to think I told you that you should meet with him less."

Rice asked a question about the culture of corruption in Iraq. And Kay explained how U.N. sanctions had turned all of Iraq into a black market, a gangster state, enforced by thugs. And Iraqi weapons scientists had lied at every level, he said, too terrified to admit that their programs were moribund.

"So they were telling the palace whatever it wanted to hear," Kay said. It struck him that Tenet had done the same thing at the White House. The CIA chief couldn't bring himself to admit doubt to the president or Congress, Kay thought.

Card asked why so many other Western intelligence agencies also misjudged Saddam's weapons programs. "Everyone was recirculating the same bad information, and treating it like it confirmed other pieces of bad information," Kay said.

He ticked off problems with the British, the Israelis, and other friendly spy services. In his view, he added, the Chinese were probably the most skillful at collecting information because they set up front companies that operated without drawing suspicion.

"Yeah, that's why they're so good at stealing our technology," Bush interjected. Cheney guffawed at the president's joke but otherwise stared sullenly at Kay across the table and said nothing.

They talked for an hour and a half, forty-five minutes longer than

Kay had been told to expect. But the president kept returning to the one question that was the most obvious and the most troubling.

"What went wrong?" Bush asked. "Why did we get it so wrong?"

Finally, Kay put down his fork and looked across the starched white linen at the president.

He and his team had uncovered an unimaginable failure of simple tradecraft, of basic analysis, and of senior leadership at the CIA, he said. The details were classified so he hadn't mentioned the scandal in public.

The CIA had depended on a single Iraqi source called Curveball for one of their most alarming prewar claims, Kay told the president. They never talked to him before the war. They never vetted him or confirmed his information. Colin Powell had highlighted his tracks at the United Nations. He, the president, had cited him in his State of the Union speech. He was why the president had announced finding weapons of mass destruction. But Curveball was a liar, a con man, an out-and-out fabricator, Kay said. The mobile weapons labs had never existed. The United States had gone to war to chase a mirage.

The president showed no reaction. He asked no follow-up questions. Bush already knew about Curveball, Kay realized.

EPILOGUE

The truth behind Curveball's lies wasn't all that complicated.

Kay Mereish, the U.N. Bravo team inspector, found the answer in the three shipping containers that she examined and photographed at Djerf al Nadaf six weeks before the 2003 invasion. After the search, she drove into Baghdad to interview the director of the company that operated the warehouse complex. He couldn't have been more engaging or helpful when she inquired about the trailers.

He told her that the Mesopotamia State Company for Seeds imported eleven shipping containers filled with German-manufactured seed processing machinery in the spring of 1997. They were trucked off to operate at seed warehouses around Iraq, he said. At her request, he provided a list.

The locations overlapped precisely with Curveball's six supposed germ truck depots, from Djerf al Nadaf to Suwayrah to Tikrit.

Over the next few weeks, Bravo team located the other eight seed trailers. Records showed that U.N. officials had approved the imports as legitimate agricultural items that did not violate trade sanctions. As far as Mereish was concerned, it was a dead end. She figured the intelligence source was a janitor or truck driver, someone who had visited the warehouses but who didn't know a fermentor from a thresher.

She sent a note to Hans Blix at U.N. headquarters in New York to advise him that Western intelligence agencies apparently had confused seed processing trailers with germ trucks. The chief weapons inspector reported the discovery deep inside a data-packed report to the U.N. Security Council on May 30, 2003, two months after the invasion. The mention drew no attention whatsoever.

"At several of the inspected sites," the report said, "sea containers with recently (United Nations-registered) imported seed-processing equipment, with some resemblance to production equipment, were present."

The CIA never saw the seed trailers. They disappeared before Jerry and the bio-babes made their six visits to Djerf al Nadaf. Looters probably carted them off. They don't appear in Killip's twenty-minute video or in Iraq Survey Group reports. But the trailers loaded with German-made equipment clearly provided the foundation for Curveball's feverish claims and the cascade of tragic misjudgments and mistakes that followed.

The Iraqi seed-processing program was real, not a cover for illicit weapons, as the CIA assumed. The Chemical Engineering and Design Center, where Curveball worked, was initially in charge. The Iraqis based their design on a German-manufactured seed purification plant in Tikrit, just as he claimed. It's most likely that Curveball visited Djerf al Nadaf in the spring of 1997, after he was fired. He would have seen the three containers, just as he told the BND, shortly after they were delivered. They carried German equipment, just as he said. The perimeter wall that blocked off the main warehouse was not yet built. His account, at least to that point, was accurate.

At that point, Curveball's story spun into fantasy. It seems certain that he drew from U.N. documents on the Internet. The final UNSCOM report to the Security Council in January 1999, eleven months before he arrived in Munich, was filled with names, places, and information about Iraq's former bioweapons program. The details filled two annexes and sixty-three pages of explicit descriptions, history, and charts. The report notes that Iraqi bio-experts referred to anthrax and other germs as Agent A, Agent B, and Agent C, just as Curveball said. The germ factory at Al Hakam, General Saadi's proposal to build mobile facilities, Taha's role as Dr. Germ, all appear in the public report.

If Curveball fused fact and fiction, others twisted and magnified his account in grotesque ways. His marginal story took on an importance it did not deserve. Senior intelligence officials irresponsibly hyped his claims and accepted unconfirmed reports. They cast aside contradictory evidence, brushed aside clear warnings, and ignored a rising clamor of skeptics. Time and again, bureaucratic rivalries, tawdry ambitions, and spineless leadership proved more important than professional integrity.

Curveball's case occupies a singular place in U.S. history. After 9/11, critics complained that U.S. intelligence and law enforcement failed to connect the dots of evidence that might have prevented the terrorist attacks. But in this case, the CIA and its allies made up the dots. Iraq never built or planned to build any mobile weapons labs. It had no other WMD. The U.S. intelligence apparatus, created to protect the nation, conjured up demons that did not exist. America never before has squandered so much blood, treasure, and credibility on a delusion.

Declaring Curveball a fabricator in the end was a cop-out for the CIA. It implied that U.S. intelligence had fallen for a clever hoax. The truth was more disturbing. The defector didn't con the spies so much as they conned themselves. George Tenet tried to please the president. Even after the case began to collapse, he and his aides held on to the flawed evidence.

After the 2003 invasion, the faulty intelligence led to multiple investigations and an orgy of finger-pointing but no real accountability.

British intelligence repudiated Curveball as a fabricator in the fall of 2004. But London's spy chiefs blamed German intelligence for the disaster. Richard Dearlove, then head of MI6, complained to a postwar parliamentary inquiry that the BND had wrongly reported that the mobile factories carried spray driers and milling equipment, thereby vastly increasing the potential threat. The review found that the defector never said it.

"The problem was not just mistranslation but incomplete reporting," said Lord Robin Butler, who directed the inquiry. Many of the German reports on Curveball, he said, were open to "some doubts" or were "seriously flawed."

German intelligence authorities refused to admit any errors or renounce Curveball as a fabricator. Since the Germans were not part of the Iraq Survey Group, they did not see the wall at Djerf al Nadaf or examine his personnel records. Some BND officials were furious when they learned of the CIA burn notice. They took it as a professional insult.

August Hanning, president of the BND, was promoted to assistant secretary in the Ministry of Internal Affairs in December 2005 after a new federal government was elected to office. His new responsibilities included counterespionage from foreign spy services, including the CIA. Ernst Uhrlau, the German intelligence overseer, replaced Hanning as BND chief. He was convinced that the CIA hyped Curveball's account to go to war. "They sexed up the intelligence," he insisted. "That's the real story."

Werner Kappel, the erudite BND official, was haunted by the case. He didn't blame the defector. "Even if Curveball is a fabricator, he is right and we were wrong because we failed to disprove it," he argued. But he defended the BND refusal to grant CIA access to the defector, and the false claim that he hated Americans.

"Frankly, I was never sure that he said, 'I don't like the Americans. I hate the Americans.' People believed it, but I don't know why. It wasn't in the reports. It wouldn't matter if he had. It meant nothing.

"If we had done it the other way around, if we had gone to the CIA and demanded to talk to an important American source, they would just laugh. They would blacklist me as an intelligence professional. They would say I am mentally unstable."

Schumann, the pugnacious chief handler, decided the troublesome case would be his last. He retired in mid-2004, soon after he was ejected from the CIA interrogation with Curveball. Meiner, the tepid analyst, took early retirement as well. Hans Pieper, his boss, died of a strange tooth infection. Gradl, the German spy in Washington, returned home to a BND posting in Bremen in mid-2005. Alex Steiner, of Munich House, moved to another DIA base known as Hapsburg House, outside Berlin, but retired in late 2005 to sell German real estate.

George Tenet resigned as director of central intelligence in June 2004, a week after the CIA declared Curveball a fabricator, President Bush later awarded him the Presidential Medal of Freedom, the nation's highest civilian award. In his 2007 book, *At the Center of the Storm*, Tenet called Curveball the "most notorious example of bad information" in the prewar intelligence. "We allowed flawed information to be presented to Congress, the President, the United Nations, and the World," he admitted. "That never should have happened." But he chiefly blamed Tyler Drumheller for embarrassing the CIA rather than the managers and analysts who mishandled the case and tried to cover up their mistakes.

James Pavitt, head of the clandestine service, followed Tenet out the door and joined a private consulting firm in Washington. John McLaughlin, Tenet's deputy, quit later that year to teach. They both insisted they had acted appropriately given what they knew at the time.

Drumheller left the CIA in early 2005, embittered about the case, and wrote a book about his career. He regretted not fighting harder to ring the alarm on Curveball. "It was unimaginable to me," he explained, "that the entire war was based on reporting from that one poor Iraqi."

His group chief, the hard-charging Margaret, became a CIA chief of station in Europe. Chris, who interrogated Curveball, also got a CIA station. McLaughlin's executive assistant, Steve, went to the National Security Council at the White House.

Kay Mereish and Dimitri Perricos returned to U.N. headquarters in New York. The Bush administration refused to let the U.N. inspectors resume their work in Iraq after the invasion. The Security Council finally disbanded UNMOVIC in June 2007. Scott Ritter, who quit the U.N. in 1998, felt bitter about his early role in the saga. "We created a mythology of the mobile labs," he said. "We postulated their existence. And they became reality. But we never found any evidence. None."

David Kay returned to his former life at a think tank in Virginia, consulting overseas, speaking at conferences, and testifying occasionally at congressional hearings. The CIA never invited him back as a graybeard or anything else. Rita, head of the bio-team, was promoted to a nonproliferation post at the National Security Council at the White House in 2004. Martha, her fellow bio-babe, returned to the CIA and a town house with a huge U.S. flag in the front window. Both Jerry and the Kid transferred from the CIA to another U.S. intelligence agency.

Hamish Killip finally won his private war against the two trailers that President Bush had called weapons of mass destruction. The final report of the Iraq Survey Group in October 2004 concluded that they could not produce biological agents. By then, U.S. troops were using the trailers to store concertina wire. Someone stole the metal nameplates off the equipment as souvenirs. The CIA concluded an internal review of the bioweapons mistakes in early 2007 but refused to release the review. The discredited White Paper from May 2003 remains on the CIA website.

Curveball continued to use a false name and live in the defector protection program near Munich. After his wife arrived in 2004, they had a daughter. But the couple bickered and the BND assigned another handler, a woman, to provide marriage counseling and other help. Curveball remained dissatisfied with his lot. Still unable to master the language, still filled with resentment, he could not find an engineering job and refused anything less. He has never recanted his story.

CHRONOLOGY

January–February 1991—Persian Gulf War.

April 1991—U.N. Security Council resolution requires Iraq to unconditionally surrender all weapons of mass destruction and to allow U.N. inspections.

1994—Curveball is recruited out of Baghdad University to work at the Chemical Engineering and Design Center.

May 1995—Secret planning begins to construct mobile biological weapons factories, according to Curveball.

July 1995—Iraq admits that it produced anthrax, botulinum toxin, and other biowarfare agents prior to 1991 war.

August 1995—Lt. Gen. Hussein Kamil, head of Iraq's WMD programs, flees to Jordan. He tells CIA that all biological and chemical weapons were destroyed in mid-1991.

September 1995—Lt. Gen. Amir Hammudi Hasan Saadi, scientific advisor to Saddam, tells U.N. inspectors that he proposed hiding germ factories on trucks, but says they were not built.

June 1996—U.N. teams supervise the complete destruction of Al Hakam, Iraq's main facility for biological warfare agents.

December 1996—A CIA report includes two handwritten notes indicating Iraq was "considering" mobile germ weapons labs. The notes are undated and unsigned.

May 1997—Satellite imagery shows a six-foot-high wall at the Djerf al Nadaf seed-processing plant.

July 1997—The first mobile germ production unit begins operations at Djerf al Nadaf, according to Curveball.

May 1998—Iraqi engineers redesign the germ trucks to improve efficiency, according to Curveball.

December 1998—An accident kills twelve technicians at Djerf al Nadaf, according to Curveball. Separately, U.N. inspectors are withdrawn and U.S. and British air strikes hit military and regime targets for four days.

November 1999—Curveball flies into Munich and applies for political asylum.

January 2000—First debriefing of Curveball by German intelligence.

May 2000—CIA doctor fears Curveball may be an alcoholic.

Late 2000—Curveball prepares a physical model of Djerf al Nadaf and draws detailed sketches.

December 2000—Then-secret National Intelligence Estimate cites "new intelligence" from Curveball "to adjust our assessment upward of the BW threat posed by Iraq."

Early 2001—Curveball displays severe emotional problems. The CIA is told Curveball is "out of control."

September 2001—German debriefings of Curveball end after his brother telephones.

October 2001—After 9/11, the CIA reassesses Curveball's reports and ramps up earlier warnings. It concludes that mobile production labs provide Baghdad "with BW capabilities surpassing the pre–Gulf War era."

April 2002—British intelligence warns the CIA that it "is not convinced that Curveball is a wholly reliable source" and that "elements of (his) behavior strike us as typical of individuals we would normally assess as fabricators."

September 2002—A German official warns CIA division chief Tyler Drumheller that Curveball is "crazy" and may be a fabricator. Drumheller warns his supervisors.

October 2002—A new National Intelligence Estimate warns with "high confidence" that Iraq "has now established large-scale, redundant and concealed BW agent production capabilities based on mobile BW facilities."

November 2002—U.N. inspections resume after four years.

December 2002—A senior CIA official calls a meeting to "resolve precisely how we judge Curveball's reporting on mobile BW labs." He decides Curveball is credible.

January 2003—The CIA station chief in Berlin warns that German intelligence "has not been able to verify" Curveball's reporting and that the defector is "problematic." In his State of the Union address, President Bush warns that Saddam has "mobile biological weapons labs."

February 2003—Secretary of State Colin Powell, addressing the U.N. Security Council, highlights the germ trucks as "one of the most worrisome things that emerges from the thick intelligence file we have" on Iraq. U.N. inspectors from Bravo Team visit Djerf al Nadaf and other sites identified by Curveball. They find no evidence to support his claims.

March 2003—War begins with "shock and awe" bombing campaign.

May 2003—U.S. military discloses the discovery of two suspected bioweapons trailers in northern Iraq. A CIA White Paper calls the trailers "strikingly similar" to those described by Curveball. "We found the weapons of mass destruction," President Bush announces in error.

June 2003—The CIA appoints David Kay as head of the Iraq Survey Group, which has replaced the Pentagon's unsuccessful hunt for WMD.

July–October 2003—The CIA "bio-babes" and other experts investigate the Curveball case.

October 2003—David Kay tells Congress that he has found no stockpiles of WMD and no signs of recent production in Iraq.

January 2004—David Kay resigns. "We were almost all wrong," he tells a Senate committee. The next day, Kay briefs President Bush about Curveball and other problems with intelligence.

February 2004—CIA chief George Tenet defends prewar intelligence in a speech at Georgetown University.

March 2004—A CIA case officer debriefs Curveball for the first time. He concludes that the Iraqi has lied about the germ trucks.

May 2004—CIA formally withdraws more than one hundred Curveball reports with a burn notice that concludes he "appears to be fabricating in this stream of reporting."

GLOSSARY

Al Hakam—Iraq's primary biological weapons factory, destroyed in 1996.

Baghdad station—The CIA operations base in Iraq.

BND—Bundesnachrichtendienst, Germany's Federal Intelligence Service.

Bravo team—UNMOVIC biological weapons experts.

BW—Biological warfare.

Camp Slayer—Iraq Survey Group headquarters.

Chemical Engineering and Design Center—Baghdad office where Curveball worked.

CIA—Central Intelligence Agency.

CW—Chemical warfare.

Defense HUMINT Service—The DIA division that handles agents, defectors, and other human intelligence sources.

DI—Directorate of Intelligence, the CIA division that analyzes foreign intelligence.

DIA—Defense Intelligence Agency, the Pentagon's chief organization for military intelligence collection and analysis.

Directorate One—The BND division that handles agents, defectors, and other human intelligence sources.

Directorate Three—The BND division that analyzes source intelligence.

Djerf al Nadaf—Iraqi complex where Curveball said he built mobile biological labs.

DO—Directorate of Operations, the CIA division that directs clandestine operations overseas.

Gang of Four—Four U.N. inspectors who helped unravel Iraq's biowarfare program in the 1990s.

Hortensia 2—Code used on BND reports sent to DIA.

HUMINT—Human intelligence.

HVT—High value target.

IAEA—International Atomic Energy Agency.

IIR—Intelligence Information Report used by DIA.

INC—Iraqi National Congress, led by Ahmed Chalabi.

INR—Bureau of Intelligence and Research at the State Department.

Langley—CIA headquarters in Virginia.

MI6—Britain's foreign intelligence service.

Military Industrialization Commission—Iraqi group that produced WMD before 1991.

Munich House—DIA operations base in Munich.

NIE—National Intelligence Estimate.

NSA—National Security Agency.

PDB—President's Daily Brief.

Perfume Palace—Iraq Survey Group headquarters at Camp Slayer.

Pullach—BND headquarters outside Munich.

SCIF—Sensitive compartmented information facility.

UNMOVIC—United Nations Monitoring, Verification, and Inspection Commission.

UNSCOM—United Nations Special Commission.

WINPAC—CIA center for Weapons Intelligence, Nonproliferation, and Arms Control.

WMD—Weapons of mass destruction.

Zirndorf—German refugee center near Nuremberg.

ACKNOWLEDGMENTS

I wrote the first story about Curveball for the *Los Angeles Times* on March 28, 2004, with Greg Miller, a good friend and superb reporter on intelligence issues. A year later, I joined forces with the incomparable John Goetz, an American investigative reporter based in Berlin, to explore the German side of the saga. The *Los Angeles Times* published our lengthy report on November 20, 2005, and it led directly to this book. I am forever indebted to John for his unflagging energy, his unerring journalistic instincts, and his crucial suggestions.

My thanks go to John Carroll and Dean Baquet, the inspirational former editors of the *Los Angeles Times,* for their unstinting support. I am immensely grateful to Douglas Frantz, the former managing editor, and Scott Kraft, the national editor, for granting me so many months away from the office. I owe much to Craig Matsuda and Bill Rempel in Los Angeles, Jeff Fleishman in Berlin, and Doyle McManus, Tom McCarthy, and Bob Ourlian in the Washington bureau for their constant encouragement and advice.

Flip Brophy, my agent at Sterling Lord Literistic, met me for coffee on a Monday and negotiated my contract with Random House that Friday, which must be a record. Sharon Skettini played backup. Claire Tisne, my fabulous editor at Random House, enthusiastically supported and steered this project from start to finish. She conceived the idea, edited each draft, and guided me throughout. I am indebted to her and Joelle Dieu. Random House hotshot Peter Gethers provided mentoring and wise counsel at all times. Gina Centrello, Dan Menaker, Jonathan Jao, Benjamin Dreyer, Rachel Bernstein, Nicole Bond, Elizabeth Paulson, Tom Perry, Amelia Zakman, Karen Fink, Gene Mydlowski, Laura Goldin, and Dennis Ambrose at Random House all proved inordinately supportive. Fred Chase was a masterful copyeditor, as was Karen

Richardson. David Gerson of Focus Features, Matthew Snyder of Creative Artists Agency and Steven Knight in London, are stars in their own right. My thanks as well to David Brady at the Hoover Institution at Stanford University, who helped support my research by naming me a media fellow.

Heartfelt thanks and affection to close friends and fellow journalists Ann Grimes, Tom Hamburger, Jan Pogue, John Walter, and Vernon Loeb for plowing through early drafts and responding with crucial suggestions. My mother, Samantha, and sister, Susan, always urged me forward. So did Danny, Michael, and Sammy Drogin. Tyler Marshall and Chris Cermak kindly helped with translations of German material. Angelique Bender and Keith Richburg offered valuable advice. I cannot thank them all enough.

I especially thank the current and former intelligence and military officers, government officials, U.N. inspectors, and other sources, named and unnamed in this book, who shared so much time and information with me in Washington and abroad during my research. They displayed remarkable patience and goodwill, answering my endless questions about spying and tutoring me in the ways of their world. I can't possibly repay their assistance, but I hope this book proves worthy of their input.

Most of all, I thank my family. Casey and Caroline, my children, offered endless good cheer, warm hugs, and card tricks. They even promised to read the book someday. My wife and best friend, Frankie, not only patiently edited all drafts—she read them aloud on long drives and sustained me with love throughout. She above all made this book, and so much more in my life, possible.

NOTES

CHAPTER 1

6   **A total of 95,113**   "Migration Report," December 1999, European Forum for Migration Studies (EFMS), University of Bamberg, Germany. For additional details, see "European Refugee Fund: Final Report on Germany," March 2006, http://ec.europa.eu/dgs/justice_home/doc/dg_eval_Germany_0306_en.pdf.

10   **After the Berlin Wall fell**   By the time Zirndorf celebrated its fiftieth anniversary in 2005, it had fed, clothed, and cared for more than 219,000 refugees, according to its records.

11   **"In the future,"**   "Migration Report," November 1999, European Forum for Migration Studies (EFMS), University of Bamberg, Germany.

CHAPTER 2

14   **He ordered his top deputies**   The most authoritative biography on Gehlen is E. H. Cookridge, *Gehlen: Spy of the Century* (London: Corgi, 1972), p. 25. See also James H. Critchfield, *Partners at the Creation: The Men Behind Postwar Germany's Defense and Intelligence Establishments* (Annapolis: Naval Institute Press, 2003).

14   **They underwent a year**   The CIA has declassified numerous documents from this period. I drew especially on Kevin C. Ruffner, *Forging an Intelligence Partnership: CIA and the Origins of the BND, 1945–49,* History Staff, Center for the Study of Intelligence, European Division, Directorate of Operations, 1999 (declassified 2002).

14   **Gehlen insisted his old**   Pieper-Georg Wieck, Clarence W. Schmitz, and Timothy Naftali, "Spies Like Us," *Foreign Affairs,* November/December 2004.

14   **Martin Bormann, Hitler's chief**   "The History of the Bundesnachrichtendienst," http://www.bnd-standortpullach.de/en/hist_bnd_geschichte_en.htm.

15   **They included at least five**   Timothy Naftali, "Berlin to Baghdad: The Pitfalls of Hiring Enemy Intelligence," *Foreign Affairs,* July/August 2004. According to Naftali, among the dozens of murderers and thugs working for

Gehlen was Konrad Fiebig, hired in 1948, who had served with Einsatzgruppe B (a mobile killing unit) in Byelorussia and was later charged with shooting eleven thousand Jews. Erich Deppner, who ran Gehlen's operations out of West Berlin, had been deputy to Wilhelm Harster, an SS brigadier general who was Heinrich Himmler's representative in the occupied Netherlands. Deppner helped his boss supervise the deportation of 100,000 Dutch Jews to the death camps and was personally responsible for executing Soviet prisoners of war interned there. Gehlen's chief Soviet expert, Emil Augsburg, had been detailed in 1939–40 to the special SS units that executed Jews and communists in Poland and later did the same thing in the western Soviet Union. See also Richard Breitman, Norman Goda, Timothy Naftali, and Robert Wolfe, *U.S. Intelligence and the Nazis* (Washington, D.C.: National Archive Trust Fund Board, 2004), p. 377.

15 **Scores of sensitive operations**   For details on this period, see David E. Murphy, Sergei A. Kondrashev, and George Bailey, *Battleground Berlin: CIA vs. KGB in the Cold War* (New Haven: Yale University Press, 1997). See also *On the Front Lines of the Cold War: Documents on the Intelligence War in Berlin, 1946 to 1961*, edited by Donald P. Steury, CIA History Staff, Center for the Study of Intelligence, Washington, DC., 1999; John Pike, Intelligence Resource Program, Federation of American Scientists, 1997, http://www.fas.org/irp/world/germany/intro/gehlen.htm.

15 **After West German authorities arrested**   David E. Murphy, Chief Eastern European Division, *Heinz FELFE Damage Assessment*, Central Intelligence Agency, February 7, 1963 (declassified June 2006).

15 **His successor, Helmut Schmidt**   "German Spies Polish Image," *Deutsche Welle*, March 27, 2003.

16 **"Ninety percent of what"**   Frank Johnson, "Spies, Strauss and the Muggeridge Factor," *The Times*, London, September 9, 1985.

17 **"like having Santa Claus"**   Bill Gertz, "German Spy Scandal Spawns U.S. Probe into Loss of Secrets," *Washington Times*, October 12, 1990.

17 **In 1996, the president**   Robin Gedye, "Spy Chief Resigns over Secrets Sale," *Daily Telegraph*, London, March 1, 1996.

17 **So did a 1999 report**   "U.S. Reportedly Tapped German Embassy Phones," Reuters, October 3, 1999.

18 **The computer discs**   For further information on Stasi operations, see the review of Hubertus Knabe, et al., "The MsF's Operations in the West," second edition (Berlin: Verlag, 1999) in Benjamin B. Fischer, "Intelligence in Recent Public Literature," Studies in Intelligence, CIA, Washington, D.C. (unclassified) https://www.cia.gov/csi/studies/vol46no2/article08.html.

19 **They publicly warned**   William Drozdiak, "The Cold War in Cold Storage: Washington Won't Part with East German Spy Files; Bonn Wants Them Back," *Washington Post*, March 3, 1999.

CHAPTER 3

20   **The Zirndorf report was rushed**   Werner Kappel is a pseudonym for a senior German intelligence officer who spoke on condition of anonymity because he holds an undercover position.

23   **The head of the interrogation**   Indictment, *United States of America v. George Trofimoff*; Case # 8:00-CR-197-T, U.S. District Court, Middle District of Florida, Tampa Division, 6-14-2000. See also CNN Transcript—Breaking News, "U.S. Attorney Holds News Conference on Retired Army Colonel Arrested on Espionage Charges," aired July 14, 2000, www.transcripts.cnn.com/TRANSCRIPTS/0006/14/bn.01.html; Tamara Lytle, "Brevard Retiree Is Accused of Espionage," *Orlando Sentinel*, June 15, 2000; Larry Dougherty, "Retired Colonel Accused of Spying," *St. Petersburg Times*, June 15, 2000; Graham Brink, "Trofimoff Spy Trial Promises Intrigue," *St. Petersburg Times*, June 6, 2001.

The case was straight out of an espionage thriller. George Trofimoff was born in Germany to impoverished Russian émigrés. His parents fled Moscow when their patron and employer, Tsar Nicholas II, was murdered with his family during the Russian revolution in 1917. Rescued by American soldiers in the final days of World War II, Trofimoff joined the U.S. Army, became a naturalized American citizen, and devoted his career to military intelligence. In 1969, Colonel Trofimoff was named chief of the United States Army Element at the Nuremberg center, part of the U.S. 66th Military Intelligence Group. It meant he was the top American in the Joint Interrogation Center.

Trofimoff's security clearance gave him access to virtually all NATO defense plans against a Soviet invasion. They included Allied military deployments, the "current state of knowledge" of Soviet and Warsaw Pact capabilities and forces, lists of all U.S. intelligence targets and priorities in the Soviet bloc, information on chemical and biological warfare threats, and intelligence reports from other defectors and refugees.

But in 1992, amid the debris of the collapsing Soviet empire, a KGB clerk named Vasili Mitrokhin tried to defect to the U.S. embassy in Tallinn, Estonia. He explained that he had secretly copied 25,000 pages of notes from KGB central archives over a twelve-year period. He concealed the notes in his clothes and shoes, smuggled them out the door, and buried them in metal cans under his dacha. Hordes of former Soviet spies and posers peddled phony or useless documents to Western intelligence then, and the CIA was swamped. The agency turned Mitrokhin down. Twice.

Mitrokhin finally convinced British intelligence of his value. He handed over his smuggled files in exchange for resettlement in England. Among the papers were notes indicating that a "career American intelligence officer" at the Joint Interrogation Center in Nuremberg had photographed thousands of classified documents and given the film to a KGB courier with an impeccable cover. The courier was a "clergyman" in the Russian Orthodox Church, the notes showed.

Suspicion quickly fell on Trofimoff. As a child, he was raised with Igor

Vladimirovich Susemihl, another son of Russian émigrés. A bearded theologian in heavy black robes, Susemihl was a prominent figure in the Russian Orthodox Church. He became archbishop of Vienna and Austria, the temporary archbishop of Baden and Bavaria, and later metropolitan of Vienna and Austria. But he led a remarkable double life. He recited prayers, tended to the Russian diaspora, and supported monasteries and charitable organizations. But he also passed NATO military secrets to the KGB, which infiltrated the Russian Orthodox Church even as it publicly persecuted it. The KGB had helped install Susemihl as a prelate, and now it controlled him.

When Trofimoff took command at the Nuremberg interrogation center, according to his later indictment, "Susemihl recruited him into the service of the KGB." He and other Soviet agents gave him "instructions for further espionage activities on behalf of the KGB" and ultimately paid him about $250,000.

Trofimoff's tradecraft was surprisingly crude. Over the years, he carted fifty thousand pages of classified material home. Then he laid them out, one by one, on a frame lit by gooseneck lamps in his basement. He photographed each with a tiny Minox camera or with a larger double-frame camera. Then he stuck the film back in its box and glued the top shut so it looked new. He delivered the exposed film to Susemihl or other KGB agents at remote villages in Austria. They greeted each other with code phrases and code names. Trofimoff was "Antev," "Markiz," and "Konsul." Susemihl was "Ikar."

Armed with details from the Mitrokhin files, German federal police arrested Trofimoff and Susemihl in 1994. But a local judge released them both when prosecutors could not show evidence of espionage in the previous five years, the applicable statute of limitations. Cleared of wrongdoing, at least in Germany, Trofimoff retired the following year, after thirty-five years of military service. He and his German-born wife moved to a gated retirement community in Melbourne, Florida.

Balding and avuncular, Trofimoff was popular with neighbors on Patriot Drive. He hosted lavish dinners and gave Bavarian knickknacks as Christmas presents. But he amassed debts that overwhelmed his military pension. To make ends meet, he took a job bagging groceries in a local Publix Super Market. On a steamy day in July 1997, Trofimoff received a letter from Igor Galkin, who identified himself as an official at the Russian embassy in Washington. "There's a problem," Galkin wrote. "Please call." He signed it, "Your old friends."

They met in a Tampa hotel and talked for six hours. Trofimoff pleaded for money and tried to convince the Russian of his bona fides. He identified photos of six KGB case officers he met in Austria and described some of the documents he had photographed. At one point, he thumped his chest over his heart and declared his loyalty to Moscow. "I'm not an American here," he said.

But Galkin was an undercover FBI agent, and hidden video cameras recorded Trofimoff's apparent confession. U.S. law has no statute of limitations for espionage. The FBI arrested Trofimoff at the Tampa Airport Hilton on June 15, 2000, a year after Susemihl died. At trial, defense lawyers argued that Trofimoff lied to Galkin. But federal prosecutors had a surprise witness: General Oleg Kalugin, who had directed Soviet spying against America during the 1980s but became a U.S. citizen after the Cold War. Kalugin testified that Trofimoff had been one of Moscow's most important spies. Trofimoff was sentenced to life in prison.

24   **"An initial impression can sometimes"**   BND document obtained by author.

27   **He was "very territorial"**   The BND made this official available on condition I not reveal his true name. Other details about him are accurate.

CHAPTER 4

29   **Iraq was much worse**   In the most notorious case, several West German companies helped design and build the Al Muthanna State Establishment in scrub desert northwest of Baghdad. Ostensibly designed as a pesticide plant, Muthanna instead became Saddam's main factory to develop, test, and produce chemical weapons. Scientists first produced mustard, the blistering agent first used in World War I, and progressed to increasingly powerful nerve gases, including sarin, tabun, and VX. After the 1991 war, German prosecutors charged ten businessmen and engineers with violating export laws or other offenses. All were acquitted or released due to lack of evidence or ill health.

29   **Some fifty-six separate inquiries**   Roger Boyes, "Germany Also Helped Build Iraq's CAB Weapons," *The Times*, London, February 17, 1998. One court case involved mobile laboratories. In July 1994, three German engineers were convicted of illegally providing $17 million worth of weapons technology to Iraq. The items included eight camouflage-painted Magirus-Deutz trucks designed as mobile labs. The defendants denied any wrongdoing and insisted the trucks went to an Iraqi agricultural project. Press reports alleged, however, that Saddam's forces used the mobile labs during chemical gas attacks on Kurdish civilians in 1988. See "Bill of Indictment," Case # 501 Js 20894/90/ F1, District Attorney's Office of the Augsburg District Court, Germany (Center for Nonproliferation Studies translation by Ralph Westbrooke), http://cns.miis.edu/research/iraq/indict.pdf. See also "Bill of Indictment Summary," Iraq Special Collection (Washington, D.C.: Center for Nonproliferation Studies), 1992, http://cns.miis.edu/research/iraq/caseintr.htm; Fred Studemann, "German Arms Laws on Trial," *Sunday Telegraph*, April 17, 1994; "German Gets 5 Years for Selling Scud Missile Components to Iraq," Deutsche Presse-Agentur, July 19, 1994, in Lexis-Nexis, http://web.leis-nexis.com/.

29   **"The Germans had the best"**   Albright's group, the Institute for Science and International Security, chiefly focused on Iraq's nuclear program. At least eleven German companies provided assistance to Iraq's unsuccessful effort to enrich uranium and build a nuclear bomb. See David Albright,

"Iraq's Acquisition of Gas Centrifuge Technology," *Case Studies of Illicit Procurement Networks* (Washington, D.C.: Institute for Science and International Security, 2003), www.exportcontrols.org/centpar2.html.

30 **"Guns of this caliber"**   Michael Smith, "2 Germans Face Trial for Role in Building 'Supergun,'" *Chicago Sun Times*, October 11, 2002. http://findarticles.com/p/articles/mi_qn4155/is_20021011/ai_n12485845.

30 **The stealthy sale proved**   For daily developments of the period, see Anthony H. Cordesman, co-director CSIS Middle East Studies Program, *Iraq in Crisis: A History from Desert Fox to June 1999*, Center for Strategic and International Studies, Washington, D.C., July 1, 1999.

CHAPTER 5

32 **"We got the pick"**   This official spoke on condition I not use his real name because he signed government secrecy agreements.

34 **One of their first official moves**   Other code names also were notable. Carl Ford, director of the Bureau of Intelligence and Research, the intelligence wing at the State Department, recalled issuing a special cryptonym to a troublesome source. "I had a guy I called Numb Nuts," recalled Ford, who spent thirty-five years in U.S. intelligence. "I put it in the form as a joke. But somewhere in the bowels of the CIA is a file about a guy named Numb Nuts." Ford left government service in October 2003.

34 **Intelligence services regularly**   For the most detailed review of how and why code names are used, see William M. Arkin, *Code Names: Deciphering U.S. Military Plans, Programs, and Operations in the 9/11 World* (Hanover, New Hampshire: Steerforth, 2005).

34 **Most classified U.S. reports**   The most extensive investigative reporting on the Curveball case appeared in the *Los Angeles Times*. See Bob Drogin and John Goetz, "How U.S. Fell Under the Spell of 'Curveball,'" *Los Angeles Times*, November 20, 2005, p. 1; Bob Drogin and Greg Miller, "Iraq Defector's Tales Bolstered U.S. Case for War," *Los Angeles Times*, March 28, 2004, p. 1; Bob Drogin and Greg Miller, "Curveball Debacle Reignites CIA Feud," *Los Angeles Times*, April 2, 2005, p. 1.

CHAPTER 6

41 **"No one . . . could control"**   *Comprehensive Report of the Special Advisor to the DCI on Iraq's WMD*, Iraq Survey Group, three volumes with addendums, Central Intelligence Agency, September 30, 2004, Vol. I, p. 45, www.cia.gov/cia/reports/iraq_wmd_2004/index.html (Hereafter *Iraq Survey Group*). When the initial postwar search in Iraq failed to find any weapons of mass destruction, President Bush ordered the CIA to take over the investigation. The final report of the Iraq Survey Group provides voluminous detail about Saddam's weapons programs and ambitions over the course of his regime. Details on the Curveball investigation may be found in Vol. III,

Annex C—*ISG Investigation of Iraq's Reported Mobile Biological Warfare Agent Production Capability*, pp. 73–78.

43 **Iraq was forced to import** Ibid., p. 207.

43 **After considering several designs** Ibid., Vol. III, Annex C, p. 74.

CHAPTER 7

44 **After the 1991 war** *Iraq's Weapons of Mass Destruction: A Net Assessment*, International Institute for Strategic Studies, London, September 9, 2002, pp. 29–40. See also Kenneth Katzman, *Iraq: Weapons Threat, Compliance, Sanctions, and U.S. Policy*, CRS Issue Brief for Congress, Congressional Research Service, Library of Congress, updated December 10, 2002, p. CRS-6; Katzman, *Iraq: Weapons Programs, U.N. Requirements, and U.S. Policy*, CRS Issue Brief for Congress, Congressional Research Service, Library of Congress, updated September 2, 2003.

44 **Unlike chemical or nuclear** For an overview of the biological challenge, see Richard Danzig, *Catastrophic Bioterrorism—What Is to Be Done?* (Washington, D.C.: Center for Technology and National Security Policy, National Defense University, August 2003). See also Col. (Dr.) Jim Davis, USAF, and Dr. Anna Johnson-Winegar, *The Anthrax Terror, DOD's Number-One Biological Threat*, http://www.globalsecurity.org/wmd/library/report/2000/davis.htm.

44 **U.N. biological inspectors** I found especially helpful Tim Trevan, *Saddam's Secrets: The Hunt for Iraq's Hidden Weapons* (London: HarperCollins, 1999).

46 **Most of the haul** *Unresolved Disarmament Issues: Iraq's Proscribed Weapons Programmes*, UNMOVIC Working Document, March 6, 2003, pp. 95–133, 151–62. See also R. Jeffrey Smith, "Iraq's Drive for a Biological Arsenal," *Washington Post*, November 21, 1997, p. A1.

46 **"Nothing remained"** UNSCOM/IAEA Sensitive, Note for the File, N. Smidovitch, August 22, 1995.

47 **Anthrax posed appalling** *Textbook of Military Medicine*, published by the Office of the Surgeon General, Borden Institute, Walter Reed Army Medical Center, Washington, D.C., 1997, pp. 643–54. The textbook describes the role of anthrax as a historical force and the source of modern microbiology. As related in Exodus in the Old Testament, the fifth and sixth plagues of ancient Egypt—diseased animals and boils—almost surely referred to anthrax in domesticated animals followed by cutaneous anthrax in humans. Virgil apparently describes the effects of anthrax in his epic *Georgics*. In 1876, British researcher Robert Koch identified *Bacillus anthracis* as the cause of anthrax, the first bacterium known to cause a disease. Five years later, French scientist Louis Pasteur developed the first live bacterial vaccine to protect against anthrax.

47 **Aflatoxins are chemical** *Aflatoxins, Foodborne Pathogenic Microorganisms and Natural Toxins Handbook*, U.S. Food and Drug Administration, Washington, D.C., http://www.cfsan.fda.gov/~mow/chap41.html.

48   **Despite experiments**   *Iraq Survey Group,* Vol. III, pp. 46–48.

48   **In the summer of 1996**   Celso L. N. Amorim, Ambassador, "Report of the First Panel Established Pursuant to the Note by the President of the Security Council on 30 January 1999 (S/1999/100), Concerning Disarmament and Current and Future Ongoing Monitoring and Verification Issues," U.N. Security Council, S/1999/356, March 30, 1999, Annex I, paragraph 23.

49   **Despite years of effort**   *Report to the President of the United States,* Commission on the Intelligence Capabilities of the United States Regarding Weapons of Mass Destruction, Washington, D.C., March 31, 2005, p. 158 (hereafter *WMD Commission Report*). In early 2004, criticism over the failure to find WMD in Iraq led President Bush to appoint a panel to review U.S. intelligence capabilities. Charles Robb, a former governor and U.S. senator from Virginia, and Laurence Silberman, a senior circuit judge on the U.S. Court of Appeals for the District of Columbia Circuit, were co-chairmen. The final report includes extensive information on Curveball, especially pp. 80–111.

For a discussion of the report, see *U.S. Intelligence Reform and the WMD Commission Report,* American Enterprise Institute for Public Policy Research (unedited transcript prepared from a tape recording), May 4, 2005, http://www.aei.org/events/filter.all,eventID.1061/transcript.asp. For an independent assessment of prewar intelligence problems, see Anthony H. Cordesman, *Intelligence and Iraqi Weapons of Mass Destruction: The Lessons from the Iraq War,* Center for Strategic and International Studies, July 1, 2003.

49   **"In 1998, when inspectors"**   John E. McLaughlin, interviewed on *Fox News Sunday,* July 18, 2004, http://www.cia.gov/cia/public_affairs/press_release/2004/pr07192004.html.

CHAPTER 8

50   **The Iraqis were building**   Many people refer to these vehicles as mobile labs. I avoid the term unless it's in a quotation. A mobile lab is used to conduct research and testing either for civilian or military purposes. U.S. intelligence believed Iraq was installing equipment on trucks to produce anthrax and other biological agents for military weapons. I call them mobile weapons labs, germ trucks, biological factories on wheels, and so on.

50   **"It was his conclusion"**   Hans Pieper is a pseudonym. The BND made this official available for an interview on condition I did not reveal his true identity.

CHAPTER 9

57   **After they built**   *Iraq Survey Group,* Vol. III, Annex C, p. 74.

58   **In the first design**   *Iraqi Mobile Biological Warfare Agent Production Plants,* CIA Intelligence Assessment, May 28, 2003, p. 4, http://www.cia.gov/cia/reports/iraqi_mobile_plants/index.html. This White

Paper may be compared with the follow-up investigation in Annex D—
Trailers Suspected of Being Mobile BW Agent Production Units, *Iraq Survey Group*, Vol. III, pp. 79–98.

59   **Curveball indicated**   *Report on the U.S. Intelligence Community's Prewar Intelligence Assessments on Iraq*, Senate Select Committee on Intelligence, S. Rept. 108–301, July 7, 2004, p. 163 (hereafter *Senate Prewar Intelligence Report*). The committee investigated the Curveball case but redacted most details in the unclassified version released to the public.

59   **German companies**   *Iraq Survey Group*, Vol. I, p. 65.

CHAPTER 10

63   **Alex Steiner**   Alex Steiner is a pseudonym for a DIA officer who spoke on condition he not be identified. All other details about him are accurate.

67   **Bernie Mueller, a U.S. intelligence**   Mueller is a pseudonym because he remains an undercover U.S. operative. All other details about him are accurate.

70   **The Iraqi appeared "clearly high-strung"**   *WMD Commission Report*, p. 91.

71   **Curveball's reporting "demonstrates"**   *Senate Prewar Intelligence Report*, p. 148.

72   **But the analysts had no idea**   Ibid., p. 163.

72   **It "looked like more corroboration"**   Ibid., p. 150.

CHAPTER 12

79   **He created a special**   See Scott Ritter, *Iraq Confidential: The Untold Story of the Intelligence Conspiracy to Undermine the UN and Overthrow Saddam Hussein* (New York: Nation Books, 2005). See also Scott Ritter, *Endgame: Solving the Iraq Problem—Once and for All* (New York: Simon & Schuster, 1999).

79   **"Look, when we go"**   Scott Ritter interview, "Spying on Saddam," *Frontline*, PBS, 1999, http://www.pbs.org/wgbh/s/frontline/shows/unscom/interviews/ritter.html.

83   **On the eve of the planned attack**   *The Use by the Intelligence Community of Information Provided by the Iraqi National Congress Together with Additional Views*, Report of the Select Committee on Intelligence, 109th Congress, 2nd Session, U.S. Senate, September 8, 2006, pp. 16–25 (hereafter *Senate INC Report*). This report provides a detailed review of the CIA's tortured relations with Ahmed Chalabi and his organization. See also David Ignatius, "The CIA and the Coup That Wasn't," *Washington Post*, May 16, 2003, p. A29; Randy Stearns, "The CIA's Secret War in Iraq," *ABC News*, February 1998, http://www.defencejournal.com/oct98/cia_secretwar.htm; Jane Mayer, "The Manipulator: Ahmad Chalabi pushed a tainted case for war. Can he survive the occupation?" *New Yorker*, June 2, 2004.

84   **They scheduled another coup**   Scott Ritter, "The Coup That Wasn't," *Guardian/UK*, September 28, 2005. See also Kenneth Katzman, Specialist in Middle Eastern Affairs, *Iraq: U.S. Regime Change Efforts and Post-Saddam Governance*, CRS Report for Congress, Congressional Research Service, Library of Congress, updated May 7, 2004, p. 13; Kenneth Katzman, *Iraq: U.S. Efforts to Change the Regime*, CRS Report for Congress, Congressional Research Service, Library of Congress, updated October 3, 2002.

84   **"There was a breakdown in trust"**   *Senate INC Report*, p. 25.

84   **"Chalabi outlined what he could"**   Drogin and Miller, "Iraqi Defector's Tales Bolstered U.S. Case for War."

CHAPTER 16

106   **"Simply stated, there is no doubt"**   Vice President Speaks at VFW 103rd National Convention, Office of the Press Secretary, White House, August 26, 2002, http://www.whitehouse.gov/news/releases/2002/08/20020826.html.

107   **The speech "went well beyond"**   George Tenet with Bill Harlow, *At the Center of the Storm* (New York: HarperCollins, 2007), p. 317.

107   **low-enriched uranium in Africa**   For an extended look at this issue, see Peter Eisner and Knut Royce, *The Italian Letter* (New York: Rodale, 2007).

107   **Turner, a Green Beret**   David Ignatius, "Where to Hide All Those Spies?" *Washington Post*, December 22, 1999, p. A33.

108   **Pavitt's spies were caught**   Pavitt became the first clandestine service chief ever to testify in a public hearing. See James L. Pavitt, Deputy Director of Operations, Central Intelligence Agency, *Submitted Testimony Before the National Commission on Terrorist Attacks upon the United States*, April 14, 2004, http://www.9-11commission.gov/hearings/hearing10/pavitt_statement.pdf.

108   **"more spies stealing more secrets"**   Jim Pavitt, Deputy Director for Operations, *Address to Duke University Law School Conference*, CIA, April 11, 2002, www.cia.gov/cia/public_affairs/speeches/pavitt_04262002.html. See also David S. Cloud, "Caught Off-Guard by Terror, the CIA Fights to Catch Up," *Wall Street Journal*, April 15, 2002, p. 1.

108   **"Every morning I am briefed"**   Remarks by the Deputy Director for Operations James L. Pavitt at the Foreign Policy Association, June 21, 2004, https://www.cia.gov/cia/public_affairs/speeches/2004/ddo_speech_06242004.html.

108   **"not James Bond or Jason Bourne"**   Ibid. In the same speech, Pavitt recounted a story from the Cold War. In mid-1977, he said, "a small furtive man, hiding near the official gas station reserved for foreign diplomats, approached an official he believed to be an American and passed him a note, quickly, carefully, under the noses of surveillance."

The man, Adolf G. Tolkachev, was a senior research scientist in the Soviet military aerospace program, and according to Pavitt, "the intelligence he provided from 1977 to 1985 saved United States taxpayers literally billions of dollars in research and development fees on look-down/shoot-down radar, aeronautics design and early stealth technology." He worked "in the basement of his office complex, in the toilets of the Lenin Library, risking his life at every turn" to pass the CIA "literally thousands of documents that were nothing short of pure gold."

Soviet authorities never let Tolkachev leave Russia. "Our officers went to tremendous lengths to elude and escape surveillance to meet him in the dead of night or early morning, quickly passing film and documents," Pavitt said. "Tolkachev, fighting his solo battle, was glad for the rare moments of contact with his allies. In the end, Tolkachev was caught, and he paid the ultimate price for his service: death in the basement of the notorious Lubyanka prison in Moscow."

It was a moving story but Pavitt omitted important details. According to former CIA counterintelligence chief Barry G. Royden's "Tolkachev, A Worthy Successor to Penkovsky," https://www.cia.gov/csi/studies/vol47no3/article02.html, the CIA was so fearful of Soviet double agents that headquarters repeatedly forbade contact with Tolkachev. He had to approach the CIA seven separate times, once by banging on the car of the station chief, before they considered his offer. Once contact began, the CIA issued him faulty communications equipment. He also demanded "several million" dollars in compensation; the agency ultimately agreed to pay him a salary equivalent to that of the U.S. president. The KGB executed Tolkachev in 1986 after Edward Lee Howard, a former CIA officer, defected and apparently betrayed him.

CHAPTER 19

119 **Lindsay Moran, an energetic case officer**   For an unusual view of the CIA, see Lindsay Moran, *Blowing My Cover: My Life as a CIA Spy and Other Misadventures* (New York: G. P. Putnam's Sons, 2005).

120 **Partly due to his lobbying**   "State Department: Issues Affecting Funding of Iraqi National Congress Support Foundation" (GAO-04-559), Report to Congressional Requesters, General Accounting Office, April 2004, p. 6.

120 **"successfully chasing after"**   *Senate INC Report*, pp. 27–28.

120 **"little of current intelligence value"**   *Iraq: Evaluation of Documents Provided by the Iraqi National Congress*, National Intelligence Council, August 9, 2002, cited in Ibid., pp. 35–36.

121 **"a continuous flow of tactical"**   Ibid., p. 31.

121 **"deliver the act of a lifetime"**   *CIA Operations Cable*, February 2003, cited in Ibid., pp. 103–4.

121 **In February that year**   Jonathan S. Landay and Warren P. Strobel, "Former CIA Director Used Pentagon Ties to Introduce Iraqi Defector," Knight Ridder Washington Bureau, July 16, 2004, http://www.realcities.com/mld/krwashington/news/special_packages/9165361.htm.

121 **known by the name al-Asaaf**   Tenet, *At the Center of the Storm*, p. 329.

121 **"We learnt our lesson"**   Marie Colvin and Nicholas Rufford, "Saddam's Arsenal Revealed," *The Sunday Times*, London, March 19, 2002.

122 **"were stored in the Republican Palace"** *WMD Association at Presidential Sites Unlikely to be Revealed by Inspections*, CIA, October 11, 2002, cited in *Senate INC Report*, p. 63.

122 **He later gave far more** The *Vanity Fair* article portrayed Harith as a master of Saddam's WMD, implausibly able to move deep inside the regime's most secret nuclear, chemical, and biological weapons facilities as well as ballistic missile sites and terrorist training camps. "The defector's testimony places Iraq on the front line of Bush's war on international terrorism," a headline warned. See David Rose, "Iraq's Arsenal of Terror," *Vanity Fair*, May 2002, pp. 120–31.

122 **The CIA, already distrustful** Extensive details about Harith's case appear in "Source Two," *Senate INC Report*, pp. 57–66.

122 **"open sores was strictly forbidden"** *Senate Prewar Intelligence Report*, p. 152.

123 **"The informant was suspicious"** *Review of Intelligence on Weapons of Mass Destruction*, Report of a Committee of Privy Counsellors, Chairman: The Rt Hon The Lord Butler of Brockwell KG GCB CVO, Ordered by the House of Commons, July 2004, p. 128 (hereafter *Butler Report*). This report provides an extensive review of British intelligence failures. For related material, see also *Report of the Inquiry into the Circumstances Surrounding the Death of Dr David Kelly C.M.G.*, by Lord Hutton, Ordered by the House of Commons, January 28, 2004.

Australia's intelligence services obtained about 97 percent of their intelligence on Iraq from other governments. But intelligence analysts in Canberra tended to be more skeptical than their counterparts in Washington and London. In April 2002, the DIO (Defence Intelligence Organisation) reported that "We still have no definitive evidence that mobile BW production facilities exist in Iraq." It added that "circumstantial evidence for their existence is mounting." On December 31, 2002, the DIO cast further doubt on CIA claims. "There has been no known offensive [BW] research and development since 1991, no known BW production since 1991 and no known BW testing or evaluation since 1991," it reported. On March 10, 2003, just before the war, the DIO still was not convinced. "Confirmation of a mobile production capability would require the discovery of semi-trailers or railcars containing BW production equipment and evidence of BW agent use. This level of evidence has not yet been found." *Intelligence on Iraq's Weapons of Mass Destruction*, Parliamentary Joint Committee on ASIO [Australian Security Intelligence Organisation], ASIS [Australian Secret Intelligence Service] and DSD [Defence Signals Directorate], A Report to the Parliament of the Commonwealth of Australia, December 2003, pp. 37–38, 61–62.

CHAPTER 20

124 **"would likely wait"** *WMD Commission Report*, p. 82.

124 **"probably continuing work"** Ibid., p. 82.

124 **"adjust our assessment upward"** *Worldwide Biological Warfare Programs: Trends and Prospects*, National Intelligence Council Update (NIE 2000-12HCX) (December 2000), p. 22, quoted in *WMD Commission Report*, p. 83.

124 **"Credible reporting from a single source"** CIA, DCI Nonproliferation Center, *New Evidence of Iraqi Biological Warfare Program* (Sir 2000-003X) (December 14, 2000), quoted in *WMD Commission Report*, p. 83; *Senate Prewar Intelligence Report*, p. 144.

125 **All such caution** Most Americans woke to the danger of bioterrorism after the 9/11 attacks. Over the next few weeks, a handful of letters laced with anthrax spores killed five people and sickened seventeen others. The fallout shut the U.S. Congress and Supreme Court, crippled mail delivery in several cities for months, and required more than $1 billion in decontamination efforts. The FBI later estimated it probably cost only $2,500 in home brewing equipment and supplies to create such chaos. The perpetrator has not been identified as of this writing. See *Anthrax in America: A Chronology and Analysis of the Fall 2001 Attacks*, Center for Counterproliferation Research (November 2002), p. 2; Allan Lengel, "Little Progress in FBI Probe of Anthrax Attacks," *Washington Post*, September 16, 2005, p. A1; Erich Lichtblau and Megan Garvey, "Loner Likely Sent Anthrax, FBI Says," *Los Angeles Times*, November 10, 2002.

125 **"continues to produce at least"** *Iraq: Mobile Biological Warfare Agent Production Capability*, CIA (WINPAC IA 2001-050X) (October 10, 2001), pp. 1, 7, quoted in *WMD Commission Report*, p. 218.

125 **each mobile unit would need a week** *Iraq Survey Group*, Vol. III, Annex D, p. 89.

125 **"We know Iraq has developed"** *WMD Commission Report*, p. 84.

125 **In the early fall of 2002** Michael Isikoff and David Corn, *Hubris: The Inside Story of Spin, Scandal, and the Selling of the Iraq War* (New York: Crown, 2006), p. 31.

126 **"We don't want the smoking gun"** "Top Bush Officials Push Case Against Saddam," *Inside Politics*, CNN, September 8, 2002, http://archives.cnn.com/2002/ALLPOLITICS/09/08/iraq.debate/.

126 **"[You] can't distinguish between Al Qaeda"** *Senate Prewar Intelligence Report*, p. 454.

126 **"The going-in assumption"** Ibid., p. 505.

126 **And virtually every paragraph** *WMD Commission Report*, p. 80.

126 **"We assess that all key aspects"** National Intelligence Estimate, pp. 5–6.

127 **According to a "credible source"** *Senate Prewar Intelligence Report*, p. 148.

127 **"potentially against the US homeland"** Ibid., p. 456.

127 **had chemical weapons** Ibid., p. 198.

127 **WINPAC chemical weapons experts were "drifting"** *WMD Commission Report*, p. 173.

128 **"seems to be exploring"** *Butler Report*, pp. 59–60.

128 **"self-sufficient in the production"**   Ibid., p. 169.

128 **Four biowarfare agents could be produced**   Ibid., p. 135.

128 **Iraq has "developed mobile laboratories"**   *Iraq's Weapons of Mass Destruction: The Assessment of the British Government,* September 24, 2002, p. 6, http://www.cabinet-office.gov.uk/iraqdossier.pdf.

128 **"Iraq was trying to acquire"**   *Butler Report,* p. 170.

128 **In the debates and in news accounts**   *Iraqi Weapons of Mass Destruction—Intelligence and Assessments,* Intelligence and Security Committee, Presented to Parliament by the Prime Minister by Command of Her Majesty, September 2003, pp. 17–19, http://www.cabinetoffice.gov.uk/publications/reports/isc/iwmdia.pdf. The inquiry revealed that one of the British government's most frightening prewar claims, that the Iraqi military could fire chemical and biological weapons within forty-five minutes of the order to use them, came "from a single uncorroborated source." The report concluded that virtually all the British informants on Iraq's WMD, including some described as subsources and sub-subsources, provided inaccurate information.

CHAPTER 21

131 **The Iraqi was "out of control"**   *WMD Commission Report,* p. 91.

131 **"had changed some of his stories"**   *Postwar Findings About Iraq's WMD Programs and Links to Terrorism and How They Compare with Prewar Assessments,* Report by the Senate Select Committee on Intelligence, September 8, 2006, p. 27 (hereafter *Senate Postwar Findings About Iraq's WMD Programs*).

131 **"presently compromised by reporting inconsistencies"**   *Senate Prewar Intelligence Report,* p. 154.

131 **"to have doubts about Curveball's reliability"**   *WMD Commission Report,* p. 91.

131 **Analysts "set that information aside"**   Ibid., p. 92.

CHAPTER 22

133 **The new U.N. teams**   For an inside account of UNMOVIC, see Hans Blix, *Disarming Iraq* (New York: Pantheon, 2004).

135 **"Meeting to Review Bidding on Curveball"**   *WMD Commission Report,* pp. 96, 221.

135 **"Although no one asked"**   Ibid., p. 97.

138 **"I want to stress"**   BND letter read to author.

138 **"with the expectation of source protection"**   *WMD Commission Report,* p. 96.

138 **"Reliability of Human Reporting"**   Ibid., p. 98.

138 **"handicapped in efforts to resolve"**   Ibid., p. 99.

139 **"the master of the case"**   Ibid., p. 97.

139 **"Confirmation/replication of the described design"**   Ibid., p. 98.

139 **Battelle works closely**   http://nationalsecurity.battelle.org/default.aspx.

In September 2001, the Pentagon separately hired SAIC, a company that does classified work, to build a mock-up of a germ truck. Each chassis carried a fake fermentor, a centrifuge, and a grinding mill. But nothing worked; it had no electricity or water. The DIA used the models to train its Chemical and Biological Intelligence Support Team, or CBIST, which would deploy to Iraq. They later sent the trailer to Fort Bragg, North Carolina, so special operations teams could learn how to recognize and disarm those they found in Iraq. William J. Broad, David Johnston, and Judith Miller, "Subject of Anthrax Inquiry Tied to Anti-Germ Training," *New York Times*, July 2, 2003, p. 1.

139 **"The fact is there was yelling"** Drogin and Miller, "Curveball Debacle Reignites CIA Feud."

CHAPTER 23

141 **"to refer to the Curveball information"** The message said that the CIA "had learned" that Bush planned to address the United Nations General Assembly on January 29, 2003, but Bush gave no such speech. He had addressed the body on September 12, 2002. *WMD Commission Report*, p. 102.

141 **"transcripts of actual questions"** Ibid., p. 102.

141 **"The source himself is problematical"** Classified CIA cable traffic (January 2003), cited in Ibid., p. 102.

142 **We are not certain that we know** "Re: [Foreign Service] BW Source," Electronic mail from Division Chief, February 3, 2003, cited in Ibid., pp. 102–3.

142 **"From three Iraqi defectors"** George W. Bush, *State of the Union Speech*, Office of the Press Secretary, January 28, 2003, http://www.whitehouse.gov/news/releases/2003/01/20030128-19.html. See also Richard A. Best Jr., Specialist in National Defense, *U.S. Intelligence and Policymaking: The Iraq Experience*, CRS Report for Congress, Congressional Research Service, Library of Congress, updated January 16, 2004.

143 **"Firsthand witnesses have informed us"** "World Can Rise to This Moment," Statement by the President, White House, February 6, 2003, http://www.whitehouse.gov/news/releases/2003/02/20030206-17.html.

143 **He already felt overwhelmed** Tyler Drumheller with Elaine Monaghan, *On the Brink* (New York: Carroll & Graf, 2006), pp. 113–14.

145 **"Oh my!" Drumheller heard** *WMD Commission Report*, p. 101. In April 2005, in response to release of the *WMD Commission Report*, McLaughlin denied that anyone raised concerns to him about Curveball before Powell's speech. He said he had "absolutely no recall" of meeting Drumheller in his office. "I am at a loss to explain why accounts of this period vary so sharply," he said. See *Statement of John E. McLaughlin Upon Release of the WMD Commission Report*, April 1, 2005, http://www.fas.org/irp/offdocs/wmd_mclaughlin.html.

146 **McLaughlin "would be grateful"** *WMD Commission Report*, p. 104.

CHAPTER 24

147 **"I believe I am still"**   *WMD Commission Report*, p. 91.
147 **"were having major handling issues"**   *Senate Prewar Intelligence Report*, p. 155.
148 **"It was obvious to me"**   Ibid., p. 156.
148 **"We sure didn't give much"**   Ibid., p. 248.
148 **"This is the *Vanity Fair* source"**   Ibid., p. 248.
148 He was **"largely unreliable"**   *Senate INC Report*, p. 59.
148 **"Much of his information"**   Ibid., p. 61.
148 **"We have determined that"**   Ibid., pp. 61–62.
149 **"Let's keep in mind the fact"**   *Senate Prewar Intelligence Report*, p. 249.
149 **"and they had heard it"**   Ibid., pp. 250–51.
150 **"Yeah, yeah, yeah"**   In April 2005, in response to release of the *WMD Commission Report*, Tenet sharply disputed Drumheller's account of their phone conversation. He called it "stunning and deeply disturbing" that he was not warned of doubts about Curveball. "It is simply wrong for anyone to intimate that I was at any point in time put on notice that Curveball was probably a fabricator," he said. See *Statement of George J. Tenet, Former Director of Central Intelligence*, April 1, 2005, http://www.fas.org/irp/offdocs/wmd_tenet.pdf. Two years later, Tenet expanded on his version of events. See Tenet, *At the Center of the Storm*, pp. 375–83.

CHAPTER 25

155 **"We lost the thread of concern"**   *Senate INC Report*, p. 65.
156 **It was, he admitted later**   Tenet, *At the Center of the Storm*, p. 375.
157 **"The material I will present"**   "Secretary of State Addresses the U.N. Security Council," White House, February 5, 2003, http://www.whitehouse.gov/news/releases/2003/02/20030205-1.html.
162 **He was "shocked"**   *WMD Commission Report*, p. 89.
162 **"have been inspected, samples taken"**   "UNMOVIC Memo Regarding Presentation by US Secretary of State to Security Council, February 5, 2003," memo dated February 11, 2003.

CHAPTER 26

166 **They gave Blix's staff**   *Butler Report*, p. 90.

CHAPTER 27

177 **"where the corn originated from"**   Daily report on the activities of the IAEA and UNMOVIC inspection teams in Iraq on February 17, 2003, cited in an annex to identical letters from Mohammed A. Aldouri, Permanent Representative of Iraq to the United Nations, addressed to Secretary-General and to the President of the Security Council, February 18, 2003, p. 4.

CHAPTER 28

181 **"You are fully aware"** Letter from Maj. Gen. Eng. Hossam M. Amin, Director General, National Monitoring Directorate, to Mr. Miroslav Gregoric, Director BOMVIC [Baghdad Ongoing Monitoring, Verification and Inspection Centre], ref: 2/1/D/292/, 5 March 2003.

181 **Two days later, on March 7** Executive Director Dr. Hans Blix, "Oral introduction of the 12th quarterly report of UNMOVIC," as delivered, U.N. Security Council, March 7, 2003, http://www.un.org/Depts/unmovic-/SC7asdelivered.htm.

181 **"If Iraq genuinely wanted to disarm"** "Secretary Powell's Remarks at U.N. Security Council Meeting," White House, March 7, 2003, http://www.whitehouse.gov/news/releases/2003/03/20030307-10.html.

182 **In an accompanying letter** Letter from General/Engineer Hossam Mohamed Amin, Director General, National Monitoring Directorate, to Mr. Miroslav Gregoric, Director BOMVIC, ref: 2/1/B/326, 15 March 2003.

182 **"enough doses to kill"** George W. Bush, *State of the Union Speech.*

183 **It was still Wednesday night** *Bush Announces Military Campaign,* March 19, 2003, transcript on CNN.com, http://www.cnn.com/2003/US/03/19/sprj.irq.war.bush.transcript/index.html.

CHAPTER 29

185 **"effects of a nerve agent"** Paul Reynolds, "Banned Weapons: Where Are They?" *BBC News Online,* April 15, 2003.

185 **"This could be the smoking gun"** Kieran Murray, "U.S. Says May Have Found Iraqi WMD Storage Site," Reuters, April 7, 2003.

185 **"suspicious glass globes"** Barton Gellman, "Odyssey of Frustration; In Search for Weapons, Army Team Finds Vacuum Cleaners," *Washington Post,* May 18, 2003, p. A1.

185 **Fox News "confirmed"** "Weapons-Grade Plutonium Possibly Found at Iraqi Nuke Complex," *FoxNews.com,* April 11, 2003, http://www.foxnews.com/story/0,2933,83821,00.html.

186 **He soon approved a plan to deploy** *Department of Defense Briefing,* Stephen A. Cambone, Under Secretary of Defense for Intelligence, May 7, 2003, http://www.defenselink.mil/transcripts/2003/tr20030507-0158.html.

187 **"only when they find people"** News transcript, *Secretary Rumsfeld Interview with the Associated Press,* U.S. Department of Defense, April 24, 2003, http://www.defenselink.mil/transcripts/2003/tr20030424-secdef0125.html.

CHAPTER 30

191 **Over the next few weeks** *Briefing on the Iraq Survey Group,* Stephen A. Cambone, Under Secretary of Defense for Intelligence, and Army Maj. Gen. Keith W. Dayton, Director for Operations, Defense Intelligence Agency,

May 30, 2003, http://www.defenselink.mil/transcripts/2003/tr20030530-0231.html.

191 **"It could have been a student project"** Bob Drogin, "Banned Weapons Remain Unseen Foe," *Los Angeles Times*, June 15, 2003, p. 1.

193 **"Believe me, it's not for lack"** Transcript, *Defense Department Special Briefing Re: Postwar Stabilization Efforts*, Briefer: Lieutenant General James Conway, Commander 1st Marine Expeditionary Force (via video teleconference from Baghdad to Pentagon Briefing Room), May 30, 2003.

CHAPTER 31

195 **A solid, light brown sludge** *Iraq Survey Group*, Vol. III, Annex D, p. 94. See also Judith Miller, "Trailer Is a Mobile Lab Capable of Turning out Bioweapons, a Team Says," *New York Times*, May 11, 2003.

195 **"capable of supporting a limited"** *Senate Postwar Findings About Iraq's WMD Programs*, p. 34.

195 **"probably the latest generation"** *Joint Task Force Twenty Report on the Field Exploitation of the Irbil Transportable Biological Warfare Agent Production Trailer*, May 2003, p. 4, cited in Ibid.

195 **"We know what we're doing"** *WMD Commission Report*, p. 241.

196 **"concluded that the unit does not"** Steven Cambone, Undersecretary of Defense for Intelligence, Pentagon Briefing, Transcript CNN Live Event/Special, May 7, 2003, http://transcripts.cnn.com/TRANSCRIPTS/0305/07/se.02.html. See also Kathleen T. Rhem, "Coalition Forces Have Mobile Iraqi Bioweapons Facility," American Forces Press Service, Department of Defense, May 7, 2003, http://www.defenselink.mil/news/newsarticle.aspx?id=29011. Press Release—Headquarters Marine Corps, Division of Public Affairs, # 0512-03-0724, May 7, 2003.

196 **Then, two days later** *Iraq Survey Group*, Vol. III, Annex D, p. 96. See also "Second Suspected Mobile Weapons Lab Found in Iraq," *CNN.com*, May 13, 2003, http:/www.cnn.com/2003/WORLD/meast/05/13/sprj.irq.mobile.lab; "U.S. Troops Find Second Biological Weapons Trailer Near Mosul," Defense Department Report, distributed by Bureau of International Information Programs, Department of State, May 13, 2003, http://www.globalsecurity.org/wmd/library/news/iraq/2003/05/iraq-030513-usia01.htm.

197 **"agreed with the conclusions"** *Senate Postwar Findings About Iraq's WMD Programs*, p. 34.

197 **He famously led a four-day standoff** Kay was rewriting protocols for nuclear reactor safeguards at the International Atomic Energy Agency in Vienna when the 1991 war ended. The IAEA needed an American who could interact with U.S. intelligence agencies in Iraq. Kay got the job. Saddam's regime still denied it had tried to build nuclear weapons. But Kay's first team, blocked from entering a suspect site, chased and photographed Iraqis carting nuclear equipment out the back gate. That hit the headlines. Soon after, a defector disclosed that Iraqi scientists had hidden crucial documents in the

Nuclear Design Center in Baghdad. Kay and his deputy, Bob Gallucci, a State Department officer, compiled a team of forty-three inspectors, nearly all U.S. and British intelligence and military operatives. They launched their raid early one morning. Kay gave the following account to the author:

> We get in there and it's crazy. The Iraqi source had said, "Whatever you do, don't take the elevator. It's known for stopping, not working, it's very dangerous." So we're running up and down eight flights of stairs. This was an unusual inspection anyway because we were searching for documents, not weapons. And the source had said the documents may be locked away. You may not have long with them.
>
> So I had two safecrackers from the CIA, people expert in surreptitious entry. Everyone in the agency wanted to be on the mission. I had very senior people just to take photographs of pages and pages of documents. They were way too senior for this, but they had kicked out younger guys. The last time some of these guys were in the field was Vietnam. They were really gung ho. Then I had a group of translators and interpreters to do triage on the documents. Based on the volume of documents we anticipated, we weren't sure we would get physical possession for very long.
>
> Our information was the valuable documents were on the top floor. That turned out to be wrong. So part of the team ran up there and I sent another part of the team to a document storage area in the basement. As it turned out, at the back was a closed door. Apparently the Iraqis had not noticed the door when they cleared things out. In one of the memos we found that day, although it was not translated until a week or so later, was a document warning the Iraqis that I was leading the mission to that building on that day and they should clear everything out and they had twenty-four hours to do it. And the Iraqi security guys replied that there simply wasn't enough time. The interesting thing was supposedly only five people in the world knew I was leading the mission that day. I still don't know where the leak was.

The team carried two sets of radios. They operated one as a decoy for Iraqi intelligence to monitor, but used an encrypted channel on the other to actually talk. At midmorning, the secure set crackled to life: *We found it*. The basement team had discovered the regime's semiannual report on the status of its nuclear weapons program. It proved without a doubt that regime officials had lied about their nuclear efforts.

> That document was so precious and of such high value. It was all in Arabic. But if you do a nuclear weapons design, there are diagrams and numbers that anyone would recognize. We knew we had a smoking gun. I didn't trust the Iraqis that we would actually succeed in getting this out. But I had one person, thank God, a military guy, who couldn't take the pressure and literally was shitting in his pants. It was dehydration and he had diarrhea and he lost control. Kiwis were our medical guys. They were going to take him back to our base to be rehydrated.
>
> On his stinking body, inside his sweaty shirt, he carried this document. Then they took this document to the airport and got on the scheduled U.N. plane to Bahrain. The German air force had supplied the

pilot. But it almost didn't take off because as the flight was taking off, a tanker truck suddenly came across the active runway. Everyone on the plane said they cleared it by a foot or two.

As we continued to carry out the inspection, the Iraqis got more and more upset. And finally (Jaffar Dhia) Jafar, who ran the nuclear program, appeared as we packed the documents into crates and tied them on top of our vehicles. Jafar was very angry. He said, "You've got to give the documents back." I said, "No, we're not giving the documents back."

The problem was these were the originals. The technology was so bad in 1991 that we had brought two Xerox machines with us, both of which promptly crapped out. And the (CIA) guys quickly discovered how time-consuming it is to take photos of individual pages. So the Iraqis surround us with military guys. And we had to make a decision. I talked to New York on satellite phone. We wouldn't cooperate with the Iraqis, wouldn't help them. But we wouldn't resist. We took pictures of them taking the documents off our cars. Then we went back to the Canal Hotel.

Around 2 a.m., my phone rings. The chief Iraqi security guy is calling from downstairs. He says, "We're prepared to turn the documents over to you now." What he didn't know is we had actually been able to number them and had a list. Of course, they didn't return all the documents.

The next day, Kay's team led a raid on another building and seized another twenty-five thousand pages. This time, all the team members stuffed papers under their clothing. Irate Iraqi officials ordered soldiers to surround the U.N. vehicles at gunpoint. They commanded Kay's team to surrender the papers. Kay refused to leave without the documents.

They baked in the open parking lot for four sweltering days and Kay became a media star. He calmly described the mounting crisis to CNN and other reporters on his satellite phone. U.N. Security Council members went into crisis mode. Colin Powell, then chairman of the Joint Chiefs, rushed up to Capitol Hill. He praised Kay's ingenuity for smuggling out what he called the "jewels of the treasure," and described the nuclear report in detail. The document had gone from a soiled undershirt in Baghdad to a packed Senate hearing in Washington in thirty-six hours. The news caused shock waves back in Baghdad, according to Kay.

> The Iraqis didn't know until then that we had found the document and didn't know we'd gotten it out of the country. And they just went ape shit. One night they came to us in the parking lot, and we always worried at night. You always kept a third of the team awake in case of any trouble. A lot of these were agency (CIA) guys, and two were special ops guys. They were ready for anything. The Iraqis said to us, "What will happen if we just move in and physically seize the documents?"
>
> We said, "Please don't do it." I said, "Look, if you're going to do it, don't move in on the whole team or people will get really hurt. Grab Gallucci and me, and beat the shit out of us and then you can take the documents. We're not asking to be beaten, but don't take on the team."
>
> The Iraqis knew I was on every damn network, radio show, and front page around the globe. They didn't know what would happen if they

seized the documents against our will. I was concerned that people on my team might get killed for slugging an Iraqi soldier in the middle of the night. In the end, nothing happened. The next morning, right before they agreed we could leave with all the documents, they came to Bob and me and asked, "Does that offer about beating you up still hold?"

Kay grinned. Sorry, the offer had expired. He had won the showdown.

For further details, see Robert Gallucci, former Deputy Executive Director of UNSCOM, *Understanding the Lessons of Nuclear Inspections and Monitoring in Iraq: A Ten-Year Review,* Sponsored by the Institute for Science and International Security, June 14–15, 2001, Lunchtime Address— Reflections on Establishing and Implementing the Post-Gulf War Inspections of Iraq's Weapons of Mass Destruction Programs, transcript date July 31, 2001.

198 **"more and more like a major find"** "Trailer Found in Iraq Believed Used for Biological Weapon Creation," NBC *Nightly News with Tom Brokaw,* May 11, 2003.

199 **"the strongest evidence to date"** *Iraqi Mobile Biological Warfare Agent Production Plants,* p. 2.

199 **But the CIA paper dismissed** Ibid., p. 5.

200 **The theme of his diplomatic tour** Mike Allen, "Bush: 'We Found' Banned Weapons; President Cites Trailers in Iraq as Proof," *Washington Post,* May 31, 2003, p. A1.

200 **"We found the weapons"** White House Transcript, *Interview of the President by TVP, Poland,* May 29, 2003, http://www.whitehouse.gov/g8/interview5.html.

200 **"We've discovered a weapons system"** White House Transcript, *Press Availability with President Bush and President Putin—St. Petersburg, Russia,* June 1, 2003, http://www.whitehouse.gov/news/releases/2003/06/20030601-2.html.

200 **"We recently found two mobile"** Transcript, "Bush Thanks Troops in Qatar," CNN *Live at Daybreak,* June 5, 2003.

200 **"We didn't just make them up"** Michael Duffy, "Weapons of Mass Disappearance," *Time,* June 1, 2003, http://www.time.com/time/magazine/article/0,9171,455828-3,00.html.

200 **"I would put before you"** Transcript, Secretary Colin L. Powell, "Interview on Fox News Sunday with Tony Snow," June 8, 2003, http://www.state.gov/secretary/former/powell/remarks/2003/21318.htm.

200/201 **"I would point out to you"** Jane Corbin, "Still Chasing Saddam's Weapons," *Panorama,* BBC-1, November 1, 2003, http://news.bbc.co.uk/nol/shared/spl/hi/programmes/panorama/transcripts/saddamsweapons.txt.

202 **The equipment "could not be used"** Jefferson Project, *Technical Engineering Exploitation Report of Iraqi Suspect BW-Associated Trailers,* June 2003 (SSCI#2003-4815), cited in *Senate Postwar Findings About Iraq's WMD Production Programs,* p. 35. See also Joby Warrick, "Lacking Biolabs, Trailers Carried Case for War," *Washington Post,* April 12, 2006, p. A1.

202 **The CIA's judgment "has not changed"** *Senate Postwar Findings About Iraq's WMD Programs*, p. 36.

202 **The analysts gave Rice two pages** "Update on Iraqi BW Trailers," CIA, June 6, 2003, cited in Ibid.

CHAPTER 32

205 **"Unless we take immediate steps"** *Statement of David A. Kay*, Former U.N. Chief Nuclear Weapons Inspector in Iraq, United Nations Special Commission on Iraq, International Atomic Energy Agency, House Armed Services Committee, September 10, 2002, http://www.house.gov/hasc/openingstatementsandpressreleases/107thcongress/02-09-10kay.html.

208 **"Are you in charge of finding the WMD?"** Massimo Calibresi and Timothy J. Burger, "Who Lost the WMD?", *Time*, June 29, 2003, http://www.time.com/time/magazine/article/0,9171,1101030707-461781,00.html. See also Tenet, *At the Center of the Storm*, p. 402.

CHAPTER 33

213 **Rumsfeld's deputy, Stephen Cambone** Cambone, Pentagon Briefing, May 7, 2003.

215 **Halliburton got the contract** For details on SCIFs, see *Physical Security Standards for Sensitive Compartmented Information Facilities*, Director of Central Intelligence Document 6/9—Manual, November 18, 2002, http://www.fas.org/irp/offdocs/dcid6-9.htm.

216 **"Dr. Kay provides the guidance"** Brigadier John Duncan Deverell OBE, Commander 145 (Home Counties) Brigade, "A Personal Experience with the Iraq Survey Group," unpublished.

218 **Scorpion officers sported nicknames** Dana Priest and Josh White, "Before the War, CIA Reportedly Trained a Team of Iraqis to Aid U.S.," *Washington Post*, August 3, 2005, p. A12. See also Josh White, "Documents Tell of Brutal Improvisation by GIs," *Washington Post*, August 3, 2005, p. A1.

CHAPTER 36

234 **The six-mile highway from Slayer** For a review of the early months of the insurgency, see Anthony H. Cordesman, "The Current Military Situation in Iraq," Center for Strategic and International Studies, Washington, D.C., November 14, 2003.

CHAPTER 37

237 **The team also searched** *Iraq Survey Group*, Vol. III, Annex C, p. 77. The survey group visited the Al Mishraq Sulfur Facility, one of the world's largest sulfur mines, about thirty miles south of Mosul. UNMOVIC inspectors had

visited the same site two months before the invasion. Intelligence also indicated bio-agent from mobile factories was buried at Habbaniyah Barracks. Ground-penetrating radar and other tests detected nothing, but looters had torn out a fence that supposedly provided a marker for the burial site. The survey group also visited a former orange grove and chicken farm known as Buetha, along the Tigris River just south of Baghdad. The U.N. inspectors had searched there too.

238 **"Anyone who told you this"** *Iraq Survey Group*, Vol. III, Annex D, Trailers Suspected of Being Mobile BW Agent Production Units, p. 92.

241 **They would "shop their good sources"** *WMD Commission Report*, p. 108.

241 **"not yet able to corroborate"** Statement by David Kay on the Interim Progress Report on the Activities of the Iraq Survey Group (ISG) Before the House Permanent Select Committee on Intelligence, House Committee on Appropriations, Subcommittee on Defense, and the Senate Select Committee on Intelligence, October 2, 2003, p. 5.

241 **The scientist had stored** "Conference Call Transcript," David Kay and Members of the Press, CIA, October 3, 2003.

241/242 **"not pleased by what I heard today"** Federal News Service—Transcript, "Press Stakeout with David Kay, Chief Weapons Inspector, Iraq Survey Group, Following his Congressional Briefings re: Progress Report on Search for Iraq Weapons of Mass Destruction; Other Participants: Senator Pat Roberts (R-KS); Senator John Rockefeller (D-WV); Rep. Porter Goss (R-FL)." Hart Senate Office Building, Washington, D.C., October 2, 2003.

242 **Speaking on the South Lawn** "President Bush, Commissioner Kerick Discuss Police Force in Iraq," White House, Office of the Press Secretary, October 3, 2003, http://www.whitehouse.gov/news/releases/2003/10/2003-1003-2.html.

242 **It was the wrong strain** For a review of Kay's report, see Bob Drogin, "Friendly Fire: What David Kay Really Found," *New Republic*, Oct. 27, 2003. See also Bob Drogin, "Experts Downplay Bioagent," *Los Angeles Times*, Oct. 17, 2003, p. 1.

CHAPTER 38

244 **"to see if false information"** Bob Drogin, "U.S. Suspects It Received False Iraq Arms Tips," *Los Angeles Times*, August 28, 2003, p. 1.

244 **He knew of "no equipment"** *WMD Commission Report*, pp. 84, 216.

248 **Curveball's best friend in college** Ibid., p. 223; Drogin and Goetz, "How U.S. Fell Under the Spell of 'Curveball.'"

CHAPTER 39

252 **They feared how** *WMD Commission Report*, p. 193.

252 **He was "read the riot act"** Ibid., p. 194.

253 **Following procedures, he referred** Ibid., p. 249.

CHAPTER 40

255 **"like a man who had suddenly"**   Rod Barton, *The Weapons Detective: The Inside Story of Australia's Top Weapons Inspector* (Melbourne: Black, 2006), p. 235.

255 **"I remain convinced"**   Stuart A. Cohen, Vice Chairman, National Intelligence Council, *Iraq's WMD Programs: Culling Hard Facts from Soft Myths*, http://www.dni.gov/nic/articles_iraq_wmd.htm. See also Stuart A. Cohen, "Myths About Intelligence," *Washington Post*, Nov. 28, 2003, p. A41.

255 **Cohen called it a "myth"**   Ibid. The Senate Select Committee on Intelligence later lambasted the drafters of the National Intelligence Estimate. Most major key judgments "either overstated, or were not supported by" the underlying intelligence. The NIE based its "judgment that 'all key aspects—research and development (R&D), production, and weaponization—of Iraq's offensive biological weapons (BW) program are active and that most elements are larger and more advanced than they were before the Gulf War' primarily on its assessment that Iraq had mobile biological production vans. . . . The reporting was largely from a single source to whom the Intelligence Community never had direct access." *Senate Prewar Intelligence Report*, pp. 23, 188–89.

257 **Bush hail the "Kay Report"**   George W. Bush, *State of the Union Address*, White House Press Office, January 20, 2004, http://www.whitehouse.gov/news/releases/2004/01/20040120-7.html.

258 **"I don't think they existed"**   Tabassum Zakaria, "Ex-Arms Hunter Kay Says No WMD Stockpiles in Iraq," Reuters, January 23, 2004.

259 **"Let me begin by saying"**   Federal News Service Transcript, Hearing of the Senate Armed Services Committee; Subject: Iraqi Weapons of Mass Destruction Programs; Chaired by: Senator John Warner (R-VA); Witness: David Kay, Former Head of the Iraq Survey Group; January 28, 2004.

259 **A week earlier, Vice President Cheney**   Juan Williams, "Cheney: U.S. to Continue Search for Iraqi WMD," *NPR Morning Edition*, January 22, 2004, http://www.npr.org/templates/story/story.php?storyId=1610113.

260 **"We are constantly having"**   Hearing of the Senate Armed Services Committee, January 28, 2004.

260 **The CIA "didn't have a clue"**   Alison Mitchell, "Sen. Shelby Faults the Intelligence Agencies," *New York Times*, September 10, 2002.

260 **CIA analysts hadn't updated**   See "DCI Statement on the Belgrade Chinese Embassy Bombing to a House Permanent Select Committee on Intelligence Committee Open Hearing," July 22, 1999, https://www.cia.gov/cia/public_affairs/speeches/1999/dci_speech_072299.html.

262 **"The situation in Iraq"**   Press briefing by Scott McClellan, James S. Brady Briefing Room, Office of the Press Secretary, White House, January 28, 2004, http://www.whitehouse.gov/news/releases/2004/01/20040128-7.html.

CHAPTER 41

263 **He began with a promise** Director of Central Intelligence George J. Tenet, "Iraq and Weapons of Mass Destruction," Speech, Georgetown University, February 5, 2004, http://www.fas.org/irp/cia/product/dci020504.html.

270 **CIA officials already were convinced** *Senate INC Report*, p. 108.

271 **Investigations "since the war"** Ibid., p. 106.

CHAPTER 42

272 **"Give David Kay credit for courage"** "Mr. Kay's Truth-Telling," *Washington Post*, January 29, 2004, p. A28.

274 **"The president of the United States"** Tenet speech at Georgetown University, "Iraq and Weapons of Mass Destruction."

EPILOGUE

279 **"At several of the inspected sites"** Thirteenth quarterly report of the Executive Chairman of the United Nations Monitoring, Verification and Inspection Commission in Accordance with Paragraph 12 of Security Council Resolution 1284 (1999), S/2003/580, May 30, 2003, p. 26.

280 **The Iraqis based their design** *Iraq Survey Group*, Vol. III, Annex D, p. 74.

280 **The germ factory at Al Hakam** UNSCOM Report on Disarmament to the United Nations Security Council, S/1999/94, January 29, 1999, p. 168, http://www.fas.org/news/un/iraq/s/990125/.

281 **British intelligence repudiated** *Butler Report*, pp. 110, 130, 527.

281 **"The problem was not just mistranslation"** E-mail to author.

282 **In his 2007 book** Tenet, *At the Center of the Storm*, pp. 328, 383.

INDEX